FTCE Reading K-12
Teacher Certification Exam

By: Sharon Wynne, M.S.
Southern Connecticut State University

"And, while there's no reason yet to panic, I think it's only prudent that we make preparations to panic."

XAMonline, INC.
Boston

Library of Congress Cataloging-in-Publication Data

Wynne, Sharon A.
  Reading K-12: Teacher Certification / Sharon A. Wynne. -2nd ed.
  ISBN 978-1-58197-659-5
  1. Reading K-12.   2. Study Guides.   3. FTCE
  4. Teachers' Certification & Licensure.   5. Careers

Disclaimer:
The opinions expressed in this publication are the sole works of XAMonline and were created independently from the National Education Association, Educational Testing Service, or any State Department of Education, National Evaluation Systems or other testing affiliates.

Between the time of publication and printing, state specific standards as well as testing formats and website information may change that is not included in part or in whole within this product. Sample test questions are developed by XAMonline and reflect similar content as on real tests; however, they are not former tests. XAMonline assembles content that aligns with state standards but makes no claims nor guarantees teacher candidates a passing score. Numerical scores are determined by testing companies such as NES or ETS and then are compared with individual state standards. A passing score varies from state to state.

Printed in the United States of America   œ-1

FTCE: Reading K-12
ISBN: 978-1-58197-659-5

Table of Contents

Great Study and Testing Tips!

What to study in order to prepare for the subject assessments is the focus of this study guide but equally important is *how* you study.

You can increase your chances of truly mastering the information by taking some simple, but effective steps.

Study Tips:

1. <u>Some foods aid the learning process</u>. Foods such as milk, nuts, seeds, rice, and oats help your study efforts by releasing natural memory enhancers called CCKs (*cholecystokinin*) composed of *tryptophan*, *choline*, and *phenylalanine*. All of these chemicals enhance the neurotransmitters associated with memory. Before studying, try a light, protein-rich meal of eggs, turkey, and fish. All of these foods release the memory enhancing chemicals. The better the connections, the more you comprehend.

Likewise, before you take a test, stick to a light snack of energy boosting and relaxing foods. A glass of milk, a piece of fruit, or some peanuts all release various memory-boosting chemicals and help you to relax and focus on the subject at hand.

2. <u>Learn to take great notes</u>. A by-product of our modern culture is that we have grown accustomed to getting our information in short doses (i.e. TV news sound bites or USA Today style newspaper articles.)

Consequently, we've subconsciously trained ourselves to assimilate information better in <u>neat little packages</u>. If your notes are scrawled all over the paper, it fragments the flow of the information. Strive for clarity. Newspapers use a standard format to achieve clarity. Your notes can be much clearer through use of proper formatting. A very effective format is called the *<u>"Cornell Method."</u>*

> Take a sheet of loose-leaf lined notebook paper and draw a line all the way down the paper about 1-2" from the left-hand edge.

> Draw another line across the width of the paper about 1-2" up from the bottom. Repeat this process on the reverse side of the page.

Look at the highly effective result. You have ample room for notes, a left hand margin for special emphasis items or inserting supplementary data from the textbook, a large area at the bottom for a brief summary, and a little rectangular space for just about anything you want.

3. <u>Get the concept then the details.</u> Too often we focus on the details and don't gather an understanding of the concept. However, if you simply memorize only dates, places, or names, you may well miss the whole point of the subject.

A key way to understand things is to put them in your own words. If you are working from a textbook, automatically summarize each paragraph in your mind. If you are outlining text, don't simply copy the author's words.

Rephrase them in your own words. You remember your own thoughts and words much better than someone else's, and subconsciously tend to associate the important details to the core concepts.

4. <u>Ask Why?</u> Pull apart written material paragraph by paragraph and don't forget the captions under the illustrations.

Example: If the heading is "Stream Erosion", flip it around to read "Why do streams erode?" Then answer the questions.

If you train your mind to think in a series of questions and answers, not only will you learn more, but it also helps to lessen the test anxiety because you are used to answering questions.

5. <u>Read for reinforcement and future needs.</u> Even if you only have 10 minutes, put your notes or a book in your hand. Your mind is similar to a computer; you have to input data in order to have it processed. *By reading, you are creating the neural connections for future retrieval.* The more times you read something, the more you reinforce the learning of ideas.

Even if you don't fully understand something on the first pass, *your mind stores much of the material for later recall.*

6. <u>Relax to learn so go into exile.</u> Our bodies respond to an inner clock called biorhythms. Burning the midnight oil works well for some people, but not everyone.

If possible, set aside a particular place to study that is free of distractions. Shut off the television, cell phone, and pager and exile your friends and family during your study period.

If you really are bothered by silence, try background music. Light classical music at a low volume has been shown to aid in concentration over other types. Music that evokes pleasant emotions without lyrics is highly suggested. Try just about anything by Mozart. It relaxes you.

7. <u>Use arrows not highlighters</u>. At best, it's difficult to read a page full of yellow, pink, blue, and green streaks. Try staring at a neon sign for a while and you'll soon see that the horde of colors obscure the message.

A quick note, a brief dash of color, an underline, and an arrow pointing to a particular passage is much clearer than a horde of highlighted words.

8. <u>Budget your study time</u>. Although you shouldn't ignore any of the material, *allocate your available study time in the same ratio that topics may appear on the test.*

Testing Tips:

1. <u>Get smart, play dumb</u>. Don't read anything into the question. Don't make an assumption that the test writer is looking for something else than what is asked. Stick to the question as written and don't read extra things into it.

2. <u>Read the question and all the choices *twice* before answering the question</u>. You may miss something by not carefully reading, and then re-reading both the question and the answers.

If you really don't have a clue as to the right answer, leave it blank on the first time through. Go on to the other questions, as they may provide a clue as to how to answer the skipped questions.

If later on, you still can't answer the skipped ones . . . *Guess.* The only penalty for guessing is that you *might* get it wrong. Only one thing is certain; if you don't put anything down, you will get it wrong!

3. <u>Turn the question into a statement</u>. Look at the way the questions are worded. The syntax of the question usually provides a clue. Does it seem more familiar as a statement rather than as a question? Does it sound strange?

By turning a question into a statement, you may be able to spot if an answer sounds right, and it may also trigger memories of material you have read.

4. <u>Look for hidden clues</u>. It's actually very difficult to compose multiple-foil (choice) questions without giving away part of the answer in the options presented.

In most multiple-choice questions you can often readily eliminate one or two of the potential answers. This leaves you with only two real possibilities and automatically your odds go to Fifty-Fifty for very little work.

5. <u>Trust your instincts</u>. For every fact that you have read, you subconsciously retain something of that knowledge. On questions that you aren't really certain about, go with your basic instincts. **Your first impression on how to answer a question is usually correct.**

6. <u>Mark your answers directly on the test booklet</u>. Don't bother trying to fill in the optical scan sheet on the first pass through the test.

Just be very careful not to miss-mark your answers when you eventually transcribe them to the scan sheet.

7. <u>Watch the clock</u>! You have a set amount of time to answer the questions. Don't get bogged down trying to answer a single question at the expense of 10 questions you can more readily answer.

THIS PAGE BLANK

COMPETENCY 1.0   KNOWLEDGE OF THE THEORIES AND UNDERLYING ASSUMPTIONS OF READING PROCESSES

Skill 1.1   Identify foundational theories and theorists of reading processes and development

Decoding

In the late 1960s and the 1970s, many reading specialists, most prominently Fries (1962) believed that successful decoding resulted in reading comprehension. This meant that if children could sound out the words, they would then automatically be able to comprehend them. Many teachers of reading and many reading texts still subscribe to this theory.

Asking questions

Another theory or approach to the teaching of reading that gained currency in the late sixties and the early seventies was the importance of asking inferential and critical-thinking questions of the children that would challenge and engage them in the text. This approach to reading went beyond the literal level of what was stated in the text to an inferential level whereby text clues were needed to make predictions and to a critical level of involving the child in evaluating the text. While asking engaging and thought-provoking questions is still viewed as part of the teaching of reading, it is only viewed currently as a *component* of the teaching of reading.

Comprehension "Skills"

As various reading theories, practices, and approaches percolated during the 1970s and 1980s, many educators and researchers in the field came to believe that the teacher of reading needed to teach a set of discrete "Comprehension Skills" (Otto et al, 1977). Therefore, the reading teacher became the teacher of each individual comprehension skill. Children in such classrooms came away with main idea, sequence, cause and effect, and other concepts that were supposed to make them better comprehenders. However, did it make them lifelong readers?

Transactional Approach

During the late 1970s and early 1980s, researchers in the field of education, psychology, and linguistics, began to examine how the reader comprehends. Among them was Louise Rosenblatt who posited that reading is a transaction between the reader and the text. It is Rosenblatt (1978) who explained successful reading as the reader constructing a meaning from the text that reflected both the reader and the text.

She described two general purposes for reading: *efferent* and *aesthetic*. Efferent reading is looking for and remembering information to use functionally. Examples would be filling out a job application, reading a story in preparation for a test, or reading a newspaper article to find out who won the state basketball championship. Aesthetic reading is done to connect one's own life to the text, to be swept away by the beauty of a poem or to respond emotionally to a book such as *Bridge to Terabithia*.

These differing purposes call for somewhat different reading strategies: One might skim the newspaper article for basketball information but read a poem closely ten times and create mental images of different passages. Lastly, when children are asked to read all fiction differently (What's the setting? What's the main conflict in the plot? There will be a test on this on Thursday!), it can thwart a child's joy in the written word and work against the student's desire to be a lifelong reader.

Bottom-up, Top-down, Interactional Theories of Reading

Bottom-up theories of reading assume that children learn from part-to-whole starting with the smallest segments possible. Instruction begins with a strong phonics approach, learning letter-sound relationships, and often using basal readers or *decodable books*. Decodable books are vocabulary-controlled using language from word families with high predictability. Thus we get sentences like "Nan has a tan fan." Reading is seen as skills-based, and the skills are taught one at a time.

Top-down theories of reading suggest that reading begins with the reader's knowledge, not the print. Children are seen as having a drive to construct meaning. This approach views reading as moving from the whole to the parts. An early top-down theory was the *whole word* approach. Children memorized high-frequency words to assist them in reading the Dick and Jane books of the '30s. Then teachers helped children discover letter-sound correspondences in what they were reading. A more recent top-down theory is the *whole language* approach. This approach was influenced by research on how young children learned language. It was thought that children could learn to read as naturally as they learned to talk. Children were surrounded by print in their classrooms, quality literature often printed in Big Books, and were viewed as writers from the start. Hence kindergarten children kept journals. Advocates of whole language viewed the "skill'em-drill'em-and kill'em" approach based on bottom-up theories as a deadly dull introduction to the world of reading.

Interactive theories of reading combine the strengths of both bottom-up and top-down approaches. Teachers need to be able to teach decoding, vocabulary, and comprehension skills to support children's drive for meaning and desire for a stimulating exchange with high-quality literary texts from their earliest days in school. Strategies include shared, guided, and independent reading; Big Books, reading, writing workshops, and the like. Today this approach is called the *balanced literacy approach.* It is considered to be a synthesis of the best from bottom-up and top-down methods.

Literacy and Literacy Learning

To be literate in the 21st century means more than being able to read and write. To live well and happily in today's society, an individual must be able to read not only newspapers and books, but e-mails, blogs, directions for how to use one's cell phone, and the like. A disconnect has evolved between the isolated reading-comprehension skills the schools are teaching and the literacy skills including listening and speaking that are crucial for employment and personal and academic success. Thornburg (1992, 2003) has also noted that technology capacities and the ability to communicate online are now integral parts of our sense of literacy.

Cooper (2004) views literacy as reading, writing, thinking, listening, viewing, and discussing. These are not viewed as separate activities or components of instruction, but rather as developing and being nurtured simultaneously and interactively. Children learn these abilities by engaging in authentic explorations, readings, projects, and experiences.

In learning how to ride a bike, the learner goes through various approximations before learning how to actually ride. The reader goes through similar approximations with the scaffold (support) of the teacher before developing his/her own independent literacy skills and capacities.

Emergent Literacy: the concept that young children are emerging into reading and writing with no real beginning or ending point. Children are introduced into the world of print as soon as their parents read board books to them at the age of one or two. When children scribble or use invented spelling during the preschool years, they reveal themselves as detectives of the written word, having watched parents and teachers make lists, write thank-you notes, or leave messages. This view of the reader assumes that all children have a drive to make meaning in print and will begin doing it almost on their own if surrounded by a print-rich environment.

Reading Readiness: an approach antithetical to emergent literacy in that it assumes that all children must have mastered a sequence of reading skills *before* they can begin to read. This approach stands in contrast to emergent literacy.

Language Acquisition: continuous and never-ending. From the perspective of this theory and research, all children come to school with a language base that the school must build on. As a consequence of the connection between oral language and reading, it is important that schools build literacy experiences around the language the child brings to the school.

Prior Knowledge, Schemata, Background, and Comprehension

Schemata are structures that represent generic concepts stored in our memory (Rumelhart, l980). Young children develop their schemata through experiences. Prior knowledge and the lack of experience in some cases influence comprehension. The more closely the reader's experiences and schemata approximate those of the writer, the more likely the reader is to comprehend the text. It is obvious that for many children from non-English-language-speaking backgrounds and perhaps for those from struggling socioeconomic family structures, schemata deficits indicate the need for intense teacher support as these children become emergent and early readers.

Often the teacher will have to model and scaffold for the child the steps to form a schemata from the information provided in a text.

Comprehension: Cooper (2004) defines comprehension as "a strategic process by which readers construct or assign meaning to a text by using the clues in the text and their own prior knowledge." Comprehension is a process in which the reader transacts with the text to construct or assign meaning. Reading and writing are both interconnected and mutually supportive. Comprehension is a strategic process in which readers adjust their reading to suit their reading purpose and the type or genre of text they are reading. Narrative and expository texts require different reading approaches because of their different text structures.

Strategic readers also call into play their metacognitive capacities as they analyze texts so that they are self aware of the skills needed to construct meaning from the text structure.

The Role of Literature in Developing Literacy

The balanced literacy approach advocates the use of "real literature," recognized works of the best of children's fiction and non-fiction trade books and winners of such awards as the Newberry and Caldecott medals, for helping children develop literacy.

Balanced literacy advocates argue that:

- Real literature engages young readers and assures that they will become lifelong readers.

- Real literature also offers readers a language base that can help them expand their expressiveness as readers and as writers.

- Real literature is easier to read and understand than grade-leveled texts.

There are districts in the United States where the phonics-only approach is heavily embedded. However, the majority of school districts would describe their approach to reading as the balanced-literacy approach, which includes phonics work as well as the use of real literature texts. To contrast the phonics and balanced-literacy approaches as opposite is inaccurate, since a balanced approach includes both.

It is important to go online and to visit the key resources of the NCTE (National Council of Teachers of English) and the IRA (International Reading Association) to keep abreast of the latest research in the field.

See also Directory on page

Skill 1.2   Identify instructional applications of theories of reading processes and development

Phonological Awareness

Phonological awareness means the ability of the reader to recognize the sounds or phonemes of spoken language. This recognition includes how these sounds can be blended together, segmented (divided up), and manipulated (switched around). This awareness eventually leads to phonics, a method for decoding language by unlocking letter-sound or grapheme-phoneme relationships.

Development of phonological skills for most children begins during the pre-K years. Indeed, by the age of five, a child who has been exposed to finger plays and poetry can recognize a rhyme. Such a child can demonstrate phonological awareness by filling in the missing rhyming word in a familiar rhyme or rhymed picture book. The procedure of filling in a missing word is called the Cloze procedure. It can be used in oral or print literacy activities.

One teaches children phonological awareness by directly pointing out the sounds made by letters singly (as in /b/) or in combination (as in /bl/), and to recognize individual sounds in words.

Phonological awareness skills include but are not limited to the following:

1. Rhyming and syllabification.
2. Blending sounds into words—such as pic-tur-bo-k.
3. Identifying beginning or initial phonemes and ending or final phonemes in short, one-syllable words.
4. Breaking words down into sounds, which is also called "segmenting" words.

5. Removing initial sounds and substituting others. An example is /bat/ minus the /b/ with an /m/ substituted becomes /mat/.

The Role of Phonological Awareness in Reading Development

Instructional methods to teach phonological awareness may include any or all of the following:

1. Auditory games during which children recognize and manipulate the sounds of words, separate or segment the sounds of words, take out sounds, blend sounds, add in new sounds, or take apart sounds to recombine them in new formations.

2. Snap game. The teacher says two words. The children snap their fingers if the two words share a sound, which might be at the beginning or end of the word. Children hear initial phonemes most easily, followed by final ones. Medial or middle sounds are most difficult for young children to discriminate. One sees this in their oral responses as well as in their invented spelling. Silence occurs if the words share no sounds. Children love this simple game and it also helps with classroom management.

3. Language games model identification of rhyming words for children. These games help inspire children to create their own rhymes.

4. Read books that rhyme such as *Sheep in a Jeep* by Nancy Shaw or *The Fox on a Box* by Barbara Gregorich.

5. Share books with children that use alliteration (words that begin with the same consonant sound) such as *Avalanche, A to Z*.

Assessment of Phonological Awareness

These skills can be assessed by having the child listen to the teacher say two words. Then ask the child to decide if these two words are the same word repeated twice or two different words.

When making this assessment make certain that the two words only differ by one phoneme, such as /d/ and /g/.

Children can be assessed on words that are not real words but are familiar to them. Words used can be make-believe words.

The Role of Phonological Processing in the Development of Individual Students

Children who are raised in homes where English is not the first language and/or where standard English is not spoken may have difficulty hearing the difference between similar-sounding words like "send" and "sent." Any child who is not in a home, day care, or preschool environment where English phonology operates may have difficulty perceiving and demonstrating the differences between English language phonemes. If children cannot hear the difference between words that "sound the same" like "grow" and "glow," they will be confused when these words appear in a print context. This confusion will, of course, impact their comprehension.

Considerations for teaching phonological processing to ELL children include recognition by the teacher that what works for the English-language-speaking child from an English-language-speaking family does not necessarily work in other languages.

Research recommends that ELL children learn to read initially in their first language. It is critical for ELL learners to speak English before being taught to read it. Research supports the theory that oral language development lays the foundation for phonological awareness.

All phonological instruction programs must be tailored to the children's learning backgrounds. Rhymes and alliteration introduced to ELL children should be read or shared with them in their first language if at all possible.

Points to Ponder

Phonological awareness is auditory.
It does not involve print.
It begins before children have learned letter-sound relationships.
It is the basis for the successful teaching of phonics and spelling.
It can and must be taught and nurtured.
It precedes and must be in place before the alphabetic principle can be taught.

Phonemic Awareness

Phonemic awareness is a specific skill within the broader category of phonological awareness. Probably developing fairly late, it is the knowledge that words are comprised of individual phonemes that can be blended. Theorist Marilyn Jaeger Adams, an early-reading researcher, has outlined five basic types of phonemic awareness tasks.

Task 1—Ability to hear rhymes and alliteration. For example, the children listen to a poem, rhyming picture book, or song and identify the rhyming words, which the teacher records or lists on chart.

Task 2—Ability to do oddity tasks (recognize the member of a set that is different [odd] among the group). For example, the children would look at the pictures of grass, a garden. and a rose, and identify the one that starts with a different sound.

Task 3—The ability to orally blend words and split syllables. For example, the children can say the first sound of a word and then the rest of the word and put it together as a single word.

Task 4—The ability to orally segment words. For example, the ability to count sounds. The child would be asked to count or clap the sounds in "hamburger."

Task 5—The ability to do phonics manipulation tasks. For example, replace the "r" sound in rose with a "p" sound.

The Role of Phonemic Awareness in Reading Development

Children who have problems with phonics generally have not acquired or been exposed to phonemic-awareness activities at home or in preschool-2. This includes extensive songs, rhymes, and read-alouds.

Instructional Methods

Since the ability to distinguish between individual sounds or phonemes within words is a prerequisite to the association of sounds with letters and manipulating sounds to blend words—another way of saying "reading"—,the teaching of phonemic awareness is crucial to emergent literacy (early childhood K-2 reading instruction). Children need a strong background in phonemic awareness in order for phonics instruction (sound-spelling relationship—printed materials) to be effective.

Instructional methods that may be effective for teaching phonemic awareness can include:

- Clapping syllables in words.

- Distinguishing between a word and a sound.

- Using visual cues and movements to help children understand when the speaker goes from one sound to another.

- Incorporating oral segmentation activities that focus on easily-distinguished syllables rather than sounds.

- Singing familiar songs (e.g.. Happy Birthday and Knick Knack Paddy Wack) and replacing key words with those with a different ending.

- Dealing children a deck of picture cards and having them sound out the words for the pictures on their cards or calling for a picture by asking for its first and last sound.

Assessment of Phonemic Awareness

Teachers can maintain ongoing logs and rubrics for assessment throughout the year of phonemic awareness for individual children. Such assessments would identify particular stated reading behaviors or performance standards, the date of observation of the child's behavior (in this context, phonemic activity or exercise), and comments.

The rubric or legend for assessing these behaviors might include the following descriptors:

- Demonstrates or exhibits reading behavior consistently.

- Makes progress/strides toward this reading behavior.

- Has not yet demonstrated or exhibited this behavior.

Depending on the particular phonemic task the teacher models, the performance task might include:

- Saying rhyming words in response to an oral prompt.

- Segmenting a word spoken by the teacher into its beginning, middle, and ending sounds.

- Counting correctly the number of syllables in a spoken word.

Phonological awareness involves the recognition that spoken words are composed of a set of smaller units such as onsets, rhymes, syllables, and sounds. Phonemic awareness is a specific type of phonological awareness that focuses on the ability to distinguish, manipulate, and blend specific sounds or phonemes within an individual word. Think of phonological awareness as an umbrella and phonemic awareness as a specific spoke under this umbrella.

Phonics deals with printed words and the learning of sound-spelling correlations, while phonemic awareness activities are oral.

In reviewing reading research and theory, new distinctions and definitions appear often. The body of reading knowledge changes over time. The information and definitions in this guide are those accepted in the year of its publication and the time of its authoring and updating. As changes occur in accepted theories, they will be made in the guides and in the certification exams.

Helen Depree and Sandra Iversen, *Early Literacy in the Classroom*: "If you believe that you learn to read by reading, you must learn to want to read. Reading to children, therefore, models both the 'how' and 'why' of reading."

Terrence Moore, Ashbrook Center, Fellow-Principal of Ridgeview Classical Schools in Fort Collins, Colorado: "The long talk that parents have put off about the ways of the world might need to be an introduction to the facts about the English alphabet."

COMPETENCY 2.0 KNOWLEDGE OF EMERGENT LITERACY

Skill 2.1 **Identify the terminology and concepts of emergent literacy (e.g., oral language development, phonological awareness, alphabet knowledge, decoding, concepts about print, motivation, text structures, written language development)**

Emergent literacy is a phrase coined by reading theorist Marie Clay to describe the literacy behaviors young children go through in order to acquire the skills associated with becoming fluent readers. Even before they reach school age, children learn language from their parents, siblings, and other significant others in their lives. Emergent readers are in the stage of reading in which the reader understands that print contains a consistent message. The reader can recognize some high-frequency words, names, and simple words in context. Pictures can be used to predict meaning. The emergent reader begins to attend to left to right directionality and features of print and may identify some initial sounds and ending sounds in words.

The terminology associated with emergent literacy includes the following:

- ✓ Oral language development. This develops before children enter school through interactions with others as they put their thoughts into words. Children also develop oral language use by listening to stories and watching children's television programs.
- ✓ Phonological awareness. The ability to recognize the sounds of spoken language and how they can be blended together, segmented, and switched/manipulated to form new combinations and words.
- ✓ Alphabet knowledge. The idea that written spellings represent spoken words.
- ✓ Decoding. "Sounding out" a printed sequence of letters based on knowledge of letter-sound correspondences.
- ✓ Concepts about print. Includes how to handle books, how to look at print, directionality, sequencing, locating skills, punctuation, and concepts of letters and words.

Text Structures. Children need to be alerted to the following text features, which may initially appear strange to them:
- ✓ a period that marks the end of a "telling sentence";
- ✓ a question mark that is at the end of a sentence that asks a question;
- ✓ an exclamation mark that is used to express surprise or excitement at the end of a sentence;
- ✓ capital letters that begin a sentence and the names of persons, places, and things;
- ✓ bold, italicized, or underlined text that highlights key ideas;
- ✓ quotation marks that show dialogue;
- ✓ a hyphen that breaks a long word up into its syllables;
- ✓ a dash that shows a break in an idea or that indicates a parenthetical element or an omission;

✓ an ellipse that shows an omission or break in the text; and
✓ a paragraph in nonfiction that indicates that a new point is being made.

Written language development. While learning how to decode words to read them fluently, students also develop their written language by learning to spell familiar words and write simple sentences and stories.

Skill 2.2   Identify instructional methods for developing emergent literacy

In order for children to develop as readers they need to be surrounded by books and be read to often. Reading aloud should be a daily activity in the classroom as a pleasurable activity to help instill a love of reading in the students. The children should also be given the opportunity to freely choose books, whether or not they can read them independently. Favorite books should be read again and again. The use of rhyming books will help the children develop a sense of word sounds. Stop at the end of a rhyming line to have the children fill in the missing word.

When reading a story, stop at various intervals and ask the students what they think will happen next. After the reading, ask them what they thought were the best or worst parts. Encourage a literary response either by asking them to talk about the story or having them draw a picture about the story and writing a sentence to describe the picture.

When reading to children, discuss the cover of the book, the title, and the author. As you do, ask them to make predictions of what they think the book will be about. Use a book that all the children can see and point to the words as you read them. Familiar items in the classroom should be labeled as well as items belonging to the students.

Encourage parents to help the children develop lists at home, such as a shopping list. There should be an ample supply of writing materials in the classroom, and the students should be encouraged to write stories and sentences. When children ask how to spell a word, encourage them to sound it out first. This will further help to develop phonemic awareness.

Reading and writing activities should be modeled for the children, and they should always be praised for their attempts.

Skill 2.3   Identify characteristics of difficulties in emergent literacy development

There are signs for teachers to look for that may tell them a particular child is experiencing difficulties in emergent literacy. Persistent baby talk, an absence of interest in listening to or reading stories, difficulty following simple directions, and failure to remember the letters of the alphabet as well as his/her own name are characteristics the teacher should pay special attention to. For most of these, intervention from other sources may be needed.

Skill 2.4   Identify methods for prevention of and intervention for emergent literacy difficulties

For children who do not speak plainly or use baby talk, the speech pathologist should be called in to make an assessment. Testing by the reading specialist or the educational psychologist may be needed to ensure that there is no underlying problem that will have an impact on normal reading development. Children who do display characteristics of difficulty in emergent literacy will need one-on-one help so that they will proceed and succeed as readers. When teaching children in small groups in guided reading, the use of leveled texts on the child's reading level is of utmost importance.

Awareness of Text Leveling

The classroom library in the context of the balanced literacy approach to reading instruction is focused on leveled books. These are books that have been leveled with the support of Fountas and Pinnell's *Guided Reading: Good First Teaching for All Children* and *Matching Books to Readers: Using Leveled Reading in Guided Reading,* K-3.

The books that are leveled according to the designations in these reference books need to be stored in bins or crates with front covers facing out. This makes them much easier for the children to identify. In that way, the children can go through the appropriate levels and find the books they are particularly interested in that are also at the right level for them to read. These are the books children can read with the right degree of reading accuracy. When young children can see the covers of the books, they are more likely to flip through them until they can independently identify an appealing book. Then they will read a little bit of the book to see if it's "just right."

"Just right" leveled books that children can read on their own need to be available for them to read during independent reading. The goal is for the more fluent readers to select books on their own. Ultimately the use of leveled books helps the children, along with the teacher, decide which books are "good" or "just right" for them.

Levels are indicated by means of blue, yellow, red, and green dot stickers at their upper right corners to indicate emergent, early, transitional, and fluent reading stages. They are then kept in containers with other "blue," "yellow," "red," and "green" books.

Other lists and resources other than Fountas and Pinnell that can be used to match children with "just right" books include the Reading Recovery level list. Ultimately, the teacher needs to individualize whatever leveling is used in the library to address the individual child learner's needs.

Awareness of the Challenges and Supports in a Text

Illustrations can be key supports for emergent and early readers. Teachers should not only use wordless stories (books that tell their narratives through pictures alone), but also make targeted use of Big Books for read-alouds so that young children become habituated to the use of illustrations as an important component for constructing meaning. The teacher should model for the child how to reference an illustration for help in identifying a word in the text the child does not recognize. Of course, children can also go on a picture walk with the teacher as part of a mini-lesson or guided reading and anticipate the story (narrative) using the pictures alone to construct meaning.

Decodability. Use literature that contains examples of letter-sound correspondences you wish to teach. First, read the literature with the children or read it aloud to them. Then take a specific example from the text and have the children reread it as you point out the letter-sound correspondence. Then ask the children to go through the now-familiar literature to find other letter-sound correspondences. Once the children have correctly made the letter-sound correspondences, have them share similar relationships they find in other works of literature.

Cooper (2004) suggests that children can become word detectives so they can independently and fluently decode on their own. The child should learn the following word-detective routines so that he or she can function as an independent fluent reader who can decode words on his/her own. First, the child should read to the end of a sentence. Then the child should search for word parts that he or she knows. The child should also try to decode the word from the letter sounds. As a last resort, the child should ask someone for help or look up the word in the dictionary.

Techniques for Determining Students' Independent, and Instructional Reading Levels

Instructional reading is generally judged to be at the 95 percent accuracy level although Taberski places it at between 92 and 97 percent. Taberski tries to enhance independent reading levels by making sure that readers on the instructional reading levels read a variety of genres and have a range of available and interesting books within a particular genre to read.

Taberski's availability for reading conferences helps her to both assess first hand her children's frustration levels and to model ongoing teacher/reader book conversations by scheduling child-initiated reading conferences when she personally replenishes their book bags.

In order to allay children's frustration levels in their reading and to foster their independent reading, it is important to some children that the teacher personally take time out to hear them read aloud and to check for fluency and expression. Children's frustration level can be immeasurably lessened if they are explicitly told by the teacher after they have read aloud that they need to read without pointing and that they should try chunking words into phrases that mimic their natural speech.

Assessment of the Reading Development of Individual Students

For young readers who are from ELL backgrounds, even if they have been born in the United States, the use of pictures validates their story-authoring and story-telling skills and provides them with equity and access to the literary discussion and book talk of their native English-speaking peers. These children can also demonstrate their storytelling abilities by drawing sequels or prequels to the story detailed in the illustrations alone. They might even be given the opportunity to share the story aloud in their native language or to comment on the illustrations in their native language.

Since many stories today are recorded in two or even three languages at once, discussing story events or analyzing pictures in a different native language is a beneficial practice that can be accomplished in the 21st century marketplace.

Use of pictures and illustrations can also help the K-3 educator assess the capabilities of children who are struggling readers if the children's learning strength is spatial. Through targeted questions about how the pictures would change if different plot twists occurred or how the child might transform the story by changing the illustrations, the teacher can begin to assess struggling reader's deficits and strengths.

Children from ELL backgrounds can benefit from listening to a recorded version of a particular story while they read along with the tape. This gives them another opportunity to "hear" the story correctly pronounced and presented and to begin to internalize its language structures. In the absence of taped versions of some key stories or texts, the teacher may want to make sound recordings.

Highly proficient readers can also be involved in creating these literature recordings for use with ELL peers or younger peers. This, of course, develops oral language proficiency and also introduces these skilled readers into the intricacies of supporting ELL reading instruction. When they actually see their tapes being used by children, they will be tremendously gratified.

COMPETENCY 3.0   KNOWLEDGE OF DECODING, ENCODING, AND
RELATED READING PROCESSES

Skill 3.1   Identify the processes and skills (e.g., graphophonemic, morphemic, syntactic, semantic) effective readers use for word recognition

Struggling Readers

Beth Antunez: "Students who cannot read by age 9 are unlikely to become fluent readers and have a greater tendency to drop out."

Among the causes of reading difficulties for some children (and adults) are auditory trauma or ear infections that affect their ability to hear speech. Such children need one-on-one support with articulation and perception of different sounds. When a child says a word such as "parrot" incorrectly, repeat it back as a question with the correct word modeled. If the child "gets" the sound correctly after your question, all is well. Extra support is all that was needed. If the child still has difficulty with pronunciation after repeated instances, then consult with a speech therapist or audiologist. Early identification of medical conditions that affect hearing is crucial to reading development.

Recognition that Phonemes are Represented by Letters and Letter Pairs

As young children begin to learn to read, they make connections between the printed letters on the page and the sounds they have heard in language. Phonemic-awareness activities are crucial for building this bridge. Students have engaged in many auditory activities. At this time, it is important the teacher use explicit and systematic methods to demonstrate to the students how these auditory sounds are represented on a page by letters or sometimes letter pairs. As this occurs, students can begin to decode text and move toward becoming proficient readers.

Use of Reading and Writing Strategies for Teaching Letter-sound Correspondence

Provide children with a sample of a single letter book (or create one from environmental sources, newspapers, coupons, circulars, magazines, or your own text ideas). Make sure that your already-published or created sample includes a printed version of the letter in both upper and lower case forms. Make certain that each page contains a picture of something that starts with that specific letter and also has the word for the picture. The book you select or create should be a predictable one in that when the picture is identified, the word can be read.

Once the children have your sample and have listened to its being read, challenge them to each make a one-letter book. Often it is best to focus on familiar consonants for the single-letter book or the first letter of the child's first name. Using the first letter of the child's first name invites the child to develop a book that tells about himself or herself and the words that he or she finds. This is an excellent way for the reading and writing workshop to enhance the teaching of the alphabetic principle. Encourage children to be active writers and readers by looking for words for their book on the classroom word wall, in alphabet books in the special alphabet-book bin, and in grade- and age-appropriate pictionaries (dictionaries for younger children that are filled with pictures).

Of course, the richest resource within the reading and writing workshop classroom for teaching and fostering the alphabetic principle lies in the use of alphabet books as anchor books for inspiring students' writing. While young children in grades K-1 will do better with the one-letter book authoring activity, children in grades 2 and beyond can truly be inspired and motivated by alphabet books to enhance their own reading, writing, and alphabetic skills. Furthermore, use of these books that have been and are being produced in a variety of formats to enhance social studies, science, and mathematical themes provides an opportunity for even young children to create a meaningful product that authenticates their content study as it enhances alphabetic skills and, of course, print awareness.

An annotated bibliography of selected alphabet books has been provided in the bibliography section of this guide. It was limited by space considerations, but the teacher can with no expense and with much pleasure catch up on the latest titles and identify those most appropriate for the grade by visiting a bookstore. Hold the print book in hand and then consider selecting an alphabet book that has a particularly inviting concept, art style, or adaptable format within the children's capacity to use as a model.

For instance, Tina Hoban uses actual color photographs of letters in her *26 Letters and 99 Cents.* Children may want to make clay letters or create letter sculptures that develop their own alphabet book similar to Hoban's. If nutrition is the science topic, children might want to examine Ehlert's very accessible *Eating the Alphabet: Fruits and Vegetables from A to Z.* This, combined with an examination of the fruits and vegetables in a local store (perhaps a pleasant walk from the school and a quick break from the routine) can yield a wonderful alphabet book on fruits and vegetables that can also include those fruits and vegetables eaten in various cultures (e.g., mangos, plantains, pomegranates).

The alphabet book can also offer the class a chance to work collaboratively using a template page created by the teacher. Completion of this collaborative work can be shared with peers in another class as well as with parents and can be kept in the classroom library as a model for the following year's class. It will, of course, recognize the authors.

Assessment throughout the Year of Graphophonemic Awareness

The teacher will want to maintain individual records of children's reading behaviors demonstrating alphabetic principle/graphophonemic awareness.

The following performance standards should be part of a record template form for each child in grades K-1 and beyond as needed (depending on ELL or special needs):

- Match all consonant and short vowel sounds.

- Read one's own name.

- Read one-syllable words and high-frequency words.

- Demonstrate ability to read and understand that as letters in words change, so do the sounds.

- Generate the sounds from all letters including consonant blends and long vowel patterns. Blend those different sounds into recognizable words.

- Read common sight words.

- Read common word families.

- Recognize and use knowledge of spelling patterns when reading: run/running, hop/hopping.

Any record kept of an individual child's progress should include each date of observation and some legend or rubric detailing the level of performance, standard acquisition, or mastery.

The following template can be used by teachers to record student progress for each child in grades K-1 and beyond as needed (depending on ELL or special needs):

Reading Progress

Skill Area	Mastered	Making Progress	Not Yet	Comments
Matches all consonant and short vowel sounds.				
Reads one's own name.				
Reads one-syllable words and high-frequency words.				
Demonstrates ability to read and understand that as letters in words change, so do the sounds.				
Generates the sounds from all letters including consonant blends and long vowel patterns. Blends those different sounds into recognizable words.				
Reads common sight words.				
Reads common word families.				
Recognizes and uses knowledge of spelling patterns when reading: run/running, hop/hopping.				

Any record kept of an individual child's progress should include each date of observation and some legend or rubric detailing the level of performance, standard acquisition, or mastery.

See also Skill 1.2

Skill 3.2   Identify the phases of word recognition within the decoding process (i.e., pre-alphabetic, partial alphabetic, full alphabetic)

The alphabetic principle is sometimes called graphophonemic awareness. This term means that written words are composed of letters (graphemes) that represent the sounds (phonemes) of written words.

Development of the Understanding that Print Carries Meaning

This understanding is demonstrated every day in the elementary classroom as the teacher holds up a selected book to read aloud to the class. The teacher explicitly and deliberately talks aloud about how to hold the book, focuses the class on looking at its cover, points to where to start reading, and sweeps her hands in the direction to begin, left to right.

When writing the morning message on the board, the teacher reminds the children that the message begins in the upper left hand corner at the top of the board to be followed by additional activities and a schedule for the rest of the day.

When the teacher invites children to make posters of a single letter such as *b* and list items in the classroom, their homes, or outside that start with that letter, the children are concretely demonstrating that print carries meaning.

Strategies for Promoting Awareness of the Relationship between Spoken and Written Language

- Writing down what the children say on a language chart.
- Highlighting the uses of print products found in the classroom such as labels, yellow sticky pad notes, labels on shelves and lockers, calendars, signs, and directions.
- Reading together big-print and oversized books to teach print conventions such as directionality.
- Practicing how to handle a book—how to turn pages, to find the top and bottom of pages, and to tell the difference between the front and back covers.
- Discussing and comparing with children the length, appearance, and boundaries of specific words. For example, children can see that the names Dan and Dora share certain letters and a similar shape.
- Having children match oral words to printed words by forming an echo chorus as the teacher reads poetry or rhymes aloud, and they echo the reading.
- Having the children combine, manipulate, switch, and move letters to change words.
- Working with letter cards to create messages and respond to the messages they create.

The Role of Environmental Print in Developing Print Awareness

An environmental print book can be created by the children that contains collaged symbols of their favorite lunch or breakfast foods. The children cut and clip symbols from the packaging of these foods and then place them in alphabetical order in their class-made book. Magazines and catalogues are another source of environmental print that is accessible with ads for child-centered products. Supermarket circulars and coupons from the newspaper are also excellent for engaging children in using environmental print as reading, especially when combined with dramatic play centers or prop boxes.

What is particularly effective in using environmental print is that it immediately invites the child from an ELL background into print awareness through the familiarity of commercial logos and packaging symbols.

Understanding the value and importance of the concepts of print for beginning readers developed out of the work of Marie Clay in New Zealand. Assessment of these skills typically occurs in kindergarten and continues into first grade as necessary. The following skills are part of the assessment process:

- Print carries a message. The students can demonstrate this skill even if unable to read the text by pretending to read. This may be demonstrated even if the child does not demonstrate any of the other concepts.

- Book organization. Students demonstrate an understanding of the organization of books by identifying the title, cover, author, left-to-right progression, top-to-bottom order, and one-to-one correspondence. Students may learn these skills individually as they become more familiar with books.

- Print Consistencies. This is the understanding that text is made up of letters that then form words that are then combined to form sentences. As beginning readers make these connections, they will next develop the concept of capital letters at the beginning and basic punctuation marks.

- Letter Identification. The final stage of the concepts of print assessment involves the identification of both uppercase and lowercase letters. More advanced students may begin to recognize some of the most common spelling patterns in beginning texts.

Have the children identify the front cover, back cover, and title page of a specific book. Model storytelling with the book held so that the audience can see the illustrations. Then have children demonstrate the skills for their peers.

Have children search through the class libraries for special features on the fronts or backs of books as they help return the books to their bins. Have the children display and talk about the special symbols they have found.

Review with the children, in an age- and grade-appropriate format, additional parts of the book during mini lessons and read-alouds. These additional parts of the book can include title pages, dedication page, table of contents, and copyright date and glossary.

Strategies for Promoting an Understanding of the Directionality of Print

In order to become proficient readers, young students need to develop a complete understanding that all print is read from left to right and top to bottom. Modeling is one of the most important strategies a teacher can use to develop this understanding in children. The use of big books, poems, and charts are strategies teachers can use in both large- and small-group instruction. Simple questions can encourage the students to pay closer attention to these skills (i.e., "We are going to read this passage. Where should I put my pointer to start reading?")

Directionality of print should also be taught during the writing process. In language-experience stories, interactive writing, and Kidwriting©, the teacher can incorporate explicit modeling and instruction in these skills. Sometimes it may be necessary to provide children with a dot at the top left corner of the paper in order to provide a visual reminder of where to begin.

Techniques for Promoting the Ability to Track Print in Connected Texts

Model directionality and one-to-one word matching by pointing to words while using a big book, pocket chart, or poem written out on a chart. As you repeatedly lead the children in this reading, they can follow along and eventually track the print and make one-to-one matches on the connected text independently. They can also practice by using a pointer or their fingers to follow the words. Children happily volunteer to be the point person. Even before Vanna White, the joy of "signifying letters" existed and has tremendous appeal for children.

Copy down a brief, familiar rhyme (perhaps from a favorite book or song) and post it in the room at child's-eye level so the children can independently walk around and read it.

Copy parts of a brief or familiar rhyme or poem on individual word cards. Then challenge the children in small groups or independently to reassemble and display them on a pocket chart. As children "play" with constructing and reconstructing this pocket chart, they will develop an awareness of directionality, one-on-one matching of print to spoken words, spacing, and punctuation.

Model interactive emergent writing with the class. While the teacher is noting down the weather, deliberately ask and have the children suggest where the first word in that report should go, top or bottom of the board? Will the first letter be upper case or lower case? What goes at the end of the sentence?

Create with the children sing-song repetitions/rules for using capitals, periods, and commas. Encourage the children to begin reciting these sing-songs as soon as they identify specific concepts of print in connected texts.

Model for children how, when pointing at words, they can start at the top and move from left to right. Tell the children that if there are more words to the sentence they are reading under the first line of print, they must go back to the left and under the previous line. Young children enjoy practicing this kinesthetic "return sweep." You might want to teach them to identify the need to do this by saying, "Don't fall asleep at the page" or "Time to get to the 'return-sweep' stage!" Post this saying and encourage them to singsong as they joyously take ownership of their reading.

Have even beginning readers "read" through the text to find letters they recognize in the story and then share some of the text that includes these specific letters to whet their appetite for reading.

Strategies for Promoting Letter Knowledge and Letter Formation

Engage the children in a Tale Trail game. Use a story they have already heard or read. Ask the children to circle certain letters and then reread the story, sharing the letters they have circled.

Give the children lots of opportunities to do letter sorts. Pass out word cards that have the targeted letter on them. Ask the children to come up and display their answers to questions like these about the letter, say *R*.

*R as the first letter—rose, rise, ran.
*R as the last letter—car, star, far.
*R with a t after it—start, heart, part, smart.
*R, two r's in the middle of a word—carry, sorry, starry.

Play "What's in a Name?" Select a student's name: "William." Copy it on a sentence strip. Have the children count the number of letters in the name and how many of them appear twice. Allow them to talk about which letter is uppercase and which letters are lowercase. Have the students chant the name. Then rewrite the name on another sentence strip. Cut the strip into separate letters and see if someone from the class can put the name back together correctly.

As you read a book with or to children, ask that they show you specific letters or lowercase or uppercase letters. Read the text first and encourage as many children as possible to come up and identify the letters. Use a big book and have felt and sandpaper letters available for display as well. If grade, age, and developmentally appropriate, have children then write the letter they identified themselves or even more fun, construct it using pipe cleaners, play dough or coded colored markers (different colors for upper and lower case letters).

Play "letter leap" with the children and have them look carefully at the room to identify labeled items that begin with a specific letter by "leaping" over to them and placing a large lettered placard next to them. Children who are advanced in letter formation can then be challenged to "leap" through the classroom when called upon to literally "letter" unlabeled objects.

Development of Alphabetic Knowledge in Individual Students

Researchers Laura M. Justice and Helen K. Ezell (2002) evaluated alphabetic knowledge and print awareness in preschool children from low-income households. In their post-tests, children who had participated in shared reading sessions that emphasized a print focus outperformed their control-group peers (other Head Start children) on three measures of print awareness: words in print, print recognition, and alphabetic knowledge.

Other researchers including Chaney (1994) have demonstrated a statistically significant and inverse relationship between household income and children's performance on measures of print awareness and the alphabetic principle. Lonigan (1999) found that substantial group differences existed on a variety of preliteracy tasks administered to 85 preschool children from lower- and middle-income households. The researchers looked at environmental print, print and book reading conventions, and alphabet knowledge. Results showed that preschool children from middle-income households showed significantly higher levels of skill across all print-awareness tasks in comparison with preschoolers from low income households.

Obviously, this data highlights the importance of extensive alphabetic-knowledge activities and print-awareness opportunities for some children from low income households in grades K-1 and even beyond if necessary.

Two other studies undertaken by Ezell and Justice (2000) suggested that structuring adult-child shared-book-reading interactions to include an explicit print-awareness and alphabetic-principle focus resulted in a substantial increase in children's verbal interactions with print.

This work highlights the importance not only of classroom and preschool emphasis on print-awareness and alphabetic-principle routines, but also the need for teachers to reach out to parents and to model for them these shared reading experiences so that family life can parallel the classroom experiences. Many schools currently have parent volunteers and reading buddy programs. Training of these volunteers, particularly in high-need, low-income communities is certainly warranted.

David J. Chard and Jean Osborn (1999) have reflected on the guidelines necessary for teachers to use in selecting supplemental phonics and word-recognition materials for addressing students with learning disabilities.

They note that an important way to help children with reading disabilities figure out the system underlying the printed word is leading them to understand the alphabetic principle. Children with learning disabilities (LD) in particular benefit from organized instruction that centers on letters, sounds, and the relations between sounds and letters. They also benefit from word-recognition-patterns instruction that offers practice with word families that share similar letter patterns.

Children who are LD also benefit from opportunities to apply what they are learning to the reading and re-reading of stories and other texts. Such texts contain a high proportion of words that reflect the letters, sounds, and spelling patterns the children are learning.

For special-needs children, a beginning reading program should include the following elements of alphabetic knowledge instruction:

1. A variety of alphabetic-knowledge activities in which the children learn to identify and name both uppercase and lowercase letters.

2. Games, songs, and other activities that help children learn to name the letters quickly.

3. Writing activities that encourage children to practice the letters they are writing.

4. A sensible sequence of letter introduction that can be adjusted to the needs of the children.

Sequence of Phonics Skills

- Letter Naming
    - Lowercase Letters
    - Uppercase Letters
- Letter Sounds
    - Continuous Sounds
    - Stop Sounds
    - Both Consonant and Vowel Sounds
- Short Vowels in CVC Words
- Short Vowels with Digraphs and –tch Trigraph
- Short Vowels and Consonant Blends
- Long Vowels
- Variant Vowels and Diphthongs
- R- and L- Controlled Vowels
- Multisyllabic Words

Explicit and Implicit Strategies for Teaching Phonics

Uta Frith has identified three phases that describe the progression of children's phonics learning from ages four through eight. These are as follow:

Logographic Phase

Children recognize whole words that have significance for them such as their own names or the names of stores they frequent or products that their parents buy. Examples are McDonald's, SuperValu, and the like. Strategies that nurture development in this phase include explicit labeling of classroom objects, components, furniture, and materials and showing the children's names in print as often as possible. Toward the end of this phase, children start to notice initial letters in words and the sounds they represent.

Analytic Phase

During this phase, children begin to make associations between the spelling patterns in the words they know and new words-they encounter. Children in this phase of reading development are able to generalize that hat and cat are going to be read in a similar manner because they recognize that the /at/ portions of the words are the same. This is helpful with word families and can be transferred to encoding words through many activities. Some teachers find it helpful to add word families or family houses to their word walls around the room. In this way, students can begin to make these generalizations more rapidly. As students find more complex words that fall into the family/house, they add them.

Orthographic Phase

In this phase, children recognize words almost automatically. They can rapidly identify an increasing number of words. Students are able to apply many different strategies in a seamless manner to help them decode unknown words. This may include phonics, structural analysis, syntax, semantics, and contextual clues. Students at this level are fluent readers with good prosody. They are making the shift from learning to read to reading to learn. It is a critical shift for children.

To best support these phases and the development of emergent and early readers, teachers should focus on elements of phonics-learning that help children analyze words for their letters, spelling patterns, and structural components. The children need to be involved in activities in which they use what they know about words to learn new ones.

The teacher needs to build on what the children know to introduce new spelling patterns, vowel combinations, and short and long vowel investigations. The teacher must do this and be aware that these will be reintroduced again and again as needed.

Keep in mind that children's learning of phonics and other key components of reading is not linear, but rather falls back to review and then flows forward to build new understandings.

Among suggested activities to support phonics instruction to address the needs of these three phases of phonics learning are:

(These activities have specifically been provided in detail so that the educator can study them and use them in the sample constructed response questions that have been provided at the end of the guide. Since the role of phonics in promoting reading development is so crucial, it is highly likely that a constructed response question on the certification test will focus on the use of such strategies. Therefore it is a good idea for the certification candidate to study them closely. As a bonus, the detail with which these strategies are set forth also makes them readily useful with classes the teacher is currently teaching).

Sorting Words

This activity allows children to focus closely on the specific features of words and to begin to understand the basic elements of letter-sound relationships. Start with one-syllable (monosyllabic) words. Have the children group them by their length, common letters, sound, and/or spelling pattern.

Prepare for the activity by writing ten to fifteen words on oaktag strips and place them randomly on the sentence strip holder. These words should come from a book previously shared in the classroom or a language experience chart.

Next begin to sort out the words with the children, perhaps by where a particular letter appears in a word. While the children sort the place of a particular letter in a given word, they should also be coached (or facilitated) by the teacher to recognize that sometimes a letter in the middle of the word can still be the last sound that we hear and that some letters at the end of a word are silent (such as "e").

Children should be encouraged to make their own categories and to share their own discoveries as they do the word sorts. The children's discoveries should be recorded and posted in the rooms with their names so they have ownership of their phonics learning.

Spelling Pattern Word Wall

One of the understandings emergent readers come to about a word is that if they know how to read, write, and spell one word, they can read, write, and spell many other words as well.

Create in your classroom a spelling-pattern word wall. The spelling word wall can be created by stapling a piece of 3" x 5" butcher block paper to the bulletin board. Then attach spelling-pattern cards around the border with thumbtacks so that the cards can be easily removed to use at the meeting area.

Once you decide on a spelling pattern for instruction, remove the corresponding card from the word wall. Then take a 1"x 3" piece of a contrasting color of butcher block paper and tape the card to the top end of a sheet the children will use for their investigation.

After the pattern is identified, the children can try to come up with other words that have the same spelling pattern. The teacher can write these on the spelling-pattern sheet, using a different color marker to highlight the spelling pattern within the word. The children are to add to the list until the sheet is full, which might take two days or more.

After the sheet is full, the completed spelling pattern is attached to the wall.

Letter Holder Making Words

Use a 2" x 3" piece of foam board to make a letter holder. On the front of the board, attach 16 library pockets–one for each letter from A to P. Use the back of the board to attach another 10 pockets for the rest of the alphabet.

Write the letter name on each pocket and use clear bookbinding tape to secure each row of cards with clear tape. Make twelve cards for each letter. On the front of each 2"x 6" strip, make a capital letter and on its back write that letter in lower case. Write consonants in, say, black marker and vowels in red marker.

Through use of this letter holder, children can experience how letters can be rearranged, added, or removed to make new words. They can use these cards also to focus as needed on letter sequences and to support them in recognizing spelling patterns in words.

The words you choose to use for this activity can be selected from Patricia Cunningham and Dorothy P. Hall's *Making Words* (1994). Select a word that is called the "secret word." Build toward the creation of that word through a focus on the smaller words within it. Words should be chosen that reflect the spelling patterns being studied by the class.

You can create letter holders for the children by folding up the bottom third of a used manila file folder and taping the ends to form a shallow pocket. Give them letter cards that are made of 2"x 6" oaktag. So, for example, if the secret word is bicycle, the children would be given the separate letter cards that would make up that word. The children keep the letters on the floor in front of them and only place them in the holder when they are actually making a word.

Making words should begin with making two-letter words and then progress as the individual child is ready to make larger words. The teacher tells the child which two letters will be used to make the word. After the instruction is given, the children select the correct letters and make the word in their folders. The teacher then writes the word down and the children check their letter-holder word against it. The teacher reviews the letter holders to see which children are "getting it" and then continues to build up words with more letters if the children are ready.

Word Splits

Splitting compound words. By working with compound words, children can actually experience bigger words that are often made up of smaller words. By working with five-to-ten compound words on oaktag cards, children can analyze letter-sound relationships and meaning.

Before children meet in a group, write five to ten words on oaktag cards and arrange them on the sentence-strip holder. After the words have been read, cut each of the words into its two smaller words and randomly arrange them on the sentence-strip holder. Allow the children to randomly take turns arranging the small words back into the original compound words. Also, encourage them to form new compound words. For example, if one of two original compound words is "rainbow" and the other is "dropping," the children should be able to come up with "raindrop." The new words the children come up with should be written on blank oaktag cards with the names of the children who came up with them attached. In this way the children can add to their growing bank of new words and have ownership of the words they have added.

Skill 3.3 Identify instructional methods for promoting the development of decoding and encoding skills

To decode means to change communication signals into messages. Reading comprehension requires that the reader learn the code within which a message is written and be able to decode it to get the message.

Although effective reading comprehension requires identifying words automatically (Adams, 1990, Perfetti, 1985), children do not have to be able to identify every single word or know the exact meaning of every word in a text to understand it. Indeed, Nagy (1988) says that children can read a work with a high level of comprehension even if they do not fully know as many as 15 percent of the words within a given text. Children develop the ability to decode and recognize words automatically. They then can extend their ability to decode to multi-syllabic words.

J. David Cooper (2004) and other advocates of the Balanced Literacy Approach, feel that children become literate, effective communicators and able to comprehend by learning phonics and other aspects of word identification through the use of engaging reading texts. Engaging text, as defined by the balanced literacy group, are those texts that contain highly predictable elements of rhyme, sound patterns, and plot. Researchers such as Jeanne Chall (1983) and Rudolf Flesch (1981) support a phonics-centered foundation before the use of engaging reading texts. This is at the crux of the phonics versus whole language/balanced literacy/integrated language arts, teaching of reading controversy.

It is important for the new teacher to be informed about both sides of this controversy as well as the work of theorists who attempt to reconcile these two perspectives, such as Kenneth Goodman (1994). There are powerful arguments on both sides of this controversy, and each approach works wonderfully with some students and does not succeed with others.

As far as the examinations go, all that is asked of you is the ability to demonstrate that you are familiar with these varied perspectives. If asked on a constructed response question, you need to be able to show that you can talk about teaching some aspect of reading using strategies from one or the other or a combination of both approaches.

This guide is designed to provide you with numerous strategies representing both approaches.

The working teacher can, depending on the perspective of his /her school administration and the needs of the particular children he or she serves, choose from the strategies and approaches which work best for the children concerned.

Blending Letter Sounds

Prompts for Graphophonic Cues

You said (the child's incorrect attempt). Does that match the letters you see?

If it were the word you just said (the child's incorrect attempt), what would it have to start with?

If it were the word you just said (the child's incorrect attempt), what would it have to end with?

Look at the first letter/s . . . look at the middle letter/s
. . . the last letter. . What could it be?

If you were writing (the child's incorrect attempt), what letter would you write first? What letters would go in the middle? What letters would go last?

A good strategy to use in working with individual children is to have them explain how they finally correctly identified a word that was troubling them. If prompted and habituated through one-on-one teacher/tutoring conversations, they can be quite clear about what they did to "get" the word.

If the children are already writing their own stories, the teacher might say to them: "You know when you write your own stories, you would never write any story that did not make sense. You wouldn't and probably this writer didn't either. If you read something that does make sense but doesn't match the letters, then it's probably not what the author wrote. This is the author's story, not yours right now, so go back to the word and see if you can find out the author's story. Later on, you might write your own story."

Letter Sound Correspondence and Beginning Decoding

Use this procedure for letter-sound investigations that support beginning decoding.

First, focus on a particular letter/s which you want the child to investigate. It is good to choose one from a shared text that the children are familiar with. Make certain that the teacher's directions to the children are clear and either focuses them on looking for a specific letter or listening for sounds.

Next, begin a list of words that meet the task given to the children. Use chart paper to list the words that the children identify. This list can be continued into the next week as long as the children's focus is maintained on the list. This can be easily done by challenging the children to identify a specific number of letters or sounds and "daring" them as a class to go beyond those words or sounds.

Third, continue to add to the list. Focus the children at the beginning of the day on the goal of their individually adding to the list. Give them an adhesive note (sticky pad sheet) on which they can write down the words they find. Then they can attach their newly found words with their names on them to the chart. This provides the children with a sense of ownership and pride in their letter-sounding abilities. During shared reading, discuss the children's proposed additions and have the group decide if these meet the requirements for the category. If all the children agree that they do meet the category, include the words on the chart.

Fourth, do a word sort from all the words generated and have the children put the words into categories that demonstrate similarities and differences. They can be prompted to see if the letter appeared at the beginning or end of the word. They might also be prompted to see that one sound could have two different letter representations. The children can then "box" the word differences and similarities by drawing colors established in a chart key.

Finally, before the children go off to read, ask them to look for new words in their own reading that they can now recognize because of the letter-sound relationships on their chart. During shared reading, make certain that they have time to share the words they were able to decode because of their explorations.

Strategies for Helping Students Decode Single Syllable Words that Follow Common Patterns and Multi-syllable Words

(This activity is presented in detail so it can actually be implemented with children in an intermediate classroom and also to provide detail for a potential constructed response question on a certification examination.)

The CVC phonics card game developed by Jackie Montierth, a computer teacher in South San Diego, for use with 5th and 6th grade students, is a good one to adapt to the needs of any group with appropriate modifications for age, grade level, and language needs.

The children use the vehicle of the card game to practice and enhance their use of consonants and vowels. Their fluency in this will increase their ability to decode words. Potential uses beyond whole-classroom instruction include use as part of the small group word-work component of the reading workshop and as part of cooperative team learning. This particular strategy also is particularly helpful for grade four but may be beyond English Language learners who are in a regular English Language classroom setting.

The card game works well because the practice of the content is implicit for transfer as the children continue to improve their reading skills. In addition, the card game format allows "instructional punctuation" using a student-centered high-interest exploration.

Card Design: The teacher can use the computer or use 5"x 8" index cards or actual card-deck sized oaktag cards to create a deck. For repeated use and durability, it is recommended that the deck be laminated.

The deck should consist of the following:

44 consonant cards (including the blends)

15 vowel cards (including 3 of each vowel)

5 wild cards (which can be used as any vowel)

6 final-e cards

The design of this project can also focus on particular CVC words that are part of a particular book, topic, or genre format. In advance of playing the game, children can also be directed to review the words on the word wall or other words on a word map.

Procedure:

The game is best introduced first as part of a mini-lesson with the teacher reading the rules and a pair of children demonstrating step by step when the game is played before the class for the first time. Have the children divide into pairs or small groups of no more than 4 per group. Each group needs one deck of CVC cards.

Have each group choose a dealer. The dealer shuffles the cards and deals 5 cards to each player. The remaining cards are placed face down for drawing during the play. One card is turned over to form the discard pile. Players may not show their cards to the other players. The first player to the left of the dealer looks at his/her cards and if possible, puts down three cards that make a consonant-vowel-consonant word. For more points, four cards forming a consonant-vowel-consonant word can be placed down. The player must then say the word and draw the number of cards he or she laid down. If he or she is unable to form a word, he/she draws a card from either the draw or discard pile. The player then discards one card. All players must have five cards at all times. Play moves to the left.

The game continues until one or more of the following happens:

1. There are no more cards in the draw pile

2. All players run out of cards.

3. All players cannot form a word

The winner is the player who has laid down the most cards during the game. Players may only lay down words at the beginning of their turn. Proper names may not be counted as words.

The game can also be played with teams of individuals in a small group of four or fewer competing against one another (excellent for special-needs or resource-room students). It can also be done as a whole-class activity where all the students are divided into cooperative teams or small groups who compete against one another. This second approach will work well with a heterogeneous classroom that includes special needs and/or ELL children.

Teachers of ELL students can do this game in the students' native language first and then transition it into English, facilitating native-language reading skills and second-language acquisition. They can develop their own appropriate decks to meet the vocabulary needs of their children and to complement the curriculum.

Using Phonics to Decode Words in Connected Text

Identifying New Words

Some strategies to share with children during conferences or as part of shared reading include the following prompts:

- Look at the beginning letter/s. What sound do you hear?

- Stop to think about the text or story. What word with this beginning letter would make sense here?

- Look at the book's illustrations. Do they provide you with help in figuring out the new word?

- Think of what word would make sense, sound right, and match the letters that you see. Start the sentence over, making your mouth ready to say that word.

- Skip the word, read to the end of the sentence, and then come back to the word. How does what you've read help you with the word?

- Listen to whether what you are reading makes sense and matches the letters (asking the child to self-monitor). If it doesn't make sense, see if you can correct it on your own.

- Look for spelling patterns you know from the spelling pattern wall.

- Look for smaller words you might know within the larger word.

- Read on a little, and then return to the part that confused you.

Use of Semantic and Syntactic Cues to Help Decode Words

Semantic Cues

Students will need to use their base knowledge of word meanings, semantics, to help them decipher unknown words or text as well as to clarify reading when it does not seem to make sense. Some prompts the teacher can use that will alert the children to semantic cues include the following:

- Does that sentence make sense?

- Which word in that sentence does not seem to fit?

- Why doesn't it fit?

- What word might make sense in that sentence?

Syntactic Cues

The first strategy good readers use from their own knowledge base to help determine misreading is syntactic cues. Syntactic cues use the order of words and the student's knowledge of the oral English language to help determine if what was read could be accurate. Some prompts the teacher can use to encourage and develop syntactic cues in reading include:

- You read (child's incorrect attempt). Does that sound right?

- You read (child's incorrect attempt). When we talk, do we talk that way?

- How would we say it?

- Recheck that sentence. Does it sound right the way you read it?

Specific Terminology Associated With Phonics

It is important to have a clear understanding of the terms associated with phonics. Here are some definitions that may be helpful in having a clear understanding of phonics development in children.

Phoneme—a phoneme is the smallest unit of sound in the English language. In print, phonemes are represented by the letter surrounded by slashes. So, /b/ represents the sound the letter b would make.

Morpheme—a morpheme is the smallest unit of grammar in the English language. In other words, it is the smallest unit of meaning, not just sounds.

Consonant Digraph—a consonant digraph comprises two consonants of the English language that make a unique sound, which neither makes when alone. Examples: ch, th, sh, and wh.

Consonant Blend—a consonant blend is two consonants together that retain their individual sounds. The two sounds go together in a seamless manner to produce a blended sound. Examples: st, br, and cl.

Schwa sound—the schwa sound is a vowel sound that is neutral. It typically occurs in the unaccented syllable of a word. An example would be the sound of the a at the end of the word sofa or the sound of e in the word "the." It is represented in print by an upside down e.

Development of Phonics Skills with Individual Students

In *On Solid Ground* (2000), researcher and educator Sharon Taberski said that it is much harder for children from ELL backgrounds and children from homes where other English dialects are spoken to use syntactic cues to attempt to self-correct.

These children, through no fault of their own, do not have sufficient experience hearing Standard English spoken to use this cueing system as they read. The teacher should sensitively guide them through by modeling the use of syntactic and semantic cues.

Highly proficient readers can be paired as buddy tutors for ELL or special-needs classroom members or to assist the resource room teacher during their reading time. They can use the CVC game developed by Jackie Montierth to support their peers and can even modify the game to meet the needs of classroom peers. Of course, this also offers the highly-proficient reader the opportunity to do a service-learning project while still in elementary school. It also introduces the learner to another dimension of reading, the role of the reader as trainer and recruiter of other peers into the circle of readers and writers.

If the highly proficient readers are motivated to do so or if their teachers so desire, the peer tutors can also maintain an ongoing reading progress journal for their tutees. This will be a wonderful way to realize the goals of the reading and writing workshop.

There are many different strategies to help children who are struggling with their phonics skill development. A beginning step is to identify the area of difficulty within phonics. A simple assessment to help determine the exact area of difficulty is the CORE Phonics Survey which can be downloaded free. Once the area of deficit has been identified, small group instruction can be developed around these areas to increase specific skills.

When working on specific phonics skills, it is important to utilize decodable texts. There are numerous publishers who offer a variety of different skills and texts for use in the classroom. If students continue to struggle, it may be necessary to utilize a more specific systematic and explicit phonics program. Some examples of these include *Wilson Reading, Early Intervention Reading*, and *Open Court*.

Reading and the ELL Learner

Research has shown that there is a positive and strong correlation between a child's literacy in his/her native language and his/her learning of English. The degree of native language proficiency and literacy is a strong predictor of English language development. Children who are literate and engaged readers in their native language can easily transfer their skills to a second language (e.g., English).

What this means is that teacher educators should not approach the needs of ELL learners in reading the same as they do native speakers. Those children whose families are not from a focused oral literacy and reading culture in the native language will need additional oral language rhymes, read-alouds, and singing as supports for reading skills development in both their native and the English language.

COMPETENCY 4.0   KNOWLEDGE OF READING FLUENCY DEVELOPMENT

Skill 4.1   Identify the components of reading fluency (i.e., accuracy, automaticity, rate, and prosody)

Most teachers would immediately equate fluency with the amount of words read correctly per minute. However, reading fluency is more than reading speed. Students must also demonstrate good prosody. Prosody is reading with expression, appropriate phrasing, and good inflection.

Prosody is generally considered a part of fluency and is considered as such on all rubrics used to evaluate reading fluency. Prosody is what takes otherwise robotic reading and makes it into something enjoyable to hear. Punctuation provides the cues for reading with appropriate prosody.

Modeling is one of the most effective strategies a teacher can use with students to increase their prosody skills. Teachers need to provide examples of good reading so students can hear appropriate prosody if they are to learn to distinguish between good and poor oral reading.

Prosody can only be developed by reading orally and hearing it, so any of the already-mentioned strategies for improving fluency can also be used to increase the prosody of the same students. It is important for students to clearly understand that reading is not a race. It is not about the number of words they can read correctly in a minute but rather the number of words they can read well.

While the majority of reading will occur silently in the student's head, it is necessary to take the time to practice reading aloud sometimes to ensure that students develop a feel for the natural flow of language so that this phrasing and expression will transfer into silent reading. If they are unable to do the task orally, the reading in their head may be just as robotic or choppy, which can negatively impact comprehension.

Skill 4.2   Identify appropriate instructional methods for developing reading fluency (e.g., practice with high-frequency words, timed readings, repeated readings, read-alouds, choral reading, books on tape)

Reading fluency has been shown to have strong correlations to comprehension skills, which is of course, the goal of any reading activity. Therefore, it is very important for students to have well-developed fluency skills. For students who do not naturally develop these skills, the teacher must provide strategies or activities to help them.

Choral Reading: Choral reading is an effective reading strategy to increase fluency. Students can read with a group or the teacher, with the less fluent ones building their fluency by reading with the more fluent readers. In this strategy, reading should be done at an appropriate pace and prosody.

Reader's Theatre: This strategy helps to bring drama into the classroom. Scripts are created with different parts for different characters. The students practice the script in small groups for a few days, and then they perform good, fluent reading for their peers. There is no preparation of costumes or set design, but students get to practice reading different parts.

Frequent Independent Reading: The more opportunity students have to practice reading, the more fluent they will become. The selections need to be on the appropriate level and the text should be enjoyable for the reader. Students need to have some independent reading time daily.

Paired Reading: Students are sometimes the best teachers and can provide effective instruction for their peers. Paired reading can be an excellent strategy for increasing reading fluency. Sometimes, students can graph the results of their words correct per minute (wcpm) with their peers so they can have a visual representation of their progress. There are different things to consider when pairing students, including reading level, ability to work together and stay on task, and appropriate materials for both partners to read.

Repeated Readings: Repeated reading of a passage is one of the most effective strategies for increasing oral-reading fluency. This can be done individually or in pairs. Tying graphing, paired reading, and repeated oral reading into one time frame within the classroom can provide teacher and students a specific strategy easily incorporated for a few minutes a day into the classroom routine.

COMPETENCY 5.0   KNOWLEDGE OF READING COMPREHENSION

Skill 5.1   Identify instructional methods and strategies to facilitate students' reading comprehension (e.g., summarizing, monitoring comprehension, question answering, question generating, use of graphic and semantic organizers, recognizing story structure, and use of multiple strategy instruction.)

Knowledge of Levels of Reading Comprehension (Literal, Inferential, and Evaluative) and Strategies for Promoting Comprehension of Informational/expository Texts at All Three Levels

Inferencing is a process that involves the reader making a reasonable judgment based on the information given and engages children to literally construct meaning. In order to develop and enhance this key skill in children, they might have a mini lesson where the teacher demonstrates this by reading an expository book aloud (i.e. one on skyscrapers for young children) and then demonstrates for them the following reading habits: looking for clues, reflecting on what the reader already knows about the topic, and using the clues to figure out what the author means/intends.

Identifying main ideas in an expository text can be improved when the children have an explicit strategy for identifying important information. They can make this strategy part of their everyday reading style, "walking" through the following exercises during guided reading sessions. The child should read the passage so that the topic is readily identifiable to him or her. It will be what most of the information is about. Next the child should be asked to be on the lookout for a sentence within the expository passage that summarizes the key information in the paragraph. Then the child should read the rest of the passage or excerpt in light of this information and also note which information in the paragraph is less important. The important information the child has identified in the paragraph can be used to formulate the author's main idea. The child reader may even want to use some of the author's own language in stating that idea.

Monitoring means self-clarifying: As one reads, the reader often realizes that what he or she is reading is not making sense. The reader then has to have a plan for making sensible meaning out of the excerpt. Cooper and other balanced literacy advocates have a stop and think strategy which they use with children. The child reflects, "Does this make sense to me?" When the child concludes that it does not, the child then either re-reads, reads ahead in the text, looks up unknown words, or asks for help from the teacher.

What is important about monitoring is that some readers ask these questions and try these approaches without ever being explicitly taught them in school by a teacher. However, these strategies need to be explicitly modeled and practiced under the guidance of the teacher by most, if not all child readers.

Summarizing engages the reader in pulling together into a cohesive whole the essential bits of information within a longer passage or excerpt of text. Children can be taught to summarize informational or expository text by following these guidelines. First they should look at the topic sentence of the paragraph or the text and ignore the trivia. Then they should search for information which has been mentioned more than once and make sure it is included only once in their summary. Find related ideas or items and group them under a unifying heading. Search for and identify a main idea sentence. Finally, put the summary together using all these guidelines.

Generating questions can motivate and enhance children's comprehension of reading in that they are actively involved. The following guidelines will help children generate meaningful questions that will trigger constructive reading of expository texts. First children should preview the text by reading the titles and subheadings. Then they should also look at the illustrations and the pictures. Finally they should read the first paragraph. These first previews should yield an impressive batch of specific questions.

Next, children should get into a Dr. Seuss mode and ask themselves a "THINK" question. Make certain that the children write down the question. Then have them read to find important information to answer their "think" question. Ask that they write down the answer they found and copy the sentence or sentences where they found the answer. Also have them consider whether, in light of their further reading through the text, their original question was a good one or not.

Once the children have answered their original "think" question, have them generate additional ones and then find their answers and judge whether these questions were "good" ones in light of the text.

Reading comprehension is the ultimate goal of any reading activity. As students progress through the grades, it becomes more important they be able to read factual information in the content areas, like science and social studies, with efficiency and solid comprehension. So much learning and teaching occurs through the use of texts, students need to be taught specific methods to gain comprehension from these books.

Typically, content area texts are nonfiction in nature and due to this fact, students can use specific strategies to help gain more insight. First, students can begin by analyzing the text itself. Looking at the organization and layout of the text can provide cues the student can use to filter non-pertinent information, ideas about specific places in the text the answers sought may be located and additional ways to connect information to prior knowledge, thus making it more meaningful in nature. This analysis of text structure is a critical skill for students to understand.

Additionally, the texts generally will have large amounts of information to convey. This can be overwhelming to students. Students will need some sort of organizational tool to take in the information necessary. Using summarizing skills, the students can take this large amount of information and put it into smaller more manageable pieces.

Another tool which may be beneficial to students is **semantic mapping**. In semantic mapping, the student begins to make the connections between the information they already know about the topic and the new information they are learning. It is typically a more graphic representation of the information, but built upon words and ideas. It generally increases knowledge and improves vocabulary development.

Other types of **graphic organizers** will also help students to acquire the information from content area texts. Mind mapping is a strategy that combines pictures and words to convey the underlying concepts of what was read. There are many different types of graphic organizers a teacher can use to support students. However, students need to be able to transfer these skills and knowledge, themselves, as well. In other words, they need to be able to create their own graphic organizers to meet the needs of the task before them. This will be the most efficient and most meaningful strategy as it is unique to them.

Skill 5.2   Identify instructional methods and strategies to increase vocabulary acquisition (e.g., word analysis, choice of words, context clues, multiple exposures)

Development of Word Analysis Skills and Strategies, Including Structural Analysis

Structural analysis is a process of examining the words in the text for meaningful word units (affixes, base words, inflected endings). There are six types of words that can be analyzed using structural-analysis strategies. They include:

1. Common prefixes or suffixes added to a known word ending with a consonant
2. Adding the suffix -ed to words that end with consonants
3. Compound words
4. Adding endings to words that end with the letter e
5. Adding endings to words that end with the letter y
6. Adding affixes to multisyllabic words

When teaching and using structural-analysis procedures in the primary grades, teachers should remember to make sound decisions regarding which to introduce and teach. Keeping in mind the number of primary words in which each affix appears and how similar they are will help the teacher make the instructional process smoother and more valuable to the students.

Adding affixes to words can be started when students are able to read a list of one-syllable words by sight at a rate of approximately twenty words correct per minute. At the primary level, there is a recommended sequence for introducing affixes. The steps in this process are as follow:
:

- Start by introducing the affix in the letter-sound correspondence format.

- Practice the affix in isolation for a few days.

- Provide words for practice that contain the affix (word lists, flash cards, etc.)

- Move from word lists to passage reading that includes words with the affix (and some from the word lists/flash cards).

1. Word Study Group

This involves the teacher taking time to meet with children from grades 3-6 in a small group of no more than 6 children for a word study session. Taberski (2000) suggests that this meeting take place next to the Word Wall. The children selected for this group are those who need to focus more on the relationship between spelling patterns and consonant sounds.

It is important that this not be a formalized traditional reading group that meets at a set time each week or biweekly. Rather the group should be spontaneously formed by the teacher based on the teacher's quick inventory of the selected children's needs at the start of the week. Taberski has templates in her book of *Guided Reading Planning Sheets.* These sheets are essentially targeted word and other skills sheets with his or her written dated observations of children who are in need of support to develop a given skill.

The teacher should try to meet with this group for at least two consecutive twenty-minute periods daily. Over those two meetings, the teacher can model a making-words activity. Once the teacher has modeled making words the first day, the children will then make their own words. On the second day, the children would "sort" their words.

Other topics for a word-study group within the framework of the balanced-literacy approach that Taberski advocates are inflectional endings, prefixes and suffixes, and/or common spelling patterns. These are covered later in this chapter.

It should be noted that this activity would be classified by theorists as a structural-analysis activity because the structural components (i.e. prefixes, suffixes, and spelling patterns) of the words are being studied.

2. Discussion Circles

Cooper (2004) believes that children should not be "taught" vocabulary and structural-analysis skills. Flesch and E.D. Hirsch, who are key theorists of the phonics approach and advocates of cultural literacy—a term coined by and associated with E. D. Hirsch), believe that specific vocabulary words at various grade and age levels need to be mastered and must be explicitly taught in schools. As far as J. David Cooper is concerned, all the necessary and meaningful (for the child and ultimately adult reader) vocabulary can't possibly be taught in schools (no apologies to Hirsch). To Cooper, it is far more important that the children be made aware of and become interested in learning words by themselves. Cooper feels that through the child's reading and writing, he or she develops a love for and a sense of "ownership" of words. All of Cooper's suggested structural-analysis word strategies are therefore designed to foster the child's love of words and a desire to "own" more of them through reading and writing.

Discussion circles is an activity that fits nicely into the balanced-literacy lesson format. After the children conclude a particular text, Cooper suggests that they respond to the book in discussion circles. Among the prompts, the teacher-coach might suggest that the children focus on words of interest they encounter in the text. These can also be words they heard when the text was read aloud. Children can be asked to share something funny or upsetting or unusual about the words they have read. When children's response to words is the center of the discussion circle, peers become more interested in word study.

3. Banking, Booking, and Filing It: Making Words My Own

Children can literally realize the goal of making words their own and exploring word structures by creating concrete objects or displays that demonstrate the words they own. Children can create and maintain files of words they have learned or are interested in learning.

The files can be categorized by the children according to their own interests. They should be encouraged to develop files using science, history, physical education, fine arts, dance, and technology content. Newspapers and web resources recommended by the teacher are excellent sources for such words. In addition, this provides the teacher with the opportunity to instruct the child in appropriate age- and grade-level research skills. Even children in grades 2 and 3 can begin simplified bibliographies and webliographies for their "found" words. Children can learn how to annotate and note the page of a newspaper, book, or URL for a particular word.

They can also copy down the word as it appears in the text (print or electronic). If appropriate, the child can place the words found for a given topic or content in an actual bank of the child's own making. The words can be printed on cards. This allows for differentiated word study and appeals to those children who are kinesthetic and spatial learners. Of course, children can also choose to create their own word books that include their specialized vocabulary along with descriptions of how they identified or hunted down their words. Richard Scarry, watch out! Scarry books can be anchor books to inspire this structural-analysis activity.

ELL learners can share their accounts in their native language first and then translate these accounts into English (with the help of the teacher) with both the native-language and the English-language versions of the word exploration posted.

4. Write out Your Words, Write with Your Words

Ownership of words can be demonstrated by having the children use them as part of their writings. The children can author a procedural narrative (a step-by-step description) of how they went about their word searches to compile the words they found for any of the activities. If the children are in grades K-1, or if the children are struggling readers and writers, their procedural narratives can be dictated. Then they can be posted by the teacher.

Children with special needs may model a word box on a specific holiday theme, genre, or science/social-studies topic with the teacher. Initially this can be done as a whole class. As the children become more confident, they can work with peers or with a paraprofessional to create their own individual or small team/pair word boxes.

Special needs children can create a storyboard with the support of a paraprofessional, their teacher, or a resource specialist. They can also narrate their story of how they found the words using a tape recorder.

5. Word-Study Museum within the Classroom

This strategy is presented in detail so it can be used by the teachers within their own classrooms. In addition, the way the activity is described and the mention at the end of the description of how the activity can address family literacy, ELL, and special-needs-children's talents, provides an example of other audiences a teacher should consider in curriculum design.

Almost every general education teacher and reading specialist will have to differentiate instruction to address the needs of special education and ELL learners. Family or shared literacy is a major component of all literacy instruction.

Children can create either single or multiple exhibits, museum style, within their classrooms celebrating their word study. They can build actual representations of the type of study they have done including word trees (made out of cardboard or foam board), elaborate word boxes and games, word-history timelines or murals, and word study maps. They can develop online animations, Kids Spiration graphic organizers, quick movies, digital photo essays, and PowerPoint presentations to share the word they have identified. The classroom or the gym or cafeteria can be transformed into a gallery space. Children can author brochure descriptions for their individual, team, or class exhibits. Some children can volunteer to be tour guides or docents for the experience. Other children can work to create a banner for the museum. The children can name the museum, themselves, and send out invitations to its opening. Invitations can be sent to parents, community, staff members, and peer or younger classes. Depending on their age and grade level, children can also develop interactive games and quizzes focused on particular exhibits. An artist or a team of class artists can design a poster for the exhibit, while other children may choose to build the exhibits. Another small group can work on signage and a catalogue or register of objects within the exhibit. Greeters who will welcome parents and peers to the exhibit can be trained and can develop their own scripts.

If the children are in grades 4-6, they can also develop their own visitor feedback forms and design word-themed souvenirs. The whole museum within the school or classroom can be captured digitally or with a regular camera. The record of this event can be hung near the word walls. Of course, the children can use many of their newly recognized and owned words to describe the event.

The word-study-museum activity can be used with either a phonics-based or a balanced-literacy approach. It promotes additional writing, researching, discussing, and reading about words.

It is also an excellent family-literacy strategy in that families can develop their own word exhibits at home. This activity can also support and celebrate learners with disabilities. It can be presented in dual languages by children who are ELL learners and fluent in more than a single language.

Relationship between Word-Analysis Skills and Reading Comprehension

The explicit teaching of word analysis requires that the teacher pre-select words from a given text for vocabulary learning. These words should be chosen based on the storyline and main ideas of the text. The educator may even want to create a story map for a narrative text or develop a graphic organizer for an expository text. Once the story mapping and/or graphic organizing have been done, the educator can compile a list of words that relate to the storyline and/or main ideas.

The number of words that require explicit teaching should only be two or three. If the number is higher than that, the children need guided reading and the text needs to be broken down into smaller sections for teaching. When broken down into smaller sections, each text section should only have two to three words that need explicit teaching. Some researchers, including Tierney and Cunningham, believe that a few words should be taught as a means of improving comprehension. It is up to the educator whether the vocabulary selected for teaching needs review before reading, during reading, or after reading.

Introduce vocabulary BEFORE READING if any of the following is true:

- Children are having difficulty constructing meaning on their own. Children themselves have previewed the text and indicated words they want to know.

- The teacher has seen that there are words within the text that are keys to reading comprehension

- The text, itself, in the judgment of the teacher, contains concepts that will be difficult for the children to grasp.

Introduce vocabulary DURING READING if the following are true:

- Children are already doing guided reading.

- The text has words that are crucial to its comprehension and the children will have trouble comprehending it if they are not helped with the text.

Introduce vocabulary AFTER READING if any of the following is true:

- The children themselves have shared words that they have found difficult or interesting.

- The children need to expand their vocabulary

- The text itself is one that is particularly suited for vocabulary building.

Strategies to support word analysis and enhance reading comprehension include the following:

- Use of a graphic organizer such as a word map

- Semantic mapping

- Semantic feature analysis

- Hierarchical and linear arrays

- Preview in context

- Contextual redefinition

- Vocabulary self-collection*

*Note: the terms used in this section are in the Glossary.)

Identification of Common Morphemes, Prefixes, and Suffixes

The purpose of this aspect of vocabulary development is to help children look for structural elements within words that they can use independently to help them determine meaning.

Some teachers choose to teach structural analysis directly, in particular those who teach by following the phonics-centered approach to reading. Other teachers, who follow the balanced-literacy approach, introduce the structural components as parts of mini lessons that are focused on the students' reading and writing.

Structural analysis of words as defined by J. David Cooper (2004) involves the study of significant word parts. This analysis can help the child with pronunciation and constructing meaning.

The terms listed below are generally recognized as the key structural-analysis components.

Root Words

This is a word from which another word is developed. The second word can be said to have its "root" in the first, such as *vis, to see,* in visor or vision. This structural component can be illustrated by a tree with roots to display the meaning for children. Children may also want to literally construct root words using cardboard trees to create word-family models.

ELL learners can construct these models for their native-language root-word families, as well as for the English language words they are learning. ELL students in the 5th and 6th grades may even appreciate analyzing the different root structures for contrasts and similarities between their native language and English.

Learners with special needs can work in small groups or individually with a paraprofessional on building root word models.

Base Words

These are stand-alone linguistic units that cannot be deconstructed or broken down into smaller words. For example, in the word *re-tell*, the base word is "tell."

Contractions

These are shortened forms of two words in which a letter or letters have been deleted and replaced by an apostrophe.

Prefixes

These are beginning units of meaning that can be added (the vocabulary word for this type of structural adding is "affixed") to a base or root word. They cannot stand alone. They are also sometimes known as "bound morphemes" meaning that they cannot stand alone as a base word. Examples are *re-, un-,* and *mis-*.

Suffixes

These are ending units of meaning which can be "affixed" or added to the ends of root or base words. Suffixes transform the original meanings of base and root words. Like prefixes, they are also known as "bound morphemes" because they cannot stand alone as words. Examples are *-less, -ful,* and *-tion.*

Compound Words

These occur when two or more base words are connected to form a new word. The meaning of the new word is in some way connected with that of the base word. Examples are *firefighter, newspaper,* and *pigtail.*

Inflectional Endings

These are suffixes that impart a new meaning to the base or root word. These endings in particular change the gender, number, tense, or form of the base or root words. Just like other suffixes, these are also termed "bound morphemes." Examples are *-s* or *-ed*.

Comments

Definitions are included because the structural-analysis components are explicitly taught in schools that advocate the phonics-centered approach and are also incorporated into the word-work component of the schools that advocate the balanced-literacy approach for instruction.

Definition questions, that is, multiple-choice questions that have only a single right answer, test whether the teacher candidate has memorized appropriate terminology. They constitute no less than 15% of the multiple-choice questions on the test. Therefore, by taking the time to learn these easy definitions, you may improve your scores.

Some of these activities are presented in detail to help answer the constructed response questions of the test.

Knowledge of Greek and Latin Roots That Form English Words

Knowledge of Greek and Latin roots that comprise English words can measurably enhance children's reading skills and can also enrich their writing.

Word Webs

Sharon Taberski (2000) does not advocate teaching Greek and Latin derivatives in the abstract to young children. However, when she comes across specific Greek and Latin roots while reading to children, she uses that opportunity to introduce children to these rich resources.

For example, during readings on rodents (a favorite of first and second graders), Taberski draws her class's attention to the fact that beavers gnaw at things with their teeth. She then connects the "dent" root or derivative to other words the children are familiar with or have experienced in their lives.The children then volunteer "*dentist," "dental," "denture."* Taberski begins to place these in a graphic organizer or word web.

When she has tapped the extent of the children's prior knowledge of "dent" words, she shares with them the fact that *dens/dentis* is the Latin word for teeth. Then she introduces the word "indent," which she has already previewed with them as part of their conventions of print study. She helps them to see that the "indenting" of the first line of a paragraph can even be related to the "teeth" Latin root in that it looks like a "print" bite was taken out of the paragraph.

Taberski displays the word web in the word wall chart section of her room. The class is encouraged throughout, say, a week's time to look for other words to add to the web. Taberski stresses that for her, as an elementary teacher of reading and writing, the key element of the Greek and Latin word-root web activity is the children's coming to understand that if they know what a Greek or Latin word root means, they can use that knowledge to figure out what other words mean.

She feels the key concept is to model and demonstrate for children how fun and fascinating Greek and Latin root study can be.

Greek and Latin Roots Word Webs with an Assist from the World Wide Web

Older children in grades 3-6 can build on this initial print activity by searching online for additional words with a particular Greek or Latin root which has been introduced in class.

They can easily do this in a way that authentically ties in with their own interests and experiences by reading reviews for a book that has been a read aloud online or by just reading the summaries of the day's news and printing out those words that appear in the stories online that share the root discussed.

The children can be encouraged to circle these instances of their Latin or Greek root and also to document the exact date and URL for the citation. These can be posted as part of their own online web in the word-wall section study area. If the school or class has a website or webpage, the children can post this data there as a special Greek and Latin root-word page.

Expanding the concept of the Greek and Latin word web from the printed page to the world wide web nicely inculcates in the child the habits of lifelong reading and researching online. This beginning expository research will serve them well in intermediate-level content work and beyond.

Use of Syllabification as a Word Identification Strategy

Strategy: Clap Hands, Count Those Syllables as They Come!! (Taberski, 2000)

The objective of this activity is for children to understand that every syllable in a polysyllabic word can be studied for its spelling patterns in the same way that monosyllabic words are studied for their spelling patterns.

The easiest way for the K-3 teacher to introduce this activity to the children is to share a familiar poem from the poetry chart (or to write out a familiar poem on a large experiential chart).

First, the teacher reads the poem with the children. As they are reading it aloud, the children clap the beats of the poem and the teacher uses a colored marker to place a tic (/) above each syllable.

Next, the teacher takes letter cards and selects one of the polysyllabic words from the poem, which the children have already "clapped" out.

The children use letter cards to spell that word on the sentence-strip holder or it can be placed on a felt board or up against a window on display. Together the children and teacher divide the letters into syllables and place blank letter cards between the syllables. The children identify spelling patterns they know.

Finally, and as part of continued small-group syllabification study, the children identify other polysyllabic words they clapped out from the poem. They make up the letter combinations of these words. Then they separate them into syllables with blank letter cards between the syllables.

Children who require special support in syllabification can be encouraged to use many letter cards to create a large butcher-paper syllabic representation of the poem or at least a few lines of the poem (in letter cards with spaces). They can be told that this is for use as a teaching tool for others. In this way, they authenticate their study of syllabification with a real product that can actually be referenced by peers.

Techniques for Identifying Compound Words

The teaching of compound words should utilize structural-analysis techniques. (See above section on structural analysis.)

Here are some other strategies for helping students to identify and read compound words.

- Use songs and actions to help children understand the concept that compound words are two smaller words joined together to make one bigger word

- Use games like concentration, memory, and go fish for students to practice reading compound words

- Use word sorts to have students distinguish between compound words and non-examples of compound words

Identification of Homographs

Homographs are words that are spelled the same but have different meanings. A subgroup within this area includes words that are spelled the same, have different meanings, and are pronounced differently. Some examples of homographs include:
- Lie
- Tear
- Bow

- Fair
- Bass

Teaching homographs can be interesting and fun for the students. Incorporate them into passages where the students can use context clues to decipher the different meanings of the homographs. Games are also a good strategy to help students understand multiple-meaning words. Jokes and riddles are usually based on homographs, and students love to make collections or books of these.

Semantic Feature Analysis: This technique for enhancing vocabulary skills by using semantic cues is based on the research of Johnson and Pearson (1984) and Anders and Bos (1986). Young children will set up a feature-analysis grid of various subject-content words, which is an outgrowth of their discussion about these words.

For instance, Cooper (2004) includes a sample of a Semantic Features Analysis Grid for Vegetables. .

Vegetables	Green	Have Peels	Eat Raw	Seeds
Carrots	-	+	+	-
Cabbage	+	-	+	-

Note: that the use of the + for yes, - for no, and possible use for + and − both if a vegetable like squash could be both green and yellow.

Teachers of children in grade one and beyond can design their own semantic analysis grids to meet their students' needs and to align with the topics the students are learning. Select a category or class of words (could be planets, rodent family members, winter words, weather words).

On the left side of the grid list at least three or more items that fit this category. The number of actual items listed will depend on the age and grade level of the children with three or four items for K-1 and up to 10-15 for grades 5 and 6. Brainstorm with the children or if better suited to the class, the teacher may list his/her own features that the items have in common. As can be noted from the example excerpted from *Cooper's Literacy: Helping Children Construct Meaning* (2004), common features such as vegetables' green color, peels, and seeds are usually fairly easy to identify.

Show the children how to insert the notations +, -, and even ? (If they are not certain) on the grid. The teacher might also explore with the children the possibility that an item could get both a + and a -. For example, a vegetable like broccoli might be eaten cooked or raw depending on taste and squash can be green or yellow.

Whatever the length of the grid when first presented to the children (perhaps as a semantic-cue lesson in and of itself tied to a text being read in class), make certain that creating and filling out the grid are not the end of the activity.

Children can use it as a model for developing their own semantic-features grids and share them with the whole class. Child-developed grids can become part of a word-work center in the classroom or even be published in a word-study games book by the class as a whole. Such a publication can be shared with parents during open school week and evening visits and with peer classes.

Contextual Redefinition

This strategy encourages children to use context more effectively by presenting them with sufficient context *before* they begin reading. It models for the children the use of contextual clues to make informed guesses about word meanings.

To apply this strategy, the teacher should first select unfamiliar words for teaching. No more than two or three words should be selected for direct teaching. The teacher should then write a sentence in which there are sufficient clues supplied for the child to successfully figure out the meaning. Among the types of context clues the teacher can use are compare/contrast, synonyms, and direct definition.

Then the teacher should present the words only on the experiential chart or as letter cards. Have the children pronounce the words. As they pronounce them, challenge them to come up with a definition for each word. After more than one definition is offered, encourage the children to decide as a whole group what the definition is. Write down their agreed-upon definition with no comment as to its accurate meaning.

Then share with the children the contexts (sentences the teacher wrote with the words and explicit context clues). Ask that the children read the sentences aloud. Then have them come up with a definition for each word. Make certain that as they present their definitions, the teacher does not comment. Ask that they justify their definitions by making specific references to the context clues in the sentences. As the discussion continues, direct the children's attention to their previously-agreed-upon definition of the word. Facilitate their discussing the differences between their guesses about the word when they saw only the word itself and their guesses about the word when they read it in context. Finally, have the children check their use of context skills to correctly define the word by using a dictionary.

Development of Word-Analysis Skills by Individual Students

This type of direct teaching of word definitions is useful when the children have dictionary skills and the teacher is aware of the fact that there are not sufficient clues about the words in the context to help the students define them. In addition, struggling readers and students from ELL backgrounds may benefit tremendously from being walked through this process that highly proficient and successful readers apply automatically

By using this strategy, the teacher can also "kid watch" and note the students' prior knowledge as they guess the word in isolation. The teacher can also actually witness and hear how various students use context skills.

Through their involvement in this strategy, struggling readers gain a feeling of community as they experience the ways in which their struggles and guesses resonate with other peers' responses to the text.

Andrew Biemiller (2003): "Knowledge of vocabulary will not guarantee vocabulary success, but lack of vocabulary knowledge can ensure failure."

Skill 5.3   Identify instructional methods and strategies for developing critical thinking (e.g., analysis, synthesis, evaluation)

Techniques critical for FCAT success include the ability to analyze, synthesize, and evaluate information. The students should practice the following activities:

Define author's purpose. Is it to inform, to entertain, or to persuade? Student activity: a title can often set the tone of the passage. Reading newspaper headings is one way to practice determining the author's purpose.

Cause and effect. Cause and effect may occur in fiction, nonfiction, poetry, and plays. Sometimes one cause will have single or multiple effects. Other times, multiple causes lead to a single effect. Creating cause-and-effect diagrams helps you identify these components.

Chronological order. Recognizing the order of events in a selection. A text that is chronologically organized features a sequence of events that unfold over a period of time. Student activity: fead a passage to the students then complete a timeline by matching the major events to their corresponding dates.

Graphic organizers. Graphic organizers help readers think critically about an idea, concept, or story by pulling out the main idea and supporting details. These pieces of information can then be depicted graphically through the use of connected geometric shapes. Readers who develop this skill can use it to increase their reading comprehension. An example of a graphic organizer is below.

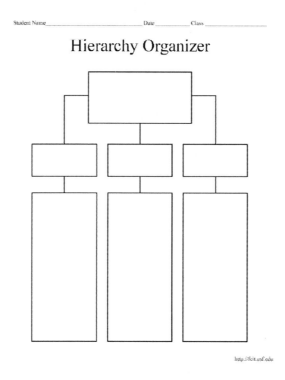

Student Name_____ Date_____ Class_____

Hierarchy Organizer

http://fcit.usf.edu

Probable passage. This is a strategy to improve comprehension, develop an awareness of story structure, and increase vocabulary development.

Student activity: prepare to read a story to the students; but before you read, hand out a chart similar to the following one or put it on the board. Ask the students: "Can you predict the story you will be reading? Use the vocabulary words from your story frame to complete the probable passage by placing words into the blanks."

Vocabulary:
Zeus
recognized
pardoned
arena
forest
bound
freed
capture
lion

Setting: _____
Characters: _____
Problem: _____
Solution: _____
Ending: _____

Selective underlining. Selective underlining is an effective tool for enhancing the recall of facts. It can be used both for initial reading and response and as a reference when studying for tests. Have students identify the main idea of various short stories and articles.

Story mapping. Story mapping is a technique used after a story has been read. It includes identifying the main elements and categorizing the main events in sequential order. A graphic representation is often used to illustrate the story structure and sequence of events.

COMPETENCY 6.0   Knowledge of content area reading and learning

Skill 6.1   Identify instructional approaches and strategies for developing and using content area vocabulary

The Relationship between Oral and Written Vocabulary Development and Reading Comprehension

Students hear and understand many words that they do not use themselves, an indication that there are two sets of words in their vocabularies. The *productive vocabulary* is the set of words they know the meanings of when they speak or read orally. *Recognition vocabulary* is the set that a student can assign meanings to when listening or reading. The latter is typically much larger than the former. The *recognition vocabulary* is developed through reading and listening, and over time many words from that set will move into the *productive vocabulary.* The goal of the teacher, then, should be to help students to enlarge both of these vocabularies as they move through the Middle School years.

There is a clear correspondence between the size of one's vocabulary and comprehension. Middle School students will be asked, probably for the first time, to read and comprehend text-book assignments. There are skills associated with developing comprehension that can be taught, but none is more important than the development of the two kinds of vocabulary. From the cradle to the grave, our vocabularies constantly grow because of our involvement with the world around us. All of us have expanded our own vocabularies enormously with the advent of computers and our use of them. A mouse is no longer just a mouse. We all know the difference between storing information and sending it or even deleting it, for that matter. These and the hundreds of other words that have entered our vocabularies in the past few years are essential to our functioning in the world as it is at the present moment.

What happens with middle schoolers is very much like that. They are ready to learn many new concepts, explore worlds they never knew existed, and move toward citizenship in a country they need to be able to navigate. What this means is that during the Middle School years, their vocabularies must be growing at a very rapid rate—not only the *recognition* but also *the productive* vocabulary.

The National Reading Panel has put forth the following conclusions about vocabulary instruction.

- ✓ There is a need for direct instruction of vocabulary items required for a specific text.
- ✓ Repetition and multiple exposure to vocabulary items are important. Students should be given items that will be likely to appear in many contexts.

- ✓ Learning in rich contexts is valuable for vocabulary learning. Vocabulary words should be those that the learner will find useful in many contexts. When vocabulary items are derived from content learning materials, the learner will be better equipped to deal with specific reading matter in content areas.
- ✓ Vocabulary tasks should be restructured as necessary. It is important to be certain that students fully understand what is asked of them in the context of reading rather than focusing only on the words to be learned.
- ✓ Vocabulary learning is effective when it entails active engagement in learning tasks.
- ✓ Computer technology can be used effectively to help teach vocabulary.
- ✓ Vocabulary can be acquired through incidental learning. Much of a student's vocabulary will have to be learned in the course of doing things other than explicit vocabulary learning. Repetition, richness of context, and motivation may also add to the efficacy of incidental learning of vocabulary.
- ✓ Dependence on a single vocabulary instruction method will not result in optimal learning.

The Panel found that a variety of methods was used effectively with emphasis on multimedia aspects of learning, richness of context in which words are to be learned, and the number of exposures to words that learners receive.

The Panel also found that a critical feature of effective classrooms is the instruction of specific words that includes lessons and activities where students apply their vocabulary knowledge and strategies to reading and writing. Included in the activities were discussions where teachers and students talked about words and their features and strategies for understanding unfamiliar words.

There are many methods for directly and explicitly teaching words. In fact, the Panel found twenty-one methods that have been found effective in research projects. Many emphasize the underlying concept of a word and its connections to other words such as semantic mapping and diagrams that use graphics. The keyword method uses words and illustrations that highlight salient features of meaning. Visualizing or drawing a picture either by the student or by the teacher was found to be effective. Many words cannot be learned in this way, of course, so it should be used as only one method among others. Effective classrooms provide multiple ways for students to learn and interact with words. The Panel also found that computer-assisted activities can have a very positive role in the development of vocabulary.

Strategies for Promoting Oral Language Development and Language Comprehension

Read-Alouds (This is the corner piece of the balanced-literacy approach for teaching reading. Therefore it is advised that the teacher candidate and new teacher read this material carefully. This may well appear as an essay topic in the Constructed Response section).

Comments:

Within the context of the balanced-literacy approach and the Literacy Block, the read-aloud is part of the whole-class activities. The book selected should be one taken from the classroom library that is appropriate for a read-aloud. Before reading the book to the class, the teacher needs to be familiar with it. The teachers should also "plan" or at least "know" what nuances of content, style, rhythm, and vocabulary will be emphasized in the reading.

In addition, specifically for the younger grades, the teacher should select a text that also enhances the development of phonemic awareness. This might include a text that can be used to teach rhyming, alliteration, or poetry.

Sometimes, read-aloud texts are selected for their tie-ins with the science, social studies, and mathematics curriculum.

Generally, teachers aim to teach one strategy during the read-aloud, which the children will practice in small groups or independently. Among these strategies for the first grader could be print strategies and talking about books.

As the teacher reads aloud, voice quality should highlight enjoyment of the read-aloud and involvement with its text. Often in a balanced-literacy classroom, the teacher reads from a specially decorated reader's chair as do the guest readers. This chair's decorativeness, complete with comfortable throw pillows or rocking-chair-style frame, is meant to set an atmosphere that will promote the children's engagement in and love for lifelong reading.

The balanced literacy approach also advocates that teachers select books children will enjoy reading aloud. Particularly accessible texts for the elementary school classroom read-alouds are collections of poetry.

Teachers must allow time for discussion during and after each read-aloud period. After the children have made comments, the teacher should also talk about the reading.

The Relationship between Oral Vocabulary and the Process of Identifying and Understanding Written Words

One way to explore the relationship between oral vocabulary and the comprehension of written words is through the use of oral records.

In *On Solid Ground: Strategies for Teaching Reading K-3*, Sharon Taberski (2000) discusses how oral reading records can be used by the K-3 teacher to assess how well children are using cueing systems. She notes that the running record format can also show visual depictions for the teacher of how the child "thinks" as the child reads. The notation of miscues in particular shows how a child "walks through" the reading process. They indicate if and in what ways the child may require "guided" support in understanding the words he or she reads aloud. Taberski notes that when children read, they need to think about several things at once. First, they must consider whether what they are reading makes sense (semantic or meaning cues). Next, they must know whether their reading "sounds right" in terms of Standard English (syntactic and structural cues). Third, they have to weigh whether their oral language actually and accurately matches the letters the words represent (visual or graphophonic cues).

In taking the running record and having the opportunity first-hand to listen to the children talk about the text, the teacher can analyze the relationship between the child's oral language and word comprehension. Information from the running record provides the teacher with a road map for differentiated cueing system instruction.

For example, when a running record is taken, a child often makes a mistake but then self-corrects. The child may select from various cueing systems when he or she self-corrects. These include: "M" for meaning, "S" for syntax, and "V" for visual. The use of a visual cue means that the child is drawing on his or her knowledge of spelling patterns. Of course, Taberski cautions that any relationship between oral language and comprehension that the teacher draws from an examination of the oral-reading records must be drawn using a series of three or more of the child's oral reading records taken over time, not just once.

A teacher can review children's running records over time to note their pattern of miscues and which cues they have the greatest tendency to use in their self-corrections. Whichever cueing system the children use to the greatest extent, it is necessary for the teacher to offer support in also using the other cueing systems to construct correct meaning. Taberski suggests that while assessing running records to determine the relationship between oral language and meaning, the children read from "just right" books.

Biemiller's (2003) research documents that children entering 4th grade with significant vocabulary deficits increasingly demonstrate reading-comprehension problems. Evidence shows that these children do not catch up; rather, they continue to fall behind.

Word Map Strategy

This strategy is useful for children grades 3-6 and beyond. The target group of children for this strategy includes those who need to improve their independent vocabulary-acquisition abilities. The strategy is essentially teacher-directed learning where children are "walked through" the process. They are helped by the teacher to identify the type of information that makes a definition. They are also assisted in using context clues and background understanding to construct meaning.

The word-map graphic organizer is the tool teachers use to complete this strategy with children. Word-map templates are available online from the Houghton Mifflin web site and from www.readwritethink.org, the website of the NCTE (see webliography section). The word map helps children visually represent the elements of a given concept.

The children's literal articulation of the concept can be prompted by three key questions: What is it? What is it like? What are some examples?

For instance, the word "oatmeal" might yield a word map with "What?": in a rectangular box a hot cereal you eat in the morning; "What is it like?": hot, mushy, salty; "What are some examples?": instant oatmeal you make in a minute, apple-flavor oatmeal, Irish Oatmeal.

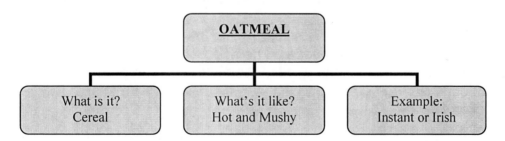

The procedure to be used in sharing this strategy with children is to select three concepts the children are familiar with. Then show them the template of a word map. Tell them that the three questions asked on the map and the boxes to fill in beneath them helps readers and writers to see what they need to know about a word. Next, help the children to complete at least two word maps for two of the three concepts that were pre-selected. Then have the children select a concept of their own to map either independently or in a small group. As the final task for this first part of the strategy, have the children, in teams or individually, write a definition for at least one of the concepts using the key things about it listed on the map. Have the children share these definitions aloud and talk about how they used the word maps to help them with the definitions.

For the next part of this strategy, the teacher should pick up an expository text or a textbook the children are already using to study mathematics, science, or social studies. The teacher should either locate a short excerpt where a particular concept is defined or use the content to write model passages of definition on his/her own.

After the passages are selected or authored, the teacher should duplicate them. Then they should be distributed to the children along with blank word-map templates. The children should be asked to read each passage and then to complete the word map for the concept in each passage. Finally, have the children share the word maps they have developed for each passage. Give them a chance to explain how they used the word in the passage to help them fill out their word map. End by telling them that the three components of the concept—class, description, example—are only three of the many components that could be chosen for any given concept.

This strategy has assessment potential because the teacher can literally see how the students understand specific concepts by looking at their maps and hearing their explanations. The maps the students develop on their own demonstrate whether they have really understood the concepts in the passages. This strategy serves to ready students for inferring word meanings on their own. By using the word-map strategy, children develop concepts of what they need to know to begin to figure out an unknown word on their own. It assists the children in grades 3 and beyond to connect prior knowledge with new knowledge.

This word-map strategy can be adapted by the teacher to suit the specific needs and goals of instruction. Illustrations of the concept and the comparisons to other concepts can be included in the word mapping for children grades 5 and beyond. This particular strategy is also one that can be used with a research theme in other content areas.

Preview in Context Strategy

This is a direct-teaching strategy that allows the teacher to guide the students as they examine words in context prior to reading a passage. Before beginning the strategy, the teacher selects only two or three key concept words. Then the teacher reads carefully to identify passages within the text that have strong context clues for the word.

Then the teacher presents the word and the context to the children. As the teacher reads aloud, the children follow along. Once the teacher has finished the read-aloud, the children re-read the material silently. After the silent re-reading, the children will be coached by the teacher to a definition of one of the key words selected for study. This is done through a child-centered discussion. As part of the discussion, the teacher asks questions that get the children to activate their prior knowledge and to use the contextual clues to figure out the correct meaning of the selected key words. Make certain that the definition of the key concept word is finally made by the children.

Next, help the children to begin to expand the word's meaning. Do this by having them consider the following for the given key concept word: synonyms, antonyms, other contexts or other kinds of stories/texts where the word might appear. This is the time to have the children check their responses to the challenge of identifying word synonyms and antonyms by having them go to the thesaurus or the dictionary to confirm their responses. In addition, have the children place the synonyms or antonyms they find in their word boxes or word journals. The recording of their findings will guarantee them ownership of the words and increase their capacity to use contextual clues.

The main point to remember in using this strategy is that it should only be used when the context is strong. It will not work with struggling readers who have less prior knowledge. By listening to the children's responses as he or she helps them define the word and its potential synonyms and antonyms, the teacher can assess their ability to successfully use context clues. The key to this simple strategy is that it allows the teacher to draw the child out and to grasp the individual child's thinking processes. The more talk from the child the better.

The Role of Systematic, Noncontextual Vocabulary Strategies

Hierarchical and Linear Arrays Strategy

The very complexity of the vocabulary used in this strategy description, may be challenging for the teacher. Yet this strategy, which is included in the Cooper (2004) literacy instruction is really very simple once it is outlined directly for children.

By "hierarchical and linear" arrays, Cooper means how some words are grouped based on associative meanings. Words may have a "hierarchical" relationship to one another. The thinking process underlying hierarchical relationships is classification. For instance, an undergraduate or a first grader is lower in the school hierarchy than the graduate student and second grader. Within an elementary school, the fifth grader is at the top of the hierarchy and the pre-K or kindergarten student is at the bottom of the hierarchy. The term doesn't need to be defined in detail to K-3 children, but might be shared with some grade- and age-appropriate modifications with children in grades 3 and beyond. It will enrich their vocabulary development and ownership of the arrays they create.

Words can have a linear relationship to one another in that they run a spectrum from bad to good; for example, from K-3 experiences, pleased-happy-overjoyed. This relationship is a serial one: The words vary along one dimension, as in seriation. These relationships can be displayed in horizontal boxes connected with dashes. Below is a way to display hierarchical relationships.

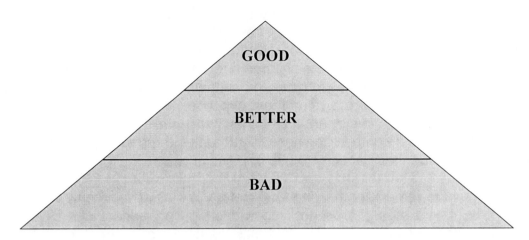

Once you get past the seemingly daunting vocabulary words, the arrays turn out to be another neat graphic organizer tool that can help children "see" how words relate to one another.

To use this graphic organizer, the teacher should pre-select a group of words from a read aloud or from the children's writing. Show the children how the array will look using arrows for the linear array and just straight lines for the hierarchy. In fact, invite some children to draw the straight hierarchy lines as it is presented so they will have a role in developing even the first hierarchical model.

Do one hierarchy array and one linear array with the preselected word with the children. Talk them through filling out (or helping the teacher to fill out) the array. After the children have had their own successful experience with arrays, they can select the words from their independent texts or familiar, previously-read favorites to study. They will also need to decide which type of array, hierarchical or linear, is appropriate. For 5th and 6th graders, this choice can and should be voiced using the now "owned" vocabulary words: "hierarchical array" and "linear array."

This strategy is best used after reading, since it will help the children expand their word banks.

Contextual Vocabulary Strategies

Vocabulary Self-Collection. This strategy is one in which children, even on the emergent level from grade 2 and up, take responsibility for their learning. It is also by definition a student-centered strategy, which demonstrates student ownership of their chosen vocabulary.

This strategy is one that can be introduced by the teacher early in the year, perhaps even the first day or week. The format for self-collection can then be started by the children. It may take the form of a journal with photocopied template pages. It can be continued throughout the year.

To start, ask the children to read a particular text or story. Invite them to select one word for the class to study from it. The children can work individually, in teams, or in small groups. The teacher can also do the self-collecting so that this becomes the joint effort of the class community of literate readers. Tell the children that they should select words that particularly interest them or which are unique in some way.

After the children have had time to make their selections and to reflect on them, make certain that they have time to share them with their peers as a whole class. When the children have shared the words they have selected, have them provide a definition for the word. Each word that is given should be listed on a large experiential chart or even in a BIG BOOK format if age- and grade-appropriate. The teacher should also share the word he or she selected and provide a definition. The teacher's definition and sharing should be somewhere in the middle of the children's recitations.

The dictionary should be used to verify the definitions. When all the definitions have been checked, a final list of child-selected (and single teacher-selected) words should be made.

Once this final list has been compiled, the children can record the words in their word journals or they may opt to record only those words they find interesting. It is up to the teacher at the onset of the vocabulary self-collection activity to decide whether the children must record all the words on the final list or can eliminate some. The decision made at the beginning by the teacher must be adhered to throughout the year.

To further enhance this strategy, children, particularly those in grades 3 and beyond, can be encouraged to use their collected words as part of their writings or to record and clip the appearance of these words in newspaper stories or online. This type of additional recording demonstrates that the child has truly incorporated the word into his/her reading and writing. It also habituates children to be lifelong readers, writers, and researchers.

One of the nice things about this simple but versatile strategy is that it works equally well with either expository or narrative texts. It also provides children with an opportunity to use the dictionary.

Assessment is built into the strategy. As the children select the word for the list, they share how they used contextual clues and through the children's response to the definitions offered by their peers, their prior knowledge can be assessed.

What is most useful about this strategy is that it documents that children can learn to read and write by reading and writing. The children take ownership of the words in the self-collection journals and that can also be the beginning of writer observation journals as they include their own writings. They also use the word lists as a start for writers' commonplace books. These books are filled with newspaper, magazine, and functional document clippings using the journal words.

This activity is a good one for demonstrating the balanced-literacy belief that vocabulary study works best when the words studied are chosen by the child.

Knowledge of Common Sayings, Proverbs and Idioms

The Fortune Cookie Strategy (Reissman, 1994). Grades 3 and up.

Just before snack-time, distribute fortune cookies to the children. Have them eat the cookies and then draw their attention to the fortunes enclosed.

First, the teacher will model by reading aloud and sharing his/her own fortune. After reading the fortune aloud, the teacher will explain what the fortune means using its vocabulary as a guide. Finally the teacher can share whether or not the teacher agrees with the statement made in the fortune.

Children can either volunteer to share their fortunes or each can read the fortune aloud, explain the saying and tell whether he or she agrees with the proverb.

Next, children can be asked to go home and interview their parents or community members to get family proverbs and common sayings.

Once the children return with the sayings and proverbs, they can each share them and explain their meaning. The class as a whole can discuss to what extent these sayings are true for everyone. Proverbs and sayings can become part of a word wall or be included in a special literacy center. The teacher can create fill in, put together, and writing activities to go with the proverbs. They tie in nicely with cultural study on the grade 3-6 level including Asian, Latin American, and African nations.

What makes proverbs particularly effective for vocabulary development are the limited number of words in their texts and the fact these short texts allow for guided and facilitated reading instruction.

This strategy also highlights in a positive way the uniqueness and commonality of the family proverbs that are contributed by children from ELL backgrounds. If possible, their proverbs can be posted in their native languages as well as in English.

Interesting websites when you are studying proverbs:

Write like a Babylonian:
http://www.upennmuseum.com/cuneiform.cgi

Write like an Egyptian:
http://www.upennmuseum.com/hieroglyphsreal.cgi

Knowledge of Foreign Words and Abbreviations Commonly Used in English (e.g. RSVP)

Foreign language in English literacy

Of course, the English language is replete with abbreviations that are shortened forms of words from other languages. Not only can this be used for expanding children's vocabulary and writing variety, but it also can help to positively highlight the bilingual and sometimes trilingual abilities of ELL students.

The teacher should develop a word-strip mix-and-match game with commonly-found foreign words and abbreviations. These items should, if possible, be cut out of newspapers and flyers to highlight their authenticity as words that are commonly encountered. Among those common words and abbreviations might be: perfume, liqueur (chocolate, of course), latte, cappuccino, pannini, brioche, and latkes. Grocery stores, local Starbucks, coffee houses, and bakeries are excellent sources for these abbreviations. To get sufficient material to start the game, just get an extra Sunday newspaper or pick up a few circulars from a large supermarket.

Model for the children how to play the game and find out the common words' or abbreviations' meanings and foreign derivations using the dictionary.

Next have the children as a whole class or in small groups work to identify the derivations of the foreign words and even map them on a world map.

As part of additional foreign-word-center activities, children can choose from a number of choices. These can include: maintaining a BIG BOOK OF FOREIGN WORDS or ABBREVIATIONS, to which everyone contributes, using the weekly food circulars and collecting labels with foreign words that can then be collaged with an accompanying product list, and authoring stories and true accounts featuring as many foreign words as possible.

What is productive about this strategy is that it enhances vocabulary development while it also highlights the extent to which the English language as spoken, used, and written in the United States, is embedded with words and terms from languages other than English. This of course makes the native language talents of the ELL child positive and important ones.

Extending a Reader's Understanding of Familiar Words

Dictionary Use:

Dictionaries are useful for spelling, writing, and reading. It is very important to expose and habituate students to the enjoyment that comes from using the dictionary.

Cooper (2004) suggests that the following be kept in mind as the teacher of grades K-6 introduces and then habituates children to a lifelong fascination with the dictionary and vocabulary acquisition. Requesting or suggesting that children look up a word in the dictionary should be an invitation to a wonderful exploration, not a punishment or busy work that has no relationship to their current reading assignment.

Model the correct way to use the dictionary for children even as late as the third through sixth grade. Many have never been taught proper dictionary skills. The teacher needs to demonstrate to the children that as an adult reader and writer, he or she routinely and happily uses the dictionary and learns new information that increases the satisfaction that is obtained from reading and writing.

Cooper believes in beginning dictionary study as early as kindergarten and this is now very possible because of the proliferation of lush picture dictionaries that can be introduced at that grade level. He also suggests that children not only look at these picture dictionaries but also begin to make dictionaries of their own at this grade level filled with pictures and beginning words. As children join the circle of lexicographers, they will begin to see themselves as compilers and users of dictionaries. Of course, this will support their ongoing vocabulary development.

In early grade levels, use of the dictionary can nicely complement the children's mastery of the alphabet. They should be given whole-class and small-group practice in locating words. As the children progress with their phonetic skills, the dictionary can be used to show them phonetic re-spelling using the pronunciation key.

Older children in grades 3 and beyond need explicit teacher demonstrations and practice in the use of guide words. They also need to begin to learn about the hierarchies of various word meanings. In the upper grades, children should also explore using special content dictionaries and glossaries in the backs of their books.

Strategies for Promoting Comprehension across the Curriculum by Expanding Knowledge of Content-Area Vocabulary

Key Words

Cooper (2004) feels that it is up to the teacher to preview the content-area text to identify the main ideas. Then the teacher should compile a list of terms related to the content thrust. These terms and words become part of the key-concepts list.

Next, the teacher sees which of the key-concept words and terms are already defined in the text. These will not require direct teaching. Words for which children have sufficient skills to determine their meaning through base, root, prefixes; or suffixes, also will not require direct teaching.

Instruction in the remaining key words, which should not be more than two or three in number, can be provided before, during, or after reading. If students have previewed the content area and identified those words they need support on, the instruction should be provided before reading. Instruction can also easily be provided as part of guided reading support. After reading support is indicated, the text offers the children an opportunity to enrich their own vocabularies.

Having children work as a whole class or in small groups on a content-specific dictionary for a topic regularly covered in their grade-level social studies, science, or mathematics curriculum offers an excellent collaborative opportunity for children to design a dictionary/word resource that can celebrate their own vocabulary learning. Such a resource can then be used with the next year's classes as well.

Development of Vocabulary Knowledge and Skills in Individual Students

Hierarchical and linear array vocabulary development strategies lend themselves well to the support of struggling learners or second-language learners. The use of the arrays allows these learners to use a visual format to "see" and diagram word relationships. Furthermore the diagrams are easy to make, and they can be illustrated. With sufficient support and modeling, many special-needs children can do simple linear and hierarchical arrays on their own. The arrays can also be attractively displayed in resource rooms and in regular-education classrooms as a demonstration of these individual students' ownership of their words.

English Language Learners should first demonstrate their capacity to fill out hierarchical and linear arrays in their native language and then work with this same format to hone their English language vocabulary development. Their native-language hierarchical relationships and arrays can be displayed in their general education classrooms. Teachers may also want to encourage children grades 3 and beyond to make connections between native words and words derived from them in English. This could be a rich "buddy" (ELL child and native English language speaker) investigation or it could be one for ELL children alone. At any rate, use of the array with the ELL child's native language makes that child a second-language vocabulary owner, which immediately includes the child positively in ongoing vocabulary development.

Cooper (2004) suggests that teachers who have children from different language backgrounds use any unscheduled or "extra" time that emerges for read-alouds.

Using the Semantic Feature Analysis Grid

Highly proficient readers can be asked to help same-grade peers or better yet younger peers with their word-analysis skills by having them work with these struggling readers on filling out teacher-developed semantic analysis grids. Some 5th and 6th grade highly-proficient readers may also evidence the aptitude and desire to create their own semantic-analysis grids for their peer or younger peer tutees. In this way, highly-proficient readers can gain insights into the field of teaching reading at an early age and younger struggling readers can have the edge taken off their struggles by working with a peer or an older student. For both sets of students, the experience is one that promotes and celebrates word-analysis skills and nurtures the concept of a literate and caring community of readers.

ELL students can also add items to the categories that reflect their cultures. For instance, Latino children can add plantains and guava to the fruits their non-Latino peers might list. This provides the ELL learners with an opportunity to enrich the knowledge base of their peers' inventory and puts the ELL learner in a positive spotlight. The easy notations on the grid make it accessible for even ELL children with limited English-language writing and speaking capacities.

Special needs learners can benefit from the grid. It can be developed by teachers, paraprofessionals, and tutors. It can be notated by the children themselves. They can also illustrate it or it can be posted or kept in the word center. The grid provides these children, who are often spatial learners, with a concrete demonstration of their word-analysis achievement.

Biemiller's research indicates that the listening vocabulary for a 6th grader who tests at the 25th percentile in reading is equivalent to that attained by the 75th percentile 3rd grader. This deficit in vocabulary presents a formidable challenge to the 6th grader's success not only on reading tests but in various content subjects in elementary school and beyond.

Skill 6.2   Identify characteristics (e.g., cause and effect, time sequence, compare and contrast, lists) and features (e.g., index, glossary, subheading) of various informational text structures

The **organization** of a written work includes two factors: the order in which the writer has chosen to present the different parts of the discussion or argument, and the relationships he or she constructs between these parts.

Written ideas need to be presented in a **logical order** so that a reader can follow the information easily and quickly. There are many different ways in which to order a series of ideas but they all share one thing in common: to lead the reader along a desired path while avoiding backtracking and skipping around in order to give a clear, strong presentation of the writer's main idea. *Some* of the ways in which a paragraph may be organized:

Sequence of events. In this type of organization, the details are presented in the order in which they occurred. Paragraphs that describe a process or procedure, give directions, or outline a given period of time (such as a day or a month) are often arranged chronologically.

Statement support. In this type of organization, the main idea is stated and the rest of the paragraph explains or proves it. This is also referred to as relative importance. There are four ways in which this type of order is organized: most to least, least to most, most-least-most, and least-most-least.

Comparison-Contrast. In this type of organization, the compare-contrast pattern is used when a paragraph describes the differences or similarities of two or more ideas, actions, events, or things. Usually the topic sentence describes the basic relationship between the ideas or items and the rest of the paragraph explains this relationship.

Classification. In this type of organization, the paragraph presents grouped information about a topic. The topic sentence usually states the general category and the rest of the sentences show how various elements of the category have a common base and also how they differ from the common base.

Cause and Effect. This pattern describes how two or more events are connected. The main sentence usually states the primary cause(s) and the primary effect(s) and how they are basically connected. The rest of the sentences explain the connection—how one event caused the next.

Spatial/Place. In this type of organization, certain descriptions are organized according to the location of items in relation to each other and to a larger context. The orderly arrangement guides the reader's eye as he or she mentally envisions the scene or place being described.

Use of Text Features (e.g. Index and Glossary) and Graphic Features (e.g. Charts and Maps) and Reference Materials

Traditionally, aspects of expository-text-reading have been taught using reference books from the school or public library—atlas, almanac, and geography books—to teach these necessary and meaningful skills.

Although these library and possibly classroom library books can be used, it is much easier to take a simple newspaper to introduce and provide children with daily ongoing, authentic experiences in learning these necessary skills as they also keep up with real-world events that affect their daily lives.

They can go on a chronological hunt through the daily newspaper and discover the many formats for schedules contained therein. For instance, some newspapers include a calendar of the week with literary, sports, social, movie and other public events. Children can also go on scavenger hunts through various sections of the newspaper and on certain days find full-blown timelines detailing famous individuals' careers, business histories, and milestones in the political history of a nation or even key movies made by a famous movie director who has been nominated for an Oscar.

The nature of newspaper reportage and the public's need to know the why and wherefore behind the stories of natural disasters, company takeovers, political downfalls, and uprisings leads newspapers to represent events graphically and to use cause/effect diagramming and comparison/contrast wording. If the teacher specifically wants to make certain that the students come away with this material, he or she can pre-clip "teaching" stories from the news for the child and introduce them in a special news center.

After children have been walked through these comparison/contrast news stories and cause/effect diagramming as it has appeared in the newspaper, they can be challenged to find additional examples of these text structures in the news or challenged to reframe or rewrite familiar stories using these text structures. They can even use desktop publishing to re-author the stories using the same text structures.

If a class participates in a local Newspaper in Education program, where the children receive a free newspaper two to three times a week, the teacher can teach index skills using the index of the newspaper and having children compete or cooperate in small groups to find various features.

Map and chart skills take on much more relevance and excitement when the children work on these skills using sports charts detailing the batting averages and pass completions of their favorite players or perhaps the box scores of their older siblings' football and baseball games. Maps dealing with holiday weather become meaningful to children as they anticipate a holiday vacation.

Skill 6.3 Identify instructional approaches and strategies for teaching study skills (e.g., note taking, summarizing, discussion, using reference materials, maps, and graphics)

When searching for information, students can become much more efficient if they learn to use a glossary and index. Students can find the necessary facts in a more rapid manner and also clarify information they may not understand on a first read.

Additionally, charts, graphs, maps, diagrams, captions, and photos in text can provide insight and clarification to concepts and ideas the author is conveying. Students may need to develop skills for correctly interpreting the information,

Content area subjects often have texts with a great deal of information, typically much more information than is necessary for students to know at one time. In cases like this, it is necessary for students to develop specific study skills to help them distinguish important from not-so-important information.

Highlighting is a difficult strategy for students to master. Even at the college level, it seems students have a hard time determining what is important and necessary. Key ideas or vocabulary are a good place to start with highlighting. Teaching students to highlight less information, rather than more, is also important. It is not a good study skill if a student highlights an entire page of information.

Outlining is a skill many teachers use to help students understand important facts. Sometimes the teacher can provide the outline to the students to use as a guide when taking their own notes. In this way, students know the important parts to focus on when reading. Developing outlines can be very difficult for some students; and for those students, mapping might be a more appropriate study aid.

Mapping involves using graphics, pictures, and words to represent the information in the text. The students can personalize and use colors and pictures that have meaning to themselves. This provides the natural bridge to prior knowledge and frames the information in a more personal way.

Note-taking skills also require direct instruction. Sometimes, in fact all too often, teachers assume students understand how to take notes based on a lecture format when, in fact, the majority of students are trying to write down everything they hear. Teachers can help in this process by taking the time to specifically teach and highlight key factors.

Test-taking is another area where students sometimes need help in skill development. Teaching students to eliminate automatic wrong answers first, and then narrowing down the choices is a start. In open-ended questions, students need to be able to restate the question in their answer and understand that they need to answer all parts of the question being asked.

The Role of Oral Language Fluency in Facilitating the Comprehension of Informational/Expository Texts

Children in the middle and secondary levels of education who are studying social-studies content have been exposed to what educators call re-enactments. This is a reader's-theater version of history and cultural study based completely on fact and established historical texts and documents.

Even young children will enjoy dramatizing a well-known historical occasion, document, or song; at the same time, they will increase their facility for comprehending expository text. They may act out the preamble to the Constitution or read aloud as a chorus the Declaration of Independence or dramatize the Battle Hymn of the Republic. This gives children an opportunity to experience the vocabulary and syntactic and semantic clues of these texts. They then must use their oral instruments (voices) to express the texts appropriately.

If the children are in grades 4 and above, they can also be asked to explain in writing how they used the words and syntactic and semantic clues to interpret their oral-language recitation. Recitation and writing can be a powerful experience for children grades 4 and up as they build their expository reading and writing skills.

Use of Writing Activities to Promote Comprehension

K-W-L Strategy

This is a graphic-organizer strategy that activates children's prior knowledge and also helps them develop their reading of expository texts. This is achieved by having the children reflect on three key questions.

Before the child reads the expository passage:
"What do I *know*?" and
"What do I or *we want* to find out?"

After the child has read the expository passage:
"What have I or *we learned* from the passage?"

What is excellent about this strategy, which is broadly used and easily implemented in almost any classroom, is that it is almost totally student-centered and powerfully focuses the child's attention on the actual reading of expository passages. The K-W-L strategy also helps the child prepare for a potential writing task.

When the teacher first introduces the K-W-L strategy, the children should be allowed sufficient time to brainstorm what all of them in the class or small group actually know about the topic. The children should have a three-columned K-W-L worksheet template for their journals and there should be a chart up front to record the responses from class or group discussion. The children can write under each column in their own journal and should also help the teacher with notations on the chart. This strategy involves the children's actually gaining experience in note taking and having a concrete record of new data and information they have gleaned from the passage about the topic.

Depending on the grade level of the participating children, the teacher may also want to channel them into considering categories of information they hope to find out from the expository passage. For instance, they may be reading a book on animals to find out more about the animal's habitats during the winter or about the animal's mating habits.

When children are working on the middle section (*want*) strategy sheet, the teacher may give them a chance to share what they would like to learn further about the topic and help them to express it in question format.

K-W-L can be introduced as early as grade 2 with extensive teacher support. It not only serves to support the child's comprehension of a particular expository text but also models for children a format for note taking. Beyond note taking, when the teacher wants to introduce report writing, the K-W-L format provides excellent outlines and question introductions for at least three paragraphs of a report.

Cooper (2004) recommends this strategy for use with thematic units and with chapters in required science, social studies, or health textbooks. In addition to its usefulness with thematic unit study, K-W-L is wonderful for providing the teacher with a concrete format to assess how well children have absorbed pertinent new knowledge within the passage (by looking at the *Learn* section). Ultimately it is hoped that students will learn to use this strategy not only under the direction of the teacher with templates of K-W-L sheets, but also on their own by informally writing questions they want to find out about in their journals and then going back to their own questions and answering them after reading.

Know	*Want/Wonder*	*Learn*
In this box, the teacher or students list the information they already know about the topic to be discussed.	In this box, the teacher or students list the questions they have about the topic, which may be answered through research or the activities already planned.	In this box, the teacher or students list what information has been learned at the *end* of the teaching process. This becomes a reflective piece for both students and teachers and can even be used as a quick assessment for the teacher to ascertain whether all predetermined objectives were met

When reading, students need to utilize as many different strategies as possible to increase their comprehension. With good comprehension being the end goal of all reading, teachers can help their students by teaching them specific features of texts that they can use to clarify or enhance their understanding.

Using specific textual features, students can begin to find information more easily, which allows them to create their own schema. Using this schema, they can analyze and organize the information in a manner that is tied directly to their own personal experience and prior knowledge. Once it is connected, it will then be easier for the students to recall and utilize the information when needed.

Most texts provide brief introductions. These introductions can be used by the reader to determine if the information they are seeking is located within the passage to be read. By reading a short passage, the student can quickly ascertain the need for a complete reading or whether a quick skim will suffice. As we teach students to write, we often spend time teaching them to write paragraphs with topic sentences and concluding sentences; however, explicit direction for using these same features to better understand text also needs to be done. These parallels can help students better understand what they are reading and also help them develop their writing skills. Understanding that topic sentences tell the main idea of the paragraph and concluding sentences restate that idea can help students' comprehension as well.

Skill 6.4   Identify instructional approaches and strategies for teaching functional literacy skills (e.g., reading labels, signs, newspapers, schedules)

Ability to Apply Reading Skills for Various Purposes

What is really intriguing about the use of newspapers as a model and an authentic platform for introducing children into the recognition and use of expository text structures, features, and references, is that the children can demonstrate their mastery of these structures by putting out their own newspapers detailing their school universe using some of these text structures.

They can also create their own timelines for projects or research papers they have done in class using newspaper models.

Application of Comprehension Strategies for Electronic Texts

If the class gets newspapers in the classroom as part of an ongoing Newspapers in Education program, it is natural and easy for the teacher to take the time to show children how the same news is covered online. All of the newspapers have e-news. Children can first do a K-W-L on what they know or think they know about e-news and then actually review their specific daily newspaper's site. With the support of the teacher or an older peer, they can examine the resource and perhaps note the following differences in electronic text:

- Use of moving pictures and video to document events
- Use of sound clips in addition to written text
- Use of music/sound effects not in printed text
- Links to other web resources and to other archived articles

Of course, this can lead to rich discussions and to further detailed web-versus-print news resource analysis. For children in grades 5 and 6, this might even include a research investigation of a particular news story or event including broadcast media coverage.

Development of Reading Comprehension Skills and Strategies of Individual Students

Both English Language Learners and struggling readers can benefit from the structure and format of the K-W-L approach. It allows them to share their prior experiences and knowledge of the topics covered in the expository text through natural conversation. It provides them with a natural device for the teacher or tutor to customize and to scaffold instruction to meet their linguistic and experiential backgrounds. Through the discussion and sharing of other children's comments, struggling readers and children from ELL backgrounds have an opportunity to learn how to use questions to "walk through" and take notes on expository writing.

Highly proficient readers can do a comparative expository news-event study between print accounts, e-news reportage, and broadcast media coverage. They can prepare charts and their own news mock-up to show the similarities and contrasts between what aspects of the event get covered in what media format. They may also want to write to actual reporters and editors from the different media to share their insights and see if these professionals are willing to respond.

Learning is not limited to one subject area. Though we often think in terms of math, reading, science, and social studies, the concepts taught in any of those subjects are truly pervasive across many others.

Students need to understand how concepts and vocabulary transfer across various subjects. Sometimes, this relationship will be obvious to the students while at other times, it will be necessary to point it out.

Understanding how the word "multiply" read in a story relates to multiplication, reproduction, and other things is important for students. This is similar in nature to the connection of prior knowledge. In this case, the learning is connected across subjects as well as to prior experiences.

Students should first be taught these types of connections, but eventually they should be encouraged to search them out on their own. It is through this process that students increase their schema. Through the process of making connections in any manner, students are taking in more knowledge and personalizing it, which is the goal of learning.

There are graphic organizers to help students see connections that can be helpful as well. However, most of the graphic organizers are for connections within text. They may need to be adapted to include other subject areas. Overall, the more connections students can make, the better off they will be in the long run.

Sharon Taberski: "If we want children to become strategic readers, then we create classrooms that reinforce the strategies we've demonstrated and allow children to practice on books that match their needs."

COMPETENCY 7.0   KNOWLEDGE OF LITERARY GENRES, ELEMENTS, AND INTERPRETATIONS

Skill 7.1   Identify the characteristics and elements of various literary genres and formats of prose and poetry (e.g., classics, multicultural literature, fables, legends, biographies)

Prose

Narrative can be defined as an interpretive story that is historically and/or culturally based. Narratives are stories, and when orally presented, they often take on a unique flavor and characteristic of the content. For example, slave narratives are often told in the "voice" and persona of 19th-century slaves. Organizationally, narratives are chronological; however, various disruptions in time-sequence can occur, sometimes very suddenly. Occasionally, narratives get side-tracked based on the specific content.

Essay: Typically a limited-length prose work focusing on a topic and propounding a definite point of view and authoritative tone. Great essayists include Carlyle, Lamb, DeQuincy, Emerson, and Montaigne, who is credited with defining this genre.

Novel: The longest form of fictional prose containing a variety of characterizations, settings, local color, and regionalism. Most have complex plots, expanded description, and attention to detail. Some of the great novelists include Austin, the Brontes, Twain, Tolstoy, Hugo, Hardy, Dickens, Hawthorne, Forster, and Flaubert.

Short Story: Typically a terse narrative with less developmental background about characters. May include description, author's point of view, and tone. Poe emphasized that a successful short story should create one focused impact. Considered to be great short story writers are Hemingway, Faulkner, Twain, Joyce, Shirley Jackson, Flannery O'Connor, de Maupassant, Saki, Edgar Allen Poe, and Pushkin

Poetry
People read poetry for many reasons, and they are often the very same reasons poets would give for writing it. Just the feel and sounds of the words that are turned by the artistic hands and mind of a poet into a satisfying and sometimes delightful experience is a good reason to read a poem. Good poetry constantly surprises. However, the major purpose a writer of poetry has for creating his works of art is the sharing of an experience, a feeling, an emotion, and that is also the reason a reader turns to poetry rather than prose in his search for variety, joy, and satisfaction.

There is another important reason that poets create and that readers are drawn to their poems: they are interpreters of life. Poets feel deeply the things that others feel or even things that may be overlooked by others, and they have the skill and inspiration to recreate those feelings and interpret them in such a way that understanding and insight may come from the experience. They often bring understanding to life's big (or even not-so-big) questions.

Children can respond to poetry at very early stages. Elementary students are still at the stage where the sounds of unusual words intrigue them and entertain them. They are also very open to emotional meanings of passages. Teaching poetry to 5th graders can be an important introduction to seeking for meaning in literature. If a 5th grader enjoys reading poetry both silently and aloud, a habit may be formed that will last a lifetime.

Drama

Drama: In its most general sense, a drama is any work that is designed to be performed by actors onstage. It can also refer to the broad literary genre that includes comedy and tragedy. Contemporary usage, however, denotes drama as a work that treats serious subjects and themes but does not aim for the same grandeur as tragedy.

Drama usually deals with characters of a less stately nature than does tragedy. A classical example is Sophocles' tragedy *Oedipus Rex,* while Eugene O'Neill's *The Iceman Cometh* represents modern drama.

Comedy: The comedic form of dramatic literature is meant to amuse and often ends happily. It uses techniques such as satire or parody, and can take many forms, from farce to burlesque. Examples include Dante Alighieri's *The Divine Comedy,* Noel Coward's play *Private Lives,* and some of Geoffrey Chaucer's *Canterbury Tales* and William Shakespeare's plays.

Tragedy: Tragedy is comedy's other half. It is defined as a work of drama written in either prose or poetry, telling the story of a brave, noble hero who, because of some tragic character flaw, brings ruin upon himself. It is characterized by serious, poetic language that evokes pity and fear. In modern times, dramatists have tried to update its image by drawing its main characters from the middle or lower classes and showing their nobility through their nature instead of their standing. The classic example of tragedy is Sophocles' *Oedipus Rex,* while Henrik Ibsen and Arthur Miller epitomize modern tragedy.

Dramatic Monologue: A dramatic monologue is a speech given by an actor, usually addressed to himself (or herself) but with the intended audience in mind. It reveals key aspects of the character's psyche and sheds insight on the situation at hand. The audience takes the part of the silent listener, passing judgment and giving sympathy at the same time. This form was invented and used predominantly by Victorian poet Robert Browning.

Children's Literature is a genre of its own and emerged as a distinct and independent form in the second half of the 18th century. *The Visible World in Pictures* by John Amos Comenius, a Czech educator, was one of the first printed works and the first picture book. For the first time, educators acknowledged that children are different from adults in many respects. Modern educators acknowledge that introducing elementary students to a wide range of reading experiences plays an important role in their mental/social/psychological development. Some of the most common forms of literature specifically for children follow:

- ✓ **Traditional Literature.** Traditional literature opens up a world where right wins out over wrong, where hard work and perseverance are rewarded, and where helpless victims find vindication—all worthwhile values that children identify with even as early as kindergarten. In traditional literature, children will be introduced to fanciful beings, humans with exaggerated powers, talking animals, and heroes that will inspire them. For younger elementary children, these stories in Big Book format are ideal for providing predictable and repetitive elements that can be grasped by these children.
- ✓ **Folktales/Fairy Tales:** Some examples: *The Three Bears, Little Red Riding Hood, Snow White, Sleeping Beauty, Puss in Boots, Rapunzel* and *Rumpelstiltskin.* Adventures of animals or humans and the supernatural characterize these stories. The hero is usually on a quest and is aided by other-worldly helpers. More often than not, the story focuses on good and evil and reward and punishment.
- ✓ **Fables:** Animals that act like humans are featured in these stories and usually reveal human foibles or sometimes teach a lesson. Example: *Aesop's Fables.*
- ✓ **Myths:** These stories about events from the earliest times, such as the origin of the world, are considered true in their own societies.
- ✓ **Legends:** These are similar to myths except that they tend to deal with events that happened more recently. Example: Arthurian legends.
- ✓ **Tall tales:** Examples: Paul Bunyan, John Henry, and Pecos Bill. These are purposely exaggerated accounts of individuals with superhuman strength.
- ✓ **Modern Fantasy:** Many of the themes found in these stories are similar to those in traditional literature. The stories start out based in reality, which makes it easier for the reader to suspend disbelief and enter worlds of unreality. Little people live in the walls in *The Borrowers* and time travel is possible in *The Trolley to Yesterday.* Including some fantasy tales in the curriculum helps elementary-grade children develop their senses of imagination. These often appeal to ideals of justice and issues having to do with good and evil; and because children tend to identify with the characters, the message is more likely to be retained.

- ✓ **Science Fiction:** Robots, spacecraft, mystery, and civilizations from other ages often appear in these stories. Most presume advances in science on other planets or in a future time. Most children like these stories because of their interest in space and the "what if" aspect of the stories. Examples: *Outer Space, All That Junk,* and *A Wrinkle in Time.*
- ✓ **Modern Realistic Fiction:** These stories are about real problems that real children face. By finding that their hopes and fears are shared by others, young children can find insight into their own problems. Young readers also tend to experience a broadening of interests as the result of this kind of reading. It's good for them to know that a child can be brave and intelligent and can solve difficult problems.
- ✓ **Historical Fiction:** *Rifles for Watie* is an example of this kind of story. Presented in a historically-accurate setting, it is about a young boy who serves in the Union Army. He experiences great hardship but discovers that his enemy is an admirable human being. It provides a good opportunity to introduce children to history in a beneficial way.
- ✓ **Biography:** Reading about inventors, explorers, scientists, political and religious leaders, social reformers, artists, sports figures, doctors, teachers, writers, and war heroes helps children to see that one person can make a difference. They also open new vistas for children to think about when they choose an occupation to fantasize about.
- ✓ **Informational Books:** These are ways children can learn more about something they are interested in or something they know nothing about. Encyclopedias are good resources, of course, but a book like *Polar Wildlife* by Kamini Khanduri shows pictures and facts that will capture the imaginations of young children.

Essays: Usually, essays take an opinion (whether it is about a concept, a work of literature, a person, or an event) and describe how the opinion was arrived at or why the opinion is a good one.

Letters: When letters are read and analyzed in the classroom, students generally are studying the writer's style or the writer's true, deep-down opinions and feelings about certain events. Often, students will find letters of famous individuals in history reprinted in textbooks.

Journals: Similar to letters, journals present very personal ideas. They give students, when available (as most people never want their journals published), an opportunity to see peoples' thought processes about various events or issues.

Biography: A form of nonfictional literature, the subject of which is the life of an individual. The earliest biographical writings were probably funeral speeches and inscriptions, usually praising the life and example of the deceased. Early biographies evolved from this and were almost invariably uncritical, even distorted, and always laudatory. Beginning in the 18th century, this form of literature saw major development. An eminent example is James Boswell's *Life of Johnson*, which is very detailed and even records conversations. Eventually, the antithesis of the grossly exaggerated tomes praising an individual, usually a person of circumstance, developed. This form is denunciatory, debunking, and often inflammatory. A famous modern example is Lytton Strachey's *Eminent Victorians* (1918).

Autobiography: A form of biography, but it is written by the subject himself or herself. Autobiographies can range from the very formal to intimate writings made during one's life that were not intended for publication. These include letters, diaries, journals, memoirs, and reminiscences. Autobiography, generally speaking, began in the 15th century; one of the first examples is one written in England by Margery Kempe. There are four kinds of autobiography: thematic, religious, intellectual, and fictionalized. Some "novels" may be thinly disguised autobiography, such as the novels of Thomas Wolfe.

Informational books and articles: Make up much of the reading of modern Americans. Magazines began to be popular in the 19th century in this country, and while many of the contributors to those publications intended to influence the political/social/religious convictions of their readers, many also simply intended to pass on information. A book or article whose purpose is simply to be informative, that is, not to persuade, is called exposition (adjectival form: expository). An example of an expository book is the *MLA Style Manual*. The writers do not intend to persuade their readers to use the recommended stylistic features in their writing; they are simply making them available in case a reader needs such a guide. Articles in magazines such as *Time* may be persuasive in purpose, such as Joe Klein's regular column, but for the most part they are expository, giving information that television coverage of a news story might not have time to include.

Newspaper accounts of events: Expository in nature, of course, a reporting of a happening. That happening might be a school board meeting, an automobile accident that sent several people to a hospital and accounted for the death of a passenger, or the election of the mayor. They are not intended to be persuasive although the bias of a reporter or of an editor must be factored in. A newspapers' editorial stance is often openly declared, and it may be reflected in such things as news reports. Reporters are expected to be unbiased in their coverage and most of them will defend their disinterest fiercely, but what a writer *sees* in an event is inevitably shaped to some extent by that writer's beliefs and experiences.

Skill 7.2   Identify appropriate criteria for choosing literature for students for specific purposes

In every classroom across the country, there are students at different reading levels. There is no such thing as one reading program to meet the needs of all students. Therefore, a reading specialist within the school must adapt and develop reading programs so that each child will experience success and develop further in reading skills. For some students, the reading material in the program is beyond their level, while for others it may be too easy.

One way to assure that all students are reading at their individual levels is to implement a guided reading program. The Fountas and Pinnel method of guided reading is one that has been accepted widely and one that has displayed major success in teaching children to read fluently and accurately. In this method, the students are assessed at the beginning of the year to see where they fit on the letter grade. Each letter in the guided reading system refers to the manner in which a book is written—(e.g.,Level A has one word on a page and pictures to correspond to the word).

Once the students are assessed, the teacher gathers each group together on a regular basis to instruct them on a specific learning objective. The classroom must be rich in print and the students must know exactly where to go to get the books they can read. Assessment takes place on a regular basis as well and students move upward as they grasp the strategies. The groups are constantly changing so that students will not get the idea that they are in the slow group or the smart group.

Additionally, it is sometimes important to simply group the students by their interests. In this way, slower readers will be able to participate with better readers and gain valuable skills from working with their peers. Also, it provides motivation and excitement when students are engaged in something that attracts their interest.

Within the content areas, the reading material may have to be rewritten so that it is in words the students can understand. The explanations may have to be more detailed, especially if the student does not have the necessary background knowledge. Evaluations and tests may also need to be different for those students, allowing them to experience success.

Finally, it is necessary to include works of literature that reflect all of society's diversity. In this way, students from diverse cultures can make more personal connections and all readers can begin to understand relationships and issues, which affect others.

Multicultural Literature

Living and working as we do in a multicultural society, it is important that teachers think beyond the classics of literature (or even simply the works of literature they personally enjoy and are familiar with) and consider literature that is (1) representative of the cultures in the country and community and most importantly in their classrooms, and (2) instructive to students about how to interact with people who are not like themselves.

When selecting multicultural literature, a few things need to be considered. First, is the literature, in general, appropriate? Second, does the literature *accurately* portray a particular culture? Third, will students be able to utilize the literature for a greater social purpose? Each of these questions is discussed below.

When selecting any piece of literature for classroom use, we want to make sure that it is appropriate, in general. Has the board of education in the teacher's district approved the text for classroom use? If that decision is left to the teacher, does the text contain violence, vulgar language, sexual explicitness, negative values, or racism? If so, teachers should strongly consider not using the text. In addition, is the text at the appropriate reading level for the class? These considerations should be given for any text, whether representative of a multicultural selection or not.

The next issue to consider when selecting multicultural literature is the extent to which the text accurately portrays other cultures. Often, in general literature, we find gross misunderstandings of cultures. If, by chance, certain students have not had opportunities to interact with others in those misrepresented cultures, they may develop incorrect perceptions. In addition, even if there is an opportunity for students to interact with people representing those cultures, will students in those cultures feel that they were portrayed correctly? If not, it could be damaging to those students, as well as the relationships they have with other students who have been given that misinformation.

Finally, we want to make sure that the literature helps students learn how to live in a multicultural society. The literature students read in classrooms could be one of the few opportunities students have to learn how to interact with people in different cultures in a variety of situations. We want to make sure that they have good role models in the literature and that the literature assists in positively developing students' habits of mind. While not all literature should serve this purpose, it is important that at various times throughout the school year, students do get some "life instruction" through their classroom reading materials.

COMPETENCY 8.0   KNOWLEDGE OF DIVERSE LEARNERS

Skill 8.1   Choose appropriate methods (e.g., differentiating instruction, modifications, accommodations) for meeting reading needs of diverse individuals and groups

Oftentimes, students absorb the culture and social environment around them without deciphering contextual meaning of the experiences. When provided with a diversity of cultural contexts, students are able to adapt and incorporate multiple meanings from cultural cues vastly different from their own socioeconomic backgrounds. Socio-cultural factors provide a definitive impact on a students' psychological, emotional, affective, and physiological development, along with a student's academic learning and future opportunities.

The educational experience for most students is a complicated and complex one with a diversity of interlocking meanings and inferences. If one aspect of the complexity is altered, it affects other aspects, which may impact how a student or teacher views an instructional or learning experience. With the current demographic profile of today's school communities, the complexity of understanding, interpreting, and synthesizing the nuances from the diversity of cultural lineages can provide many communication and learning blockages that could impede the progress of students.

Teachers must create personalized learning communities where every student is a valued member of and contributor to the classroom experiences. In classrooms where socio-cultural attributes of the student population are incorporated into the fabric of the learning process, dynamic interrelationships are created that enhance the learning experience and the personalization of learning. When students are provided with numerous academic and social opportunities to share, everyone in the classroom benefits from bonding through shared experiences and having an expanded viewpoint of a world experience and culture that vastly differs from their own.

Researchers continue to show that personalized learning environments increase the learning effect for students, decrease drop-out rates among marginalized students, and decrease unproductive student behavior that can result from constant cultural misunderstandings or miscues between students. Promoting diversity of learning and cultural competency in the classroom for students and teachers creates a world of multicultural opportunities and learning. When students are able to step outside their comfort zones and share the world of a homeless student or empathize with an English Language Learner (ELL) student who has just immigrated to the United States and is learning English for the first time and is still trying to keep up with the academic learning in an unfamiliar language, then students grow exponentially in social understanding and cultural connectedness.

Personalized learning communities provide supportive learning environments that address the academic and emotional needs of students. As socio-cultural knowledge is conveyed continuously in the interrelated experiences shared cooperatively and collaboratively in student groupings and individualized learning, the current and future benefits will continue to present the case and importance of understanding the "whole" child, inclusive of the social and the cultural context.

Knowledge of levels of reading comprehension and strategies for promoting comprehension of imaginative literary texts at all levels

Sharon Taberski (2000) recommends that initially strategies for promoting comprehension of imaginative literary texts be done with the whole class.

Here are Taberski's four main strategies for promoting comprehension of imaginative literary texts. She feels that if repeated sufficiently during the K-3 years and even if introduced as late as grade 4, these strategies will serve the adult lifelong reader in good stead.

Strategy One: "Stopping to Think"—reflecting on the text as a whole.
As part of this strategy, the reader is challenged to come up with the answer to these three questions:
1. What do I think is going to happen? (Inferential)
2. Why do I think this is going to happen? (Evaluative and inferential)
3. How can I prove that I am right by going back to the story? (inferential)

Taberski recommends that teachers introduce these key strategies with books that can be read in one sitting and recommends the use of picture books for these instructive strategies.

Taberski also suggests that books that are read aloud and used for this strategy also contain a strong storyline, some degree of predictability, a text that invites discussion, and a narrative with obvious stopping points.

Strategy Two: story mapping, for promoting comprehension of imaginative/literary texts.

For stories to suit this strategy, they should have distinct episodes, few characters, and clear-cut problems to solve. In particular, Taberski tries to use a story where a single, central problem or issue is introduced at the beginning of the story and then resolved or at least followed through by the close of the story. To make a story map of a particular story, Taberski divides the class into groups and asks one group of children to illustrate the characters in the book. Another group of children are asked to draw the setting while a third and fourth group of children tackle problem and resolution. The story map may also help children hold their ideas for writing together in the writing workshop as they take their reading of an author's story to a new level.

Strategy Three: The character-mapping strategy also used by Taberski focuses the children as readers on the ways in which the main character's personal traits can determine what will happen in the story. Character mapping works best when the character is a non-stereotypical individual, has been featured perhaps in other books by the same author, has a personality that is somewhat predictable, and is capable of changing behavior as a consequence of what happens. Using writing to share, deepen, and expand understanding of literary texts is a cornerstone of the balanced literacy approach.

Strategy Four: Taberski advocates the teacher's reading sections of stories aloud and then pausing to reflect on what's happened in the story and model writing down a response to it. The teacher can use a chart to record his/her response to the events or characters of the story and the children can contribute their comments as well. Later on, the children can start reflective reader's notebooks or journals recording their reactions to their readings independently.

The best types of texts for this type of response are those that relate to age-appropriate issues for young children (i.e. homework, testing, bullies, and friendship), a plot that can be interpreted in different ways, a text that is filled with questions, and a text full of suspense or wonder.

Development of Literary Response Skills

Literary response skills are dependent on prior knowledge, schemata, and background. Schemata (the plural of schema) are those structures that represent concepts stored in our memory.

Without schemata and experiences to call upon as they read, children have little ability to comprehend. Of course, the reader's schemata and prior knowledge have more influence on the comprehension of plot or character information that is implied rather than directly stated.

Prior Knowledge

Prior knowledge can be defined as all of an individual's prior experiences, learning, and development that precede his/her entering a specific learning situation or attempting to comprehend a specific text. Sometimes prior knowledge can be erroneous or incomplete. Obviously, if there are misconceptions in a child's prior knowledge, these must be corrected so that the child's overall comprehension skills can continue to progress. Prior knowledge of children includes their accumulated positive and negative experiences both in and out of school.

These might come from wonderful family travels, watching television, visiting museums and libraries, visiting hospitals or prisons, and surviving poverty. Whatever the prior knowledge that the child brings to the school setting, the independent reading and writing the child does in school immeasurably expands his/her prior knowledge and hence broadens his/her reading comprehension capabilities.

The teacher must consider as he/she prepares to begin any imaginative/literary text the following about the students' level of prior knowledge:

1. What prior knowledge needs to be activated for the text or theme or for the writing to be done successfully?
2. How independent are the children in using strategies to activate their prior knowledge?

Holes and Roser (1987) have suggested five techniques for activating prior knowledge before starting an imaginative/literary text:

1. Free Recall: Tell us what you know about...
2. Unstructured Discussion: Let's talk about...
3. Structured Question: Who exactly was Jane Aviles in the life of the hero of the story?
4. Word Association: When you hear these words—hatch, elephant, who, think—what author do you think of?
5. Recognition: Mulberry Street. What author comes to mind?

Previewing and predicting and story mapping are also excellent strategies for activating prior knowledge.

Development of Literary Analysis Skills

There are many exciting ways to sensitize and to teach children about the features and formats of different literary genres.

Strategy One: Genre Switch—Reader and Writer Transformation

This strategy should be introduced as a read-aloud with young children or with children who are struggling readers. In a similar fashion, it would be introduced as a read-aloud for ELL learners. Older children in grades 3-6 might just be "started off" by a teacher prompt and do the required reading on their own.

To begin, the teacher selects a book from a particular genre. If it is close to Halloween, a goblin or suspense story will do well. The teacher begins to read the story with the open invitation to the students to determine, as the story is being read, what type of story it is and what makes it that type of story. Older children take notes in their reading journals while younger children and those more in need of explicit teacher support contribute their ideas and responses as part of the discussion in class. Their responses are recorded on a chart.

As the reading continues, the story-type components are listed on the chart. Most of the responses are those that have been elicited from the children.

At some point in what is either an oral read-aloud, guided reading, or independent reading, the teacher directs the children's attention to the components that have emerged on the chart. They then use these components, which are generally components of character—setting, plot, style, conflict, language—to identify the story genre.

The teacher provides the children with an opportunity to expound at length on why this story is an example of the genre they have identified. Once they have done so, the teacher challenges them to consider how this story with its set of given characters, plot, and setting would be changed if the genre were different. The teacher can challenge the class as a whole with the idea of changing the story to a radically different genre—i.e. from suspense to a fairy tale or a comedy—or allow the children to come up with another genre.

Then, depending on the children's developed writing abilities, they might be given time to rewrite the story on their own or re-tell it in class prior to writing and illustrating it.

In the balanced-literacy approach, this transformation of the story into another genre is done as part of the Writing Workshop component, which uses the same reading material as the source for writing. The strategy results in the children's experiencing an in-depth analysis of a particular genre as well as hands-on writing (or telling, if they cannot yet write or cannot yet write in English) or restyling that basic plot and characters into another genre. This authenticates the children's participation as readers and writers.

Strategy Two: Analyzing Story Elements

Story elements include plot (including conflict and resolution), setting (including time and place), characters (flat and round/static and dynamic), and theme (the main idea of the story). Students can use graphic organizers such as story maps, compare/contrast displays, and sequence boxes to display their understanding of these critical features of fiction.

Strategy Three: Analyzing Character Development

Characters in children's literature may be flat or round. A flat character is one-dimensional and is often defined by one characteristic. Rosie in *Rosie's Walk* is an example. A round character seems like someone you know, such as Jesse in *Bridge to Terabithia*. Static characters do not change from the beginning to the end of the story, while dynamic ones do. Characters reveal themselves through their actions, their interactions, and through what they say.

Strategy Four: Interpreting Figurative Language

Similes are direct comparisons between two things using "like" or "as." "Her eyes were like stars" is a simile. Metaphors are indirect comparisons, such as "The earth is a big blue marble." Personification is giving human characteristics to non-animal beings. Frances, Shrek, or the animals in *Mr. Gumpy's Outing* are all examples of personification.

Strategy Five: Identifying Literary Allusions

Children can understand allusions best when they read a lot. A literary allusion when it appears in a story is also called *intertextuality*, which is when a reference, character, or symbol from one story appears in or is alluded to in another. Many recent popular children's books use literary allusions, from the Ahlbergs' *Each Peach Pear Plum* to Jon Scieszka's *The True Story of the Three Little Pigs*. Note that any character or plot element can become an allusion, not just references from fairy tales.

Strategy Six: Analyzing the Author's Point of View

In fiction, point of view is the vantage point from which the narrator tells the story. We determine point of view by asking where the narrator is standing in relation to the characters? Is the narrator inside or outside of the story? If inside, is the narrator one of the characters? This is *first person point of view.* If outside, can the narrator "see" into anyone else's mind besides his/her own? If the narrator cannot see into the mind and heart of other characters, then the point of view is *third person limited.* If the narrator can see what other characters are thinking and feeling, it is *third person omniscient point of view.*

Use of Comprehension Strategies Before, During, and After Reading

Cooper (2004), Taberski (2000), Cox (2005) and other researchers recommend a broad array of comprehension strategies before, during, and after reading.

Cooper (2004) suggests a broad range of classroom posters on the walls plus explicit instruction to give children prompts to monitor their own reading. An example follows: My Strategic Reading Guide

1. Do I infer/predict important information, use what I know, think about what may happen or what I want to learn?

2. Can I identify important information about the story elements?

3. Do I generate questions and search for the answers?

4. Does this make sense to me? Does this help me meet my purpose in reading?

5. If lost, do I remember fix-ups such as re-read, read further ahead, look at the illustrations, ask for help, think about the words, and evaluate what I have read?

6. Do I remember to think about how the parts of the stories that I was rereading came together?

Storyboard panels, which are used by comic-strip artists, artists who do advertising campaigns, and television and film directors, are perfect for engaging children K-6 in a variety of comprehension strategies before, during, and after reading. They can storyboard the beginning of a story, read aloud, and then storyboard its predicted middle or end. Of course, after they experience or read the actual middle or ending of the story, they can compare and contrast what they produced with its actual structure. They can play familiar literature-identification games with a buddy or as part of a center by storyboarding one key scene or characters from a book and challenging a partner or peer to identify the book and characters correctly.

Use of Oral Language Activities to Promote Comprehension

Retelling

Retelling needs to be very clearly defined so that the child reader does not think that the teacher wants him or her to spill the *whole* story in the retelling. Children should be able to talk comfortably and fluently about the stories they have just read. They should be able to tell the main things that happened in the story.

When children retell a story to a teacher, the teacher needs ways to assess their understanding. Ironically, teachers can use some of the same strategies they recommend to children to assess their understanding of a book that is not familiar to the teacher. These strategies include the following:

1. Back cover reading

2. Scanning the table of contents

3. Looking at the pictures

4. Reading the book jacket

If the child can explain how the story turned out and provide examples to support these explanations, try not to interrupt with too many questions. Children can use the text of the book to reinforce what they are saying and they can even read from it if they wish. It is also important to note that some children need to reread the text twice and they need to understand that it is quite possible that the second reading is just as enjoyable as the first one was.

When the teacher plans to use the retelling as a way of assessing the child, then the following ground rules must be set and made clear to the child. The teacher explains the purpose of the retelling to determine how well the child is reading at the outset of the conference.

The teacher maintains in the child's assessment notebook or assessment record what the child is saying in phrases, not sentences. Just enough is recorded to indicate whether the child actually understood the story. The teacher also tries to analyze from the retelling why the child cannot comprehend a given text if that is the case. If the child's accuracy rate with the text is below 95 per cent, then the problem is at the word level, but if the accuracy rate for the text is above 95 per cent, the difficulty lies at the text level.

Development of the Reading Comprehension Skills and Strategies of Individual Students

ELL students bring to their classrooms different prior-knowledge concerns than do their native English-language-speaking peers. Some of the ELL students have extensive prior knowledge in their native language and can read well on or above their chronological age level in that language. Other ELL students come to the United States from cultures where reading was not emphasized or circumstances did not give families native-language literacy opportunities.

Rigg and Allen (1999) offer the following four principles regarding the literacy development and prior knowledge of ELL learners:

1. In learning a language you learn to do the things you want to do with people who are speaking that language.

2. A second language, like the first, does not develop linearly, but rather globally.

3. Language can develop in rich context.

4. Literacy develops parallel to language, so as speaking and listening for the second language develop, so do writing and reading.

As far as retelling, it needs to be noted that second-language learners have the problem of not bringing rich oral English vocabulary to the stories they are decoding. Therefore, often they sound the stories out well, but cannot explain what they are about because they do not know what the words mean.

Use of Oral-Reading Fluency in Facilitating Comprehension

At some point it is crucial that just as the nervous, novice bike rider finally relaxes and speeds happily off, so, too, must the early reader integrate graphophonic cues with semantic and structural ones. Before this is done, the oral quality of early readers has a stilted beat to it, which of course does not promote reading engagement and enjoyment.

The teacher needs to be at his/her most dramatic to model for children the beauties of voice and nuance that are contained in the texts whose print they are tracking so anxiously. Children love nothing more than to mimic their teacher and can do so legitimately and without hesitation if the teacher takes time each day to recite a poem with them. The poem might be posted on chart paper and be up on the wall for a week.

First the teacher can model the fluent and expressive reading of this poem. Then with a pointer, the class can recite it with the teacher. As the week progresses, the class can recite it on their own.

Use of Writing Activities to Promote Literary Response and Analysis

In addition to the activities already mentioned, the activities below will promote literary response and analysis:

- Have children take a particular passage from a story and retell it from another character's perspective.

- Challenge children to suggest a sequel or a prequel to any given story they have read.

- Ask the children to recast a story in which the key characters are male into one where the key characters are female (or vice versa). Have them explain how these changes alter the narrative, plot, or outcome.

- Encourage the children to transform a story or book into a reader's-theater format and record it complete with sound effects for the audio-cassette center of the classroom.

- Have the children produce a newspaper as the characters of a given story would have reported the news in their community.

- Transform the story into a ballad poem or a picture-book version for younger peers.

- Give ELL children an opportunity to translate stories into their native language or to author in English with a buddy a favorite story that was originally published in their native language.

Skill 8.2   Select appropriate resources to reflect and address student diversity in the classroom and community

Reading specialists must have a large amount of materials available to them to be able to meet the needs of the various students they may encounter. A typical classroom will contain children from a variety of cultural backgrounds with a variety of reading abilities and personal interests. Therefore, a reading specialist must gather materials that reflect an appropriate diversity of culture, level, and interest.

Exposing children to a rich array of materials from both mainstream and non-mainstream cultures will keep them engaged with reading and develop their understanding of the world. It is essential to provide materials that address the experiences of members of the specific cultural groups present in a particular classroom. Find books authored or illustrated by writers and artists from these cultures and contact local museums or cultural organizations for advice about other materials to acquire. Materials dealing with important cultural traditions, holidays, and folklore can capture students' interest and help them preserve their cultural identities. Naturally, avoid any materials that express negative biases or cultural stereotypes. Beyond this, be sure also to provide materials that reflect mainstream culture. Help children from mainstream culture explore their own backgrounds and immigrant ancestry by reading materials that deal with cultures that have become mainstream. In general, use resources to explore and celebrate the differences in cultures, but also highlight in the materials universal themes that are common to all cultures.

Selecting materials to meet the instructional needs of students at a variety of reading levels is important as well. Assessment data, including running records, provide the basis for beginning instruction. In most cases, texts should be leveled according to some standard. Many people use the Fountas and Pinnell leveling system or the Developing Readers Assessment system. Either one will provide lists of books and their corresponding levels; in fact, most major publishing companies provide this information for all of their materials. Knowing these levels will be helpful in meeting the instructional needs of students in a more efficient manner.

Matching young children with "just right" books fosters independent reading, no matter how young they are. The teacher needs to have an extensive classroom library of books. Books that emergent readers and early readers can be matched with should have fairly large print, appropriate spacing so the reader can easily see where words begin and end, and few words on each page so the young reader can focus on top-to bottom, left-to-right, and the one-to-one match of word to print.

Illustrations for young children should support the meaning of the text, and language patterns and predictable text structures should make these texts appealing to young readers. Most important of all, the content of the story should relate to the children's interests and experiences as the teacher knows them.

Only after all these considerations have been addressed can the teacher select "just right" books from an already-leveled bin or list. In a similar fashion, when the teacher is selecting books for transitional and fluent readers, the following ideas need to be taken into account:

The book should take at least two sittings to read so children can get used to reading longer books. The fluent and transitional reader needs to deal with more complex characters and more intricate plotting. Look for books that set the stage for plot development with a compelling beginning. Age appropriateness of the concepts, plot, and themes is important so that the child will sustain interest in the book. Look for book features such as a list of chapters to help children navigate through the book. Series books are wonderful to introduce at this point in their development

Finally, you should provide children with materials that relate to their diverse interests. Familiarize yourself with various genres of literature, including those that specifically appeal to the students with whom you are working. Locate materials that supplement their current content-area learning. Give them interest surveys to gain insight into their minds and help you understand what motivates them. In addition, most students respond well to activities that involve computers and other electronic devices. Technological advances make possible not only activities and games on compact discs, but also web-based reading-support programs. These sites can be bookmarked for ease of use with various groups of students.

There are many accepted methods for organizing diverse classroom materials. For example, books can be organized by level, author, genre, series, topics, or other ways that seem helpful to both teacher and student. Crates can be purchased rather inexpensively or boxes could be used to hold the books. Labeling each container may be time-consuming at the outset but the time will be well-spent in the long run. Supportive materials such as lesson plans, worksheets, and activity guides can be stored in filing cabinets labeled by book title or kept in the same storage container as the books. Keeping all materials together can be difficult to manage but is the most efficient way to organize an overwhelming amount of information.

COMPETENCY 9.0 KNOWLEDGE OF READING ASSESSMENTS

Skill 9.1   Identify measurement concepts, characteristics, and uses of norm-referenced, criterion-referenced, and performance-based assessments

Characteristics and Uses of Criterion-Referenced and Norm-Referenced Tests to Assess Reading Development and Identify Reading Difficulties

Criterion-Referenced Tests

These tests measure against criteria or guidelines that are uniform for all the test takers. Therefore, by definition, no special questions, formats, or considerations are made for the test taker who is either from a different linguistic/cultural background or is already identified as a struggling reader/writer. On a criterion-referenced test, it is possible that a child test-taker can score 100% because the child may have been exposed to and has already mastered all the concepts taught. A child's score on such a test may indicate which of the concepts the child has already been exposed to and what he or she needs additional review or support to master.

Two criterion-referenced tests that are commonly used to assess children's reading achievement are the Diagnostic Indicators of Basic Early Literacy Skills (DIBELS) and the Stanford Achievement Test. DIBELS measures progress in literacy from kindergarten to grade three. It can be downloaded from the Internet free at dibels.uoregon.edu. The Stanford is designed to measure individual children's achievement in key school subjects. Subtests covering various reading skills are part of this test. Both DIBELS and the Stanford Achievement Test are group-administered. *Degrees of Reading Power (DRP)* assesses how well children understand the meaning of written text in real life situations and is supposed to measure the process of children's reading, not the products of reading such as identifying the main idea and author's purpose. *CTPIII* s a criterion-referenced test that measures verbal and quantitative ability in grades 3-12. It helps differentiate among the most capable students, i.e., those who rank above the 80th percentile on other standardized tests. This is a test that emphasizes higher-order thinking skills and process-related reading comprehension questions.

Norm-Referenced Tests

These tests measure the test-takers against one another. Scores on these tests are reported in percentiles. Each percentile indicates the percent of the testing population whose scores were the same as or lower than a particular child's score. Percentile is defined as a score on a scale of 100 showing the percentage of a distribution that is equal to it or below it. This type of state-standardized norm-referenced test is being used in most districts today in response to the No Child Left Behind Act. While this type of test does not help track the individual student's progress in his/her ongoing reading development, it does permit comparisons across groups. There are many more standardized norm-referenced tests to assess children's reading than there are criterion-referenced. In these tests, scores are based on how well a child does compared to others, usually on the local, state, and national level. If the norming groups on the tests are reflective of the children being tested (e.g. same spread of minority, low income, gifted students), the results are more trustworthy.

One of the best known norm-referenced tests is the *Iowa Test of Basic Skills*. It assesses student achievement in various school subjects and has several subtests in reading. Other examples of norm-referenced tests used around the country are the *Metropolitan Achievement Tests*, the *Terra Nova-2*, and the *Stanford Diagnostic Reading Test-4*. These are all group tests. An individual test that reading specialists use with students is the *Woodcock Reading Mastery Test*.

Skill 9.2 Identify appropriate oral and written methods for assessing individual student progress (e.g., informal reading inventories, fluency checks, think alouds, rubrics, running records, story retelling, and portfolios)

The Characteristics and Uses of Formal and Informal Assessments

Informal Assessments

A running record of children's oral-reading progress in the early grades K-3 is a pivotal informal assessment. It supports the teacher in deciding whether a book a child is reading is matched to his/her stage of reading development. In addition, this assessment allows the teacher to analyze a child's miscues to see which cueing systems and strategies the child uses and to determine other systems the child might use more effectively. The running record also offers a graphic account of a child's oral reading.

Generally, a teacher should maintain an annotated class notebook with pages set aside for all the children or individual notebooks for each child. One of the benefits of using running records as an informal assessment is that they can be used with any text and can serve as a tool for teaching rather than as an instrument to report on children's status in class.

Another good point about using running records is that they can be taken repeatedly and frequently by the teacher, so the educator can truly observe a pattern of errors. This in turn provides the educator with sufficient information to analyze the child's reading over time. As any mathematician or scientist knows, the more samples of a process you gather over time, the more likely you are to get an accurate picture.

Using the notations Marie Clay developed and shared in her *An Observation Study of Early Literacy Achievement*, Sharon Taberski offers in her book, *On Solid Ground*, a lengthy walk through keeping a running record of children's reading. She writes in the child's miscue on the top line of her running record above the text word. Indeed, she records all of the child's miscue attempts on the line above the text word. Sharon advises the teacher to make all the miscue notations as the child reads, since this allows the teacher to get additional information about how and why the child makes miscue choices. Additionally, the teacher should note self corrections (coded SC) when the child is monitoring his/her own reading, crosschecking information, and using additional information.

As part of the informal assessment of primary-grade reading, it is important to record the child's word insertions, omissions, requests for help, and attempts to get the word. In informal assessment the rate of accuracy can be estimated by dividing the child's errors by the total words read.

Results of a running-record assessment can be used to select the best setting for the child's reading. If a child reads from 95%–100% correct, the child is ready for independent reading. If the child reads from 92% to 97% right, the child is ready for guided reading. The child who reads below 92% needs a read-aloud or shared-reading activity. Note that these percentages are slightly different from those one would use to match books to readers.

One of the increasingly popular and meaningful forms of informal assessment is the compilation of the literacy portfolio. What is particularly compelling about this type of informal portfolio is that artists, television directors, authors, architects, and photographers use portfolios in their careers and jobs. This is an authentic format for documenting children's literacy growth over time. The portfolio is not only a significant informal assessment tool for the teacher, but a vehicle and format for the child reader to take ownership of his or her progress over time. It models a way of compiling one's reading and writing products as a lifelong learner, which is the ultimate goal of reading instruction.

Portfolios can include the following six categories of materials:

Work samples: These can include children's story maps, webs, K-W-L charts, pictures, illustrations, storyboards, and writings about the stories they have read.

Records of independent reading and writing: These can include the children's journals, notebooks, or logs of books read with the names of the authors, titles of the books, dates completed, and pieces related to books completed or in progress.

Checklists and Surveys: These include checklists designed by the teacher for reading development, writing development, ownership checklists, and general-interest surveys.

Self Evaluation Forms: These are the children's own evaluations of their reading and writing progress framed in their own words. They can be simple templates with starting sentences such as:
- ✓ I am really proud of the way I _____
- ✓ I feel one of my strengths as a reader is _____
- ✓ To improve the way I read aloud I need to _____
- ✓ To improve my reading I should _____

Generally, at the beginning of a child's portfolio in grade 3 or above, there is a letter to the reader explaining the work that will be found in the portfolio and from fourth-grade level up, children write a brief reflection detailing their feelings and judgments about their growth as readers and writers.

When teachers are maintaining the portfolios for mandated school administrative review, district review, or even for their own research, they often prepare portfolio summary sheets. These provide identifying data on the children and then a timeline of their review of the portfolio contents plus professional comments on the extent to which the portfolio documents satisfactory and ongoing growth in reading.

Portfolios can be used beneficially for child/teacher and of course, parent/teacher conversations to review the child's progress, discuss areas of strength, set future goals, make plans for future learning activities and evaluate what should remain in the portfolio and what needs to be cleared out for new materials.

Rubrics

Holistic scoring involves assessing a child's ability to construct meaning through writing. It uses a scale called a *rubric*, which can range from 0 to 4.

0—This indicates the piece cannot be scored. It does not respond to the topic or is illegible.

1—The writing responds to the topic but does not cover it accurately.

2—This piece of writing responds to the topic but lacks sufficient details or elaboration.

3—This piece fulfills the purpose of the writing assignment and has sufficient development (which refers to details, examples, and elaboration of ideas).

4—This response has the most details, best organization, and the best-expressed reaction to the original writer's piece.

Miscue Analysis

This procedure allows the teacher to look at reading process. By definition, the miscue is an oral response different from the text being read. Sometimes miscues are also called unexpected responses or errors. By studying a student's miscues from an oral-reading sample, the teacher can determine which cues and strategies the student is correctly using or not using in constructing meaning. The teacher can then customize instruction to meet the needs of this particular student.

Informal Reading Inventories (IRI)

These are a series of samples of texts prearranged in stages of increasing difficulty. Listening to children read through these inventories, the teacher can pinpoint their skill level and the additional concepts they need to work on.

Techniques for Assessing Particular Reading Skills

Sharon Taberski recommends that the teacher build in one-on-one time for supporting individual children as needed in considering what makes sense, sounds right, and matches the letters.

She has noted that emergent and early readers tend to focus on meaning without adequate attention to graphophonic cues. She suggests using the following prompts for children who are having problems with graphophonic cues:

- ✓ Does what you said match the letters?

- ✓ If the word were what you said ___, what would it have to start with?

- ✓ Look carefully at the first letters..., then look at the middle letters..., then look at the last letters. What could it be?

- ✓ If it were ____, what would it end with?

Oral retellings can be used to test children's comprehension.

Children who are retelling a story to be tested for comprehension should be told what the purpose is when they sit down with the teacher.

It is a good idea to let the child start the retelling on his or her own because then the teacher can see whether he or she needs prompts to retell the story. Many times more experienced readers summarize what they have read. This summary usually flows out along with the characters, the problem of the story, and other details.

Other signs that children understand what they are reading when they give an oral retelling include their use of illustrations to support the retelling, references to the exact text in the retelling, emotional reaction to the text, making connections between the text and other stories or experiences they have had, and giving information about the text without the teacher's asking for it.

Skill 9.3   Interpret assessment data (e.g., screening, progress monitoring, diagnostic) to guide instructional decisions

When using running records as a form of informal assessment as to the progress a student is making, it is important to study the types of errors the child is making. In this way, you can examine the student's strategies and errors for purposes of planning instruction, monitoring progress, and assessing skill levels. Even if they are not using a running record, teachers can use even more informal methods of using the errors a student makes to find significant ways to help the student improve.

Miscue analysis can be multi-faceted and provide both the teacher and reader with a wealth of important information. First, examining the methods a student uses to figure out unknown words helps the teacher understand which methods require further instruction or just fine tuning. Typically, students use phonics skills (letter/sound correspondence), contextual clues (the other words in the sentence/passage), semantic analysis, or structural-analysis techniques to solve problems in reading. The reader becomes more proficient by using not just one of these methods but by using a combination of all of them.

After collecting the running record, teachers can then evaluate which of the strategies the students are using with success. Tallying is one method to use; in this way, the educator can see strategies used by the student and whether one is more dominant than others. This method will also help to point out weak strategies that require more instruction. After this analysis, the teacher can develop an instructional plan to address vulnerable areas and increase a more balanced problem-solving approach for the student.

Additionally, the teacher can look at the students' ability to monitor their own reading and comprehension. Observing these self-monitoring attempts allows the teacher to determine whether the students recognize when they make a mistake. This is a very important skill for readers to develop. Once they realize something does not make sense, they can go back and apply a correction strategy and improve comprehension. This becomes more important as the complexity of text increases.

Self-corrections by students show maturity of reading skills. However, students who make many self-corrections lack fluency in reading and will eventually lose some comprehension. Self-correction is an important step for readers, but as with any other learning process, we want students to pass through it rapidly and move on to fluency.

Skill 9.4   Use individual student-reading data to differentiate instruction

See Competencies 4.0, 5.0 and 6.0

Regularly assess students' fluency, reading comprehension, and mastery of content-area information. Use this data to determine areas where students need further instruction or intervention and to select texts appropriate for their current reading level. Students will vary in their reading abilities, and to avoid boredom and develop as readers they may need to receive small group, differentiated instruction and targeted intervention. Set up Reading Centers in your classroom: a Teacher-Led Center where students can work in groups with you and Independent Student Centers where students can work in small groups, pairs, or individually. Set skill targets for students based on their current reading abilities and tailor their instruction to help meet these goals. Some students may need extra guidance in certain areas, while others who have mastered these areas may profit from enrichment activities.

Examine the data you have collected for each student for areas of weakness and achievement and use this and your observations of each student to organize the class into flexible groups. These groups will vary in size (smaller for struggling readers) and in how often they meet with you in the Teacher-Led Center and how long each session with you lasts. Different lesson structures will meet the needs of each group. Some groups will need Skills-Focused Lessons developed by you to give them further practice with specific elements such as decoding strategies, vocabulary building, fluency, phonemic awareness, reading comprehension strategies, and so on. You may need to reteach these elements explicitly or just provide students more concentrated practice with them. However you structure a lesson, it must be targeted to meet the specific needs of this particular group of students, must fit the timeslot you have available for sessions in the Teacher-Led Center, and must engage the students interactively.

A second lesson structure to use with groups in the Teacher-Led Center is Guided Reading. In this type of lesson you pick a text that is appropriate to the skill level of a group, introduce it to the group, read it with students, discuss it, and teach and use reading strategies. Because this type of lesson focuses more on discerning the meaning of a text, it will most likely work better with more fluent readers. A Guided Reading lesson gives you an excellent opportunity to monitor students' comprehension of a text, but does not really allow you to work on word analysis skills with struggling students. Therefore, you may in some cases want to mix aspects of both kinds of lessons, depending on each group's current needs.

Activities for the Independent Student Centers should be as varied as the needs of your students. Sometimes students will benefit from individual practice with a skill, while at other times they will learn better working with a skill in pairs or groups or being tutored by a peer who has already mastered the skill. For example, does a student struggle to read fluently? Have him or her take turns reading with a partner or reading chorally. Depending on what skill each student is struggling to master, provide pairs or groups with passages that allow them to practice specific fluency skills such as reading dialogue, reading with feeling, or interpreting punctuation. In addition, know the text readability of classroom textbooks and other classroom resources and match students to these texts accordingly. Then say a student is able to read a passage fluently, but does not comprehend what he or she has read. You might give that student extra individual practice with reading strategies such as summarizing, monitoring comprehension, or using a graphic organizer. When possible, pair a student struggling with reading comprehension with a partner who has mastered this skill and have students work through a text together until both understand what it means. Finally, suppose a student is able to decode content-area texts but unable to use or retain the information in the texts. You can assign this student more individual practice interpreting the text structures of different content-area texts and have him or her work on study skills such as note-taking or using reference materials. In all cases, check student-reading data periodically to ensure that progress is being made toward the clearly stated skill targets.

Skill 9.5 Evaluate the appropriateness (e.g., curriculum alignment, cultural bias) of assessment instruments and practices

Concepts of Validity, Reliability, and Bias in Testing

Validity is how well a test measures what it is supposed to measure. Teacher-made tests are therefore not generally extremely valid although they may be an appropriate measure for the validity of the concept the teacher wants to assess for his/her own children's achievement.

Reliability has to do with the consistency of the test. This is measured by whether the test will indicate the same score for the child who takes it more than once.

Bias in testing occurs when the information within the test or the information required to respond to a multiple-choice question or constructed response (essay question on the test) is information that is not available to some test takers who come from a different cultural, ethnic, linguistic or socio-economic background than do the majority of the test takers. Since they have not had the same prior linguistic, social, or cultural experiences that the majority of test takers have had, these test takers are at a disadvantage in taking the test and no matter what their actual mastery of the material taught by the teacher, cannot address the "biased" questions. Generally other "non-biased" questions are given to them and eventually the biased questions are removed from the examination.

To solidify what might be abstract to the reader, on a recent reading test in one school system, the grade-four reading-comprehension multiple-choice test had some questions about the well-known fairy tale about the gingerbread boy. These questions were simple and accessible for most of the children in the class. But two children who were recent arrivals from the Dominican Republic had learned English there. They were reading on grade-four level, but in their Dominican grade school, the story of the gingerbread boy was not a major one. Therefore, a question about this story on the standardized reading test demonstrated examiner bias and was not fair to these test takers.

Characteristics and uses of Group versus Individual Reading Assessments

In assessment, tests are used for different purposes. They have different dimensions or characteristics whether they are given individually or in a group and whether they are standardized or teacher-made. The chart below shows the relationships of these elements.

	Standardized	**Teacher-made**
Individual	*Characteristics* • is uniformly administered *Uses* • is best for younger children • helps with placement for special services	*Characteristics* • has more flexibility *Uses* • assists teaching decisions • used for diagnostic purposes
Group	*Characteristics* • is uniformly administered • is time efficient *Uses* • permits comparisons across groups • used for policy decisions by administrators	*Characteristics* • has high face validity • is time efficient *Uses* • informs teach-reteach & enrichment decisions • documents students' learning

COMPETENCY 10.0 KNOWLEDGE OF PRINT AND NONPRINT MEDIA

Skill 10.1 **Identify criteria for selecting and evaluating both print and nonprint media (e.g., Internet, software, trade books, textbooks, DVDs, videos, interactive computing) for instructional use**

Because there is such an array of print and nonprint media available for instructional use these days, it is essential that only the most pertinent and useful materials be provided to students. Before deciding to use any product, ask yourself first what this product will bring to the classroom and then consider whether another product might do a better job at this task. Keeping the following criteria in mind will allow you to evaluate which materials best suit your current purposes:

- Is the content of the product relevant? Will it help students meet the objectives of your content-area curriculum?
- Does the product meet the general abilities of your students? Think about whether the product might be too easy or too advanced for students to read, watch, or use.
- Is the content of the product accurate, comprehensive, and up-to-date? Are facts presented in an objective way? When an issue is discussed, are both sides presented fairly? Is the product free from bias?
- Is the product suitable for your audience? Does it contain any taboos, caricatures, stereotypes, or other negative, offensive, or inappropriate content?
- Is the format of the product appropriate? Do your students have any learning styles or special needs that should be taken into account? For example, if you are working with visual learners, a video or DVD might serve your purpose better in some cases than a trade book or magazine article would, while auditory learners might benefit from using audiotapes.
- Is the product of good quality? Is the cost of purchase or use worth the benefit to be gained from using the product? Does it come well-recommended or has it been nominated for or won any awards?

Skill 10.2   Identify appropriate use of print and nonprint media to match students' needs and interests within the instructional unit.

Variety captures and sustains students' interest in a topic, and it makes sense to take advantage of the wide assortment of print and nonprint media on hand. In addition, in a world where more and more information is being conveyed through electronic hypertext and images, students must become media literate as part of their education. That said, it is important to be selective and have valid reasons for incorporating different kinds of media into the classroom. Your primary focus should always be on teaching the curriculum, a purpose that may sometimes be best served by websites or DVDs, but may other times be met with a simple library book. Be sure not to overload students with too many products at a time, and make sure that even products that you offer for fun still educate students in some way.

The primary appropriate use for any kind of media in the classroom is direct instruction of specific, content-area knowledge. Many materials can be used for this task—textbooks, trade books, magazines, newspapers, videos or DVDs—but whichever you choose should contain accurate and ideally comprehensive information and should match the current developmental level of your students.

Sometimes a main source benefits from being supplemented by a product that offers additional information about a topic or a different viewpoint on an issue. A website can offer a more in-depth and complex exploration of a subject. A CD can allow students to listen to a piece of music or a speech they have only read about. A video or DVD can let them watch a performance or view historical footage. It is not enough, however, just to expose students to supplementary print and nonprint media products. Be sure to urge them to think about what they have gained from each product. What additional information have they gathered? How does the way in which information is presented in each product affect their understanding of a topic? Seize every possible opportunity to help students develop their abilities to compare and contrast different types of media and to evaluate media products with a critical eye.

A final beneficial use for print and nonprint media is to allow students to explore these different kinds of media themselves to pursue personal interests in areas related to the main topic of the current instructional unit. Researching a topic with your guidance will prepare students for using different kinds of media and doing their own research down the line. Do set limits so that students' research remains focused on matters connected to the curriculum, and mind that students do not become exposed to inappropriate content.

COMPETENCY 11.0 KNOWLEDGE OF CLASSROOM ENVIRONMENTS THAT SUPPORT READING

Skill 11.1   Identify the characteristics and purposes of various reading programs (e.g., core reading program, supplemental reading program, intensive intervention program)

The core reading program is designed to meet the needs of students who are reading on grade level. For the most part, these programs are arranged sequentially in grade levels with the text becoming increasingly more difficult in word choice and content with each level. The problem with relying on this reading program alone is that it probably will not meet the needs of all the students in the class. A core reading program is also called a "basal reading program" and adoption of such a reading program should adhere to certain characteristics:

- It should be based on current research and methodologies.

- It should provide explicit instruction in phonemic awareness, phonics, decoding, word recognition, spelling, vocabulary, comprehension and writing.

- Opportunities for students to discuss the reading in class should be built into the program.

For many students, a supplemental reading program is essential. This could take the form of extra reading to challenge students with advanced reading skills or to provide them with an opportunity to read more on a theme or topic, whether it is discussed in class or of interest to the student. The purpose is to provide extra instruction to students who may need it by supporting and extending the core reading program. Like the core reading program, the supplemental programs should provide instruction in phonics, comprehension, fluency, and vocabulary. It could take the form of practice reading texts that expand on mini-lessons the teacher delivers in class.

An intense intervention program is intended for students who are experiencing difficulty in developing as fluent readers. With such a program, the teacher can provide a small group of students or an individual student with explicit, systematic instruction to help the student read at grade level. The focus is usually on phonics, fluency, and comprehension. The intent is to allow teachers to meet the needs of students who are struggling with the core reading program.

Skill 11.2 **Identify appropriate classroom organizational formats (e.g., literature circles, small groups, individuals, workshops, reading centers, multiage groups) for specific instructional objectives**

Due to the diverse nature of classrooms, teachers must employ various strategies to differentiate learning in order to meet the needs of all the learners. In order to differentiate the instruction, teachers need to use strategies that will best suit the students.

Literature Circles

A small group of students (no more than 5) choose a book they will read. Each person in the group is assigned a role, which changes at intervals so that each person gets to play each role. The group is temporary, depending on the book. The groups meet on a regular basis to discuss the reading and they use written notes or drawings to help guide their discussions. Once students become more familiar with literature circles, they may abandon the use of roles and have an open dynamic discussion. The teacher becomes a facilitator and although he/she does evaluate the group, the students also engage in self-assessment. Once the book is read and discussed, the group members share with the whole class and a different book is chosen.

Small Groups

Small groups are essential in a classroom so that the teacher can give instruction on topics that particular students need. It can be a completely new strategy or a reteaching of one that a few students have not yet fully grasped. These groups can be used for reading or writing instruction. Some examples of small groups within a classroom include:
- Partner reading and writing
- Literacy centers
- Group investigations
- Peer editing
- Guided reading groups

Workshops

Workshops provide the students with the chance to learn and practice new strategies in a small group setting. For example, in a writing workshop, one group of students could be working on pre-writing, another could be working on a first draft and yet another could be working on revising, editing, or publishing. In a reading workshop, students can be reading, writing a response to the reading, or working on a project to display to the class.

Reading Centers
In reading centers, the teacher can have several books that students read and respond to. There may be activities for students to practice reading strategies, listen to a taped reading, or be taught mini-lessons on various strategies.

Multiage Groups
When there are students at different grade levels who have the same problems, small groups may be formed to provide explicit instruction to meet their needs. This type of grouping would only take place at a set time so that there is no interruption of the daily schedule and so students will not miss out on important instruction within their own grade levels.

Skill 11.3   Identify methods and strategies (e.g., explicit and systematic instruction, scaffolding, modeling) to integrate reading, writing, speaking, listening, viewing, and presenting across the curriculum

Conspicuous Strategies. As an instructional priority, conspicuous strategies are a sequence of teaching events and teacher actions used to help students learn new literacy information and relate it to their existing knowledge. Conspicuous strategies can be incorporated in beginning reading instruction to ensure that all learners have basic literacy concepts. For example, during storybook reading, teachers can show students how to recognize the fronts and backs of books, locate titles, or look at pictures and predict the story, rather than assuming that children will learn this through incidental exposure. Similarly, teachers can teach students a strategy for holding a pencil appropriately or checking the form of their letters against an alphabet sheet on their desks or the classroom wall.

Mediated Scaffolding. Mediated scaffolding can be accomplished in a number of ways to meet the needs of students with diverse literacy experiences. To link oral and written language, for example, teachers may use texts that simulate speech by incorporating oral language patterns or children's writing. Or teachers can use daily storybook reading to discuss book-handling skills and directionality-concepts that are particularly important for children who are unfamiliar with printed texts. Teachers can also use repeated readings to give students multiple exposures to unfamiliar words or extended opportunities to look at books with predictable patterns as well as provide support by modeling the behaviors associated with reading. Teachers can act as *scaffolds* during these storybook reading activities by adjusting their demands (e.g., asking increasingly complex questions or encouraging children to take on portions of the reading) or by reading more complex texts as students gain knowledge of beginning literacy components.

Strategic Integration. Many children with diverse literacy experiences have difficulty making connections between old and new information. Strategic integration can be applied to help link old and new learning. For example, in the classroom, strategic integration can be accomplished by providing access to literacy materials in classroom writing centers and libraries. Students should also have opportunities to integrate and extend their literacy knowledge by reading aloud, listening to other students read aloud, and listening to tape recordings and videotapes in reading corners.

Primed Background Knowledge. All children bring some level of background knowledge (e.g., how to hold a book, awareness of directionality of print) to beginning reading. Teachers can utilize children's background knowledge to help children link their personal literacy experiences to beginning reading instruction, while also closing the gap between students with rich and students with impoverished literacy experiences. Activities that draw upon background knowledge include incorporating oral language activities (which discriminate between printed letters and words) into daily read-alouds, as well as frequent opportunities to retell stories, look at books with predictable patterns, write messages with invented spellings, and respond to literature through drawing.

Emergent literacy research examines early literacy knowledge and the contexts and conditions that foster that knowledge. Despite differing viewpoints on the relation between emerging literacy skills and reading acquisition, strong support was found in the literature for the important contribution that early childhood exposure to oral and written language makes to the facility with which children learn to read.

Reading, writing, listening and speaking are the four main components of language arts at any grade level. They are interrelated and they complement each other. By ensuring that all four of these strands are woven into your language arts classes, you can ensure that you provide a balance of experiences to give students the instruction and support that they need. With such a balance, the students are able to integrate all of the English language processes and build on their prior knowledge and experiences.

Speaking and listening may be viewed as separate from reading and writing, but all four form the main communication system of the English language. They are interdependent and all other forms of communication depend on the ability to speak and listen. They are also the foundation for many other language skills, which is why teachers should provide ample opportunities for students to speak and listen in class as part of the daily routine. Classrooms are places where talk flows freely and by taking advantage of this talk to find out where students are in their thinking about topics, themes, and responses to literature, teachers can easily assess this component of language arts. When students can express ideas in their own words, it helps them to make meaning of their experiences with reading.

Although students don't have a lot of problems with speaking in class, listening is something that needs to be nurtured and taught. Good listeners will respond emotionally, imaginatively, and intellectually to what they hear. Students need to be taught how to respond to presentations by their classmates in ways that are not harmful or derogatory in any way. There are also different types of listening that the teacher can develop in the students:

- Appreciative listening to enjoy an experience

- Attentive listening to gain knowledge

- Critical listening to evaluate arguments and ideas

Within the classroom setting, many opportunities will present themselves for students to speak and listen for various purposes and often these may be spontaneous. Activities for speaking and listening should be integrated throughout the language arts program, but there should also be times when speaking and listening are the focus of the instruction. By incorporating speaking and listening into the language arts program, students will begin to see the connection between the two and therefore, be able to improve their reading skills with more efficiency. Some of the ways that speaking and listening can be integrated include:

- Conversations
- Small group discussions
- Brainstorming
- Interviewing
- Oral reading
- Readers' Theatre
- Choral speaking
- Storytelling
- Role playing
- Booktalks
- Oral reports
- Class debates
- Listening to guest speakers

Skill 11.4   Choose effective techniques (e.g., selecting text at the appropriate level, matching text to student interest) for improving attitudes toward reading and for motivating students to engage in reading events

With a little preparation and dedication you can motivate students to read more and with better focus. Students who see the act of reading only as required schoolwork will read texts begrudgingly and not put in the time needed reading outside the classroom to become truly accomplished readers. The following techniques can stimulate an interest in and passion for reading:

- Start by creating a classroom environment that in every aspect encourages the act of reading. Surround students with images of people reading. Gather a classroom library composed not just of books, but of magazines, newspapers, encyclopedias and other reference books, and of less complex texts such as advertisements, cartoon strips, posters, and simple sets of instructions or directions. Collect anything you think will get children at all levels reading.

- Students are more likely to read a text if it appeals to their personal interests. Give students surveys to discover areas in which they are particularly interested or about which they already know many things. Listen to your students as they talk amongst themselves and draw upon their experiences and discussions. Fill your classroom library with texts that relate to student interests and help them use the library to find other intriguing works.

- • Because students who are unmotivated to read are likely to be stymied in general by the process of book selection, make this process easier for them by offering lists of suggested texts, geared toward their personal interests or related to current classroom topics.

- Seize the moment. Often student interest in a topic will arise organically as part of a spirited classroom discussion. Use this interest to urge students to read more about the topic. For example, if students become involved in a debate about an issue, take the opportunity to provide them with texts and articles supporting both sides of the issue. If students have questions about a subject your class is exploring, encourage them to read more about the subject on their own in order to find some answers.

- Help students build a track record of successful reading experiences. The more positive experiences students have with reading, the more likely they are to continue to read. Students may become bored with reading works that are too easy or repelled by works that are too hard. Do your best to know the readability of all classroom texts, and monitor all students' current reading levels so that you can match them with works that they will be able to read successfully and with pleasure.

- Maintain a balanced relationship with students. If students feel forced to read or unsure of what you want from them, they may start resenting you and refuse to read or become confused and stumble over their assignments. Press constantly for students to succeed, but do not push them to read at a level, pace, or duration beyond their current capabilities. Set clear goals for students and communicate your expectations to them so that they know where they stand at all times. Monitor students' progress and mark occasions when they meet goals or master new reading skills.
- Model enthusiasm yourself about reading. If you are excited about something you are reading, share your feelings with your students. Sometimes talking about the books or other texts that you as a teacher are reading will kindle a similar interest in your students. Knowing that you are a reader as well, for pleasure as well as for work, models for the students what you would like for them to become.

COMPETENCY 12.0   KNOWLEDGE OF RESEARCH

Skill 12.1   Identify characteristics (e.g., validity, reliability) of scientifically based reading research

Scientifically based research uses systematic and empirical methods that use experimentation and observation. The collection of data and rigorous analysis of this data is necessary in order to address the hypothesis of the research and to justify the conclusion. All researchers must use the same measurements although they may be in different classrooms and with varying groups of students. The conclusions must be reviewed by a journal or a panel of independent experts. In addition, the results must be replicable.

Also, the results of formal testing are confidential. The teacher will relay the results to the students and parents/guardians; however, in order to release the testing results to any other persons, whether they are professionals in the field of education or if they are in the medical field, the parents/guardians must sign a release paper and agree to let others see the results. They also must be informed as to how the test results will be used.

All tests must have a purpose. The utility of the test will give the teacher an idea of where the student is in regard to understanding the concepts associated with language arts: reading, writing, listening, speaking, viewing, and representing.

Terminology for standardized testing

Achievement Test: a standardized test designed to determine what learning has occurred as a result of classroom instruction.

Alternative Assessment: assessment that differs from the traditional, standardized, norm-referenced, or criterion-referenced test that utilizes open-ended questions, working out problems, performing a task, or producing work that is different from pencil-and-paper tests.

Benchmark: an established standard of student performance on a scale.

Cut Score: score used to determine the minimum level of performance needed to pass a test.

Grade Equivalent: a score that determines the approximate grade level of a student based on an average score. For example, a student with a grade equivalent of 5.5 is said to be able to function at the midpoint of grade 5.

Item Analysis: analyzing the answers students give to questions on a test to determine the proportion of students giving the same answer

Mean: one of the ways of representing a group with a single score. The scores of all the students in a class are added up and divided by the number of students in the class to find the class average. However, this can be affected by extremely high and low scores.

Median: the middle value in a list ordered from smallest to largest.

Norm: the average score of a specified class of persons on a specified test.

Norm group: a random group of students selected by a tester to complete a test to establish the percentiles of performance to be used in establishing standards.

Normal Curve Equivalent: a score that ranges from 1–99 that is used by testers to compare different tests for the same group of students and between different groups of students taking the same test. An NCE is a normalized test score of 50 with a standard deviation of 21.06. For comparative purposes, an NCE should be used instead of percentiles.

Percentile: a ranking score from 1–99 with a median score of 50. A percentile rank indicates the percentage of a reference or norm group obtaining scores equal to or less than the test-taker's score. A percentile score does not refer to the percentage of questions that the student answered correctly. It refers to the student's standing relative to the standard of the norm group.

Profile: how well an individual performs on a group of assessments compiled on a graph.

Quartile: the breakdown of an aggregate of percentile rankings broken down into four categories (0.25, 25-50, 50-75, 75-100).

Quintile: the breakdown of an aggregate of percentile rankings broken down into five categories (1-20, 20-40, 40-60, 60-80. 80-100).

Raw Score: the original result a student obtains on a test, such as the number of questions answered correctly.

Scaled Score: the mean score for each grade and content area.

Stanine: a method of scaling test scores on a nine-point standard with a mean of 5 and a standard deviation of 2.

Skill 12.2   Identify findings from current reading research (e.g., National Reading Panel Report, Preventing Reading Difficulties in Young Children)

Research projects undertaken over the last few years have attempted to examine and draw conclusions from a myriad of past findings so that future plans for reading programs can be supported by informed judgments. Two significant publications generated by such projects are <u>Preventing Reading Difficulties in Young Children</u> by the National Research Council (NRC) Committee and "Teaching Children to Read," a report by the National Reading Panel (a committee composed of scientists, reading teachers, educational administrators, and parents). The NRC publication studied previous research to identify what skills children must master to be able to read and what environments and interactions help and hinder the acquisition of these skills. However, as the NRP points out, "the NRC Committee did not specifically address 'how' critical reading skills are most effectively taught and what instructional methods, materials, and approaches are most beneficial for students of varying abilities," and the NRP subsequently prepared and published its own findings dealing with those areas. Taken together, these two publications offer a wealth of information to teachers, parents, and anyone else concerned with the development of literacy in children.

The primary aim of the committee that created <u>Preventing Reading Difficulties in Young Children</u> was to convert the wealth of information contained in previous research into practical advice and guidance for anyone assisting children in developing literacy and then pass on their recommendations to this audience. In this way, what was before an overwhelming mass of data has been transformed into a useful tool and placed in the hands of those who most need it. The report emphasizes the importance of researching and understanding literacy development and the obligation that reading experts (from government agencies, private foundations, and so on) are under to spread this information to others (parents, people in the community) who can and must put theory into practice. Only through being informed will people be able to give children the support they need from the start to succeed as readers, especially those children identified to be particularly at risk. In brief, the report discusses the process by which children learn to read, identifies groups likely to have reading difficulties and predictors for whether a child will successfully learn to read or not, provides information about ways to prevent reading difficulties in early childhood, describes instructional and organizational strategies for helping children once they enter school, and then discusses who can best help children improve as readers and suggests some recommendations for practice and further research.

Ultimately <u>Preventing Reading Difficulties in Young Children</u> concludes that early intervention is essential. It calls for organizations and the government to educate the public about methods of fostering literacy so that parents and other members of the community can help young children develop a stronger foundation for future accomplishments. It also calls for children with reading difficulties, especially those belonging to groups known to be at risk, to be diagnosed as early as possible, and for all children to be exposed to an environment rich in language and literacy, where they are urged to share and discuss books, play with oral language, and be made aware of the connections between the written and spoken word.

In turn, "Teaching Children to Read" explains the specific methodological standards used by NRP subgroups to research and study various topic areas and describes their findings in these areas, which were alphabetics, fluency, comprehension, teacher education and reading instruction, and computer terminology and reading instruction. After discussing which strategies and methods of instruction they found most and least useful, the subgroups offered suggestions for further research. In general, they concluded that reading instruction should include phonemic awareness, phonics, guided oral reading, and learning how and when to apply targeted reading strategies.

Skill 12.3 Identify reliable sources of reading research (e.g., peer-reviewed journals, technical reports)

It is imperative for teachers to keep up on the current research regarding validated methods for teaching reading. This can be best done through membership in professional organizations such as the International Reading Association (IRA), the National Reading Conference (NRC), or the National Council of Teachers of English (NCTE). Membership in these or other similar organizations will help the professional stay current.

Educational journals often focus on literacy research. These are available at your school if your district has a subscription. As the reading specialist, you should have a subscription to these, which include:
- *The Reading Teacher*
- *Educational Leadership*
- *Adolescent Learning*
- *Reading Research Quarterly*
- *Language Arts*

An important publication in 2000 is the *Report of the National Reading Panel "Teaching Children to Read."* The Panel has sponsored research and publications that can be accessed at http://www.nationalreadingpanel.org.

In addition, experts are writing about the findings of research on literacy.. Consider the writings of the following:
- Marie Clay
- Donald Graves
- Regie Routman
- Susan Taberski
- Lucy Culkins

Skill 12.4 Identify the purpose, procedure, and application of teacher action research

Teacher-action research is carried out by teacher practitioners in the classroom to help them evaluate their own performance. Teachers who engage in this research have a desire to improve their teaching by examining how students learn best and then by making decisions about what changes they can make to help them. As researchers in the classroom, teachers raise questions about their own teaching and how it affects the students' success. Student work becomes part of the data that is analyzed.

Teacher research is voluntary and ethical. It also becomes public because teachers meet with one another to discuss the research and the findings. To get started, teachers must have questions based on their own curiosity. The investigation takes the form of systematically recording what happens in the classroom with the students. Teachers also reflect on their practice and make changes as they see fit, documenting these as well as the results.

Articulation of theories is an essential element of action research. Teachers become critical mentors of one another as they analyze the data. Reflections become part of the process as teachers write about what they find difficult, what they need to change, and what practices have been successful.

COMPETENCY 13.0   KNOWLEDGE OF READING PROGRAM
                    SUPERVISION AND ADMINISTRATION

Skill 13.1   Identify the purposes and practices for involving family
               members, community members, and other professionals in
               reading efforts

Oftentimes in schools, parents, grandparents, and other people involved in
children's lives want to take a more active role. They also often have an opinion
on the appropriate method for teaching students how to read. Sometimes this
can lead to controversy and misunderstandings.

It is important to provide opportunities for the public to come into the school and
participate in activities to encourage reading. During these programs, it is
important to share tidbits of information about the methodologies and strategies
being implemented. In this way, the public can begin to understand the
differences in reading instruction today as compared to what probably occurred
when they attended school. Adults often comment on changes they see in
current educational trends.

Taking the time to educate parents and other family members not only will help to
achieve better understanding and open communication, but it can also provide
more support for students than the school alone would ever be able to provide.

Some strategies for educating parents and family members include the following:

- Bingo games where the correct answer on the bingo board is a fact about
  reading instruction

- Small parent workshops offered on various topics

- Newsletter pieces or paragraphs

- Meetings with individual parents

- Inviting parents in to observe lessons

- Small pieces of information shared during social times when parents are
  invited into the school

Communicating general information about reading and appropriate reading
instruction is important. It is just as important to share more specific information
about students with parents, other school personnel, and the community.

Developing a variety of reporting procedures is discussed in skill 14.5. However, once you have the reports and have gathered the information, the next step involves finding appropriate methods to share this information with the people that need the data. Again, depending on the audience, the amount and type of information may change.

Some ways to share information with parents/guardians include:

- Individual parent meetings
- Small group meetings
- Regular parent updates through phone calls
- Charts and graphs of progress sent home
- Notes to parents

Some ways to share information with school personnel include:

- Faculty meetings
- PowerPoint or other presentations
- E-mail
- Conferences
- School-board presentations
- Graphs and charts

Skill 13.2   Interpret reading information, regulations, and assessment data to administrators, staff members, policy makers, media, students, parents, and the community

A primary task of a reading specialist is to make clear and meaningful to non-specialists information and data that might otherwise seem overwhelming and/or incomprehensible. By continuing your professional development through attending in-services and keeping up-to-date with current research about literacy development, you can provide pertinent advice and facts to parents, administrators, policy makers, and even members of the media. Your efforts to interpret reading information, regulations, and assessment data to these audiences can help them make informed decisions that will affect your students, your school, your community, and perhaps even the nation.

Information about reading includes being familiar with specialized reading terms, knowing current conclusions about what children must learn to be able to read at different levels and how best to teach them these skills, and understanding when and how to intervene if children are struggling with reading skills. Reading regulations include matters such as what national and statewide academic content standards children are to meet, how their achievements are to be assessed to determine if they are meeting these standards, what the expectations are for children with disabilities or children whose native language is not English, how these students are to be tested, and what training requirements must be met by reading specialists. Finally, interpreting assessment data means knowing how to read the results of different tests, being able to explain what the results say about the achievements of the students who have taken a test, and what should or should not be done in response to the results.

Different audiences need these things interpreted for them for different reasons. Parents need your help understanding what their children should be learning and how they can assist in this process. You should reach out to parents to educate them, send home learning activities for students to complete with parents, and check periodically that parents understand what you are asking them to do to develop their children's reading skills and that they are working toward these goals. At other times, you may need to clarify for parents which reading standards their children are struggling to master or explain to parents an assessment you have made about their child so that they understand why you might be recommending a particular course of action.

You may act as a different type of resource for administrators and fellow staff members at your school. By maintaining memberships in professional organizations, reading journals published by these organizations, and attending professional reading council meetings and state or national conferences, you can stay abreast of current research into reading and, in turn, convey the most important things you have learned to your fellow teachers in professional development sessions with them. You may be called upon to use your knowledge of current regulations and your interpretation of assessment data to help school committees plan curriculums, select textbooks, diagnose and plan interventions for at-risk students, and initiate school reform programs. Your school will need particular curriculum frameworks in place if students are to pass tests that demonstrate their mastery of content described by standards, and you must use your knowledge to tell your school how to put these in place.

In addition, you may need to deal with your community, government, and society at large. You might hold awareness sessions to help educate the community about how to foster literacy. Standards are important to understand because schools and school districts will be held accountable for achievements of students. At times you might need to work with state and national governments and committees to set reasonable standards and determine which will be tested (*i.e.* all standards or just the highest-priority standards). You can be a valuable resource for policy makers without a background in reading. And finally, you can work to educate the media and get local reporters to write constructive articles that inform the community about important issues relating to school reform, school reading programs, and how best to cultivate literacy in children.

Skill 13.3 Use school-related data to identify the content and process of ongoing high-quality staff development

Frequent and well-organized professional development makes teachers more likely to assimilate the latest research findings into their teaching and leads, therefore, to a concomitant and significant improvement in student achievement. Because of this relationship between professional development and student performance, it is often best to use data about student performance to determine areas where teachers can benefit from focused study. Identifying gaps between standards and students' abilities to master these standards helps schools target areas where more teaching will be needed and allows schools to plan future professional development opportunities where teachers can learn ways to improve their methods of instruction in these weak areas.

Sometimes a school may examine a large pool of student performances (from a set of schools or even across a state) and identify shared weaknesses, such as a widespread inability to master phonemic awareness. Once a school has identified a few such major problem areas, it can arrange for professional development opportunities that provide teachers with information about the latest research in these areas. Teachers can then use this information to adjust their teaching to focus on improving student performance in these areas.

At other times, a school may look at student data to identify any classes where students do not seem to be mastering skills at an acceptable pace. In these cases, a school may find that a particular teacher needs more training or supervision to be able to teach certain reading content and skills adequately. After determining the areas where this teacher's students appear to be struggling, a school can set up supplementary targeted training sessions for the teacher, have other teachers supervise this teacher or coach him or her on how to teach this content, and review the teacher's lesson plans to help him or her improve his or her instruction.

When using student data in this way, a school must 1.) make sure to use a reliable method of measuring whether students have met performance goals and 2.) take into account the abilities of the students and where a class's reading and language skills were before the teacher began instructing them. Classroom observations are useful in deciding whether a teacher is helping students learn to their full potential, or whether the students would master content better if the teacher improved his or her teaching methods through targeted professional development. In addition, a school must 3.) make sure to gather and analyze data relating to *all* the reading skills that must be mastered at each level so as not to overlook any weak areas that could be the topic of upcoming professional development sessions.

Skill 13.4   Select and evaluate instructional materials for reading

When it comes to instructing students, the reading specialist understands the importance of providing materials the student can actually read. It would be inappropriate to give a college level book on astrophysics to a struggling eighth-grade reader.

The difficulty comes from determining which books students can read. For decades, researchers have developed ways to examine the words in a story and determine for what level of reader it is appropriate. Frye developed his own readability formula and graph. These types of devices gave teachers a general grade level for which the books would be appropriate.

Typically, readability formulas examine a combination of words per line, syllables per one-hundred word sample, and other features to decide the reading level of the word.

In more recent times, other methods for leveling books have been developed. Fountais and Pinnel developed their own method, which uses alphabetic descriptors. "A level" books are at the lowest level and as the texts become more difficult, the letters progress sequentially. This method eliminates the grade's being mentioned so knowing they are reading several grade levels below their current grade does not additionally discourage students who may be behind.

Skill 13.5   Identify criteria for evaluating the effectiveness of a reading program

Because an effective reading program must be organized carefully to follow a certain schedule and sequence of skills (its instructional design) and must teach information in so many different areas (its instructional content), there are many aspects of any proposed program that must be examined before a school can feel confident about using this program with its students. Certain criteria must be used to evaluate these aspects to determine the value of a program. For a start, four main questions must be answered:

1.) When tested in controlled and carefully designed experiments, has the program shown evidence of working to improve student literacy?
2.) Is the program based on recent and proven research findings about reading?
3.) Is the instruction in the program precise, well-ordered, and appropriate to the level being taught?
4.) When the program was tested, was it used in environments with students similar to those in your school?

If you are satisfied that the program meets in general the criteria listed above, you can then examine its instructional design and content in more detail. Assess the design by examining lessons from several parts of the program to see how clearly instructional strategies are taught, how much practice students are given with the content of each lesson, how well-aligned to the skills being taught the assessment of each lesson is, and how comprehensively differentiated the instructional materials are (*i.e.* is a range of materials available to meet the needs of students at a variety of levels, including those with special needs and those who are advanced). In addition, you should also look at a series of lessons all together in a row to see how well each lesson builds on the one before it.

In general, any program of good quality will contain instruction in most or all of the following areas: phonemic awareness, phonics, fluency, vocabulary, and text comprehension. Your specific assessment of the instructional content of a program will depend upon the level you will be teaching. For example, a Kindergarten program should cover instruction in areas such as phonemic awareness, letter-sound association, decoding, irregular words, and listening comprehension, while a Third Grade program should cover instruction in areas such as decoding and word recognition, concept vocabulary, fluent passage reading, and reading comprehension.

Examine state and national standards and your school's requirements to determine the exact material and skills students are to master at your level in each area, and then check that the program you are examining contains organized instruction in each of these subtopics. For example, the phonemic awareness portion of a Kindergarten program should meet requirements such as focusing first on learning initial sounds, then final sounds, and then medial sounds.

Skill 13.6   Use school data and program-evaluation results to identify methods to modify and improve curriculum and instruction

As a reading specialist, one job duty you will be asked to participate in may be updating your school's reading curriculum and modifying its reading instruction. Curriculums should be living, changing works in progress. Keeping them current and filled with relevant information is important for teachers to be able to continue to provide adequate education. Sometimes curriculums are revised because state departments of education have updated and changed the state standards or because new information has arisen through research. Another reason for updated curriculums, however, is that analysis of school data (such as testing scores) or evaluation of your current program has exposed weaknesses. Generally, when figuring out how to improve curriculum and instruction, you will gather information in an assessment phase and then make judgments and decisions about your findings in an evaluation phase. Ideally, this process will be ongoing.

When examining school data to determine what (if any) changes should be made to improve curriculum and instruction, you must make sure the data you are examining is comprehensive by looking at multiple sources of data, such as the children's demographic backgrounds, the qualifications of the staff working with the children, how a program is being implemented in the classroom, what information the program is covering, and the quality of the classroom environment. To be most effective, evaluations should be ongoing and curriculum and instruction flexible so that the curriculum may be tweaked as soon as possible to better align it with standards or to meet students' current needs and so that students may receive immediate intervention if they are shown to be struggling in an area. Some methods for assessment that are most useful are 1.) screening early in the school year for at-risk students, 2.) using diagnostic tools to determine the best course of intervention with a particular student, 3.) monitoring over time how well students are progressing toward specific grade level goals, and 4.) comparing student performances on state performance assessments with national scores.

Once issues with curriculum and/or instruction have been identified, methods to modify and improve them can be used such as adding new content to deepen students' understanding in an area, offering additional services to students such as tutoring opportunities or after-school instruction, and providing teachers with targeted professional development opportunities to enhance their abilities to teach skills students are struggling to master. Other strategies include asking a reading coach to assist in directed student interventions, moving and regrouping students to reduce teacher-student ratios, and adding new technology resources to supplement the current curriculum and instruction.

Skill 13.7   Determine effective methods for training and monitoring paraprofessionals, tutors, and volunteers

Communication is probably the most important factor when working with a paraprofessional. Open dialogue can prevent miscommunications and provide valuable input and ideas as to how a student is progressing. Gathering data from another person who is working with the child can help to reaffirm ideas or thoughts as well as provide the next steps in the instructional process. Teaching the paraprofessional how to keep notes and documentation on students will help him or her become an effective teacher; it will also help the managing teacher by adding information about the student. Occasionally, it is important to touch base with the paraprofessional to ensure that lesson plans are being implemented as described.

This can be a sensitive area for both the teacher and paraprofessional. It is important to provide feedback without being punitive or seeming judgmental. With proper training and open communication, a successful working relationship can be achieved. When providing feedback it can help to follow the following suggestions:

- Observe informally first. This can be achieved by working in the same room when the instruction is being delivered and seems less threatening than a formal observation.

- Provide feedback in the form of additional instruction in the manner in which lessons should be delivered. In this way, there is no blame; it simply becomes a new lesson, not a mistake.

- Provide praise frequently.

- Use open communication to ask the paraprofessional for suggestions, indicating that those opinions are valuable to you.

- Provide professional training for paraprofessionals.

- Hold regular meetings to discuss the students both of you are working with.

- Listen carefully and make time for any questions the paraprofessional may have even if it interrupts your schedule.

- Encourage leadership and decision-making by the paraprofessional as skills increase.

Schools, particularly at the elementary level, have a wealth of adults who want to be an active part of the child's education. Parent volunteers and other adults want to come into the schools and are often willing to help with a broad range of activities the teacher needs help with. These may include copying, giving individual assessments, reading with children, tutoring, gathering and making materials, and many others.

Putting these adults to use in the classroom can be a tremendous benefit, particularly in the area of reading. However, it is important to guide and train both tutors and volunteers. Taking a few minutes at the onset can save time and effort later. This can be done on an individual basis, or school-wide tutoring training sessions can be offered.

It can be a time-saving device to train all adults interested in providing tutoring services at one time. They can work in small groups to develop their skills; and as a specialist, your time is only taken once for the training. It is important to provide the materials for the tutors in order to maximize their time with the students. This involves organization and a lot of forethought before the actual tutoring begins. There are various resources available to obtain the materials for tutoring, but it is a time-consuming process the first year.

Finding a communication method between the tutors and yourself is also important. One strategy that works well and is rather inexpensive involves a bagged book system. In this strategy, the book and activities to complete with the student are kept in a plastic bag with the child's and tutor's name on it. Inside the bag, a communication notebook with some general questions can be left. The tutor writes the answers to the guided questions about the activity completed with the student. In this way, the teacher can review the answers as materials are changed for the next tutoring session.

Overall, it is important to take the time and effort to be organized for volunteers and tutors before inviting them into the classroom to maximize their use and the benefits they provide.

GLOSSARY

These definitions are critical for success on all multiple-choice questions on the examinations. Proper use of these terms is also crucial for success in writing a constructed response involving balanced literacy.

Ability Grouping. Grouping of children with similar needs for instructional purposes. Ability groups do not remain constant throughout the year but change as the children's needs within them change.

Alliteration. Occurs when words begin with the same consonant sound, as in *Peter Piper picked a peck of pickled peppers.*

Alphabetic Principle. The idea that written spellings represent spoken words.

Anchor Book. A balanced literacy term for a book that is purposely read repeatedly and used as part of both the reading and writing workshop.
It is a good idea to use certain books that become the children's familiar and cherished favorites for both reading and inspiring children's writing.

Assonance. Repetition of stressed vowel sounds within words with different end consonants.

Authentic Assessment Assessment activities that reflect the actual workplace, family, community, and school curriculum.

Balanced Literacy Lesson Format. The Balanced Literacy Approach has its own specific format for the delivery of a literacy lesson, whether it is a reading or writing-workshop lesson. The format begins with a 10-15 minute mini-lesson delivered by the teacher to the whole class. This mini-lesson is then followed by a thirty-minute small-group lesson (the children break into small groups to work). It concludes with a 10-minute share session during which the whole class reconvenes to share what they have done in the small groups. This format is often referred to as the whole-small-whole group approach.

Benchmarks. School, state, or nationally-mandated statements of expectations for student learning and achievement in various content areas.

BICS. (Basic Interpersonal Communication SKills (An ELL/Bilinguial-Education term). Learning second-language skills and becoming proficient in a second language through face to face interaction-translation through speaking, listening, and viewing.

Blending. The process of hearing separate phonemes and being able to merge them together to read the word.

Book Features. Children need to be familiar with the following book features: front and back cover; title and half-title page; dedication page; table of contents; prologue and epilogue; and foreword and after notes. For factual books, children need to be familiar with labels, captions, glossary, index, headings and subheadings of chapters, charts and diagrams, and sidebars.

Checklist. An assessment form that lists targeted learning and social behaviors as indicators of achievement, knowledge, or skill. They can be professionally- or teacher-prepared.

Cinquain. A five-line poem that can be read and then used as a model for writing. Generally, line 1 of this format is a single word; line 2 has 2 words that describe the title of line 1; line 3 is comprised of 3 words that are movement words; line 4 has 4 words that express feeling; and line 5 has a single word that is a synonym for line 1's single word.

Comprehension. This occurs when the reader correctly interprets the print on the page and constructs meaning from it. Comprehension depends on activating prior knowledge, cultural and social background of the reader, and the reader's ability to use comprehension-monitoring strategies.

Concepts About Print. Include such things as the following: book handling, looking at print, directionality, sequencing, locating skills, punctuation, and concepts of letters and words.

Consonant Digraphs. Two consecutive consonants that represent one new speech sound. In the word "digraph" the *ph,* which sounds like /f/ is a digraph.

Contexts. Sentences deliberately prepared by the teacher that include sufficient contextual clues for the children to decipher meaning.

Contextual Redefinition. Using context to determine word meaning.

Cooperative Reading. Children read with a partner or buddy. It can be silent or oral reading.

Crisscrossers. An ELL term for second-language learners who have a positive attitude toward both first-language and second-language learning. These second-language learners, children from ELL backgrounds, are comfortable navigating back and forth between the two languages as they learn.

Cues. As they self-monitor their reading comprehensions, readers integrate various sources of information or cues to help them construct meaning from text and graphic illustrations.

Decoding. "Sounding out" a printed sequence of letters based on knowledge of letter/sound correspondences.

Diphthongs. Two vowels in one syllable where the two sounds are heard. For instance, in the word *house* both the "o" and the "u" are heard.

Directionality. Children use their fingers to indicate left-to-right direction and return-sweep to the next line.

Differentiated Instruction. The need for the teacher, based on observation of individual student's work, progress, test results, fluency, and other reading/literacy behaviors, to provide modified instruction and alternative strategies or activities. These activities are specifically developed by the teacher to address the individual student's needs.

Early Readers. Recognize most high-frequency words and many simple words. They use pictures to confirm meaning. Using meaning, syntax, and phonics, they can figure out most simple words. They use spelling patterns to figure out new words. They are gaining control of reading strategies. They use their own experiences and background knowledge to predict meanings. They occasionally use story language in their writing. This stage follows emergent reading.

Emergent Readers. The stage of reading in which the reader understands that print contains a consistent message. The reader can recognize some high-frequency words, names, and simple words in context. Pictures can be used to predict meaning. The emergent reader begins to attend to left to right directionality and features of print and may identify some initial sounds and ending sounds in words.

Encode. To change a message into symbols. For example, readers encode oral language into writing.

English as a Second Language. A way of teaching English to speakers of other languages using English as the language of instruction.

Expository Text. Non-fiction that provides information and facts. This is what newspapers, science, mathematics, and history texts use. Currently there is much focus, even in elementary schools, on teaching children how to comprehend and author expository text. They must produce brochures, guides, recipes, and procedural accounts on most elementary grade levels. The teaching of reading of expository texts requires working with a particular vocabulary and concept structure that is very different from that of narrative text. Therefore, time must be taken to teach the reading of expository text and contrasting it with the reading of narrative text.

First Language. An ELL term for the language any child acquires in the first few years of life. It is through this acquired language that the child develops phonological and phonemic awareness.

Fluent Readers. These are able to identify most words automatically. They can read chapter books with good comprehension. They consistently monitor, cross-check, and self-correct reading. They can offer their own interpretations of text based on personal experiences and prior reading experiences. Fluent readers are capable of reading a variety of genres independently. Furthermore, they can respond to texts or stories by sharing pertinent examples from their lives. They can also readily make connections to other books they have read. Finally, they are capable of beginning to create spoken and written text in the style of a particular author.

Formal Assessment. A test or an observation of performance done under controlled and regulated conditions.

Functional Reading. The reading of instructions, recipes, coupons, classified ads, notices, signs, and other documents required to be read to function in society and correctly interpret them.

Grade Equivalent/Grade Score. A score transformed from a raw score on a standardized test into the equivalent score earned by an average student in the norming group.

Graphic Organizers. Graphic organizers express relationships among various ideas in visual form including sequence, timelines, character traits, fact and opinion, main idea and details, and differences and likenesses. Graphic organizers are particularly helpful for visual learners.

Guided Reading. One of the key modes of instruction in the balanced-literacy-theory approach. The teacher "guides" the children through silent reading of a text by giving them prompts, target questions, and even helping the child start an answer to a specific prompt or question. At the end of each guided-reading section or excerpt of the text, the child stops to talk with the teacher about the text. By definition, guided reading is an interactive discussion between the child and the teacher. This mode of reading instruction is generally used when children need extra support in constructing meaning because the text is complex or because their current independent-reading capacities are still limited.

High Frequency. Frequently used words. These words appear many more times than do other words in ordinary reading material. Examples of such words are *as, in, of*, and *the*. These words are also sometimes called service words and are part of sight vocabulary words. A classic best-known high frequency word list was generated by Dolch (1936).

Independent Reading. A set period of time within the daily literacy block when children read books with 95%–100% accuracy on their own. This reading of books by themselves that they can understand without teacher support promotes lifelong literacy and love of learning. This in turn enhances reading mileage, builds fluency, and helps children orchestrate integrated cue strategies.

Informal Assessment. Observations of children made under informal conditions. These can include kid-watching, checklists, and individual child/teacher conversations.

Informal Reading Inventory (IRI). A series of reading excerpts that can be used to determine a child's reading strengths and needs in comprehension and decoding. Many published reading series have an IRI to go with their series.

Justified Print. The variable positioning of print on the page so that each line ends either a sentence or a phrase. Both right and left margins form a straight line vertically.

Kid Watching. Term used by the balanced-literacy approach for the teacher's deliberate, detailed, and recorded observations of individual student and class literacy behaviors, often done during small-group work. The teacher then reconfigures lessons on these observations to meet the students' individual and group needs.

Kinesthetic. Learning is tactile as contrasted with an activity where the learner sits still or attempts to sit still in one place. Cutting and moving syllable or word strips or using sandpaper letters are kinesthetic activities.

Language Experience. Children giving dictation to the teacher who writes their words on a chart or their drawings. This shows children that words can be written down.

Learning Logs. Daily records of what students have learned.

Listening Post. Sets of headphones attached to a single tape player. Children can go to centers where they listen to audiotapes of books while reading the same book in print. These posts are in many libraries as well.

Literature Circles. A group discussion involving four to six children who have read the same work of literature (narrative or expository text). They talk about key parts of the work, relate it to their own experience, listen to the responses of others, and discuss how parts of the text relate to the whole.

Manipulation. Moving around or switching sounds within a word or words within a phrase or sentence.

Meaning Vocabulary. Words whose meanings children understand and can use.

Miscue. An oral reading error made by a child in which what the child perceives differs from the actual printed text.

Miscue Analysis. The teacher keeps a detailed running record of the errors or inaccurate attempts of a child reader during a reading assessment. This helps the teacher know what help the child needs to avoid such errors.

Monitoring Reading. Various strategies that children use to monitor their own reading. For example, are they maintaining fluency by bringing prior knowledge to the story to make predictions, using these predictions to do further checking, searching, and self-correcting as the story progresses, and using problem-solving word-study skills to make links from known words to unknown words?

Morphemes. The smallest units of meaning in words. There are two types of morphemes: free morphemes, which can stand alone, such as *love,* and bound morphemes, which must be attached to another morpheme to carry meaning, such as *ed* in *loved.*

Narrative Text. One of the two basic text structures. The narrative text tells or communicates a story. Narrative texts are novels, short stories, and plays. Some poems are narratives as well. The narrative text needs to be taught differently than the expository text because of its structure.

One-to-One Matching. Matching one spoken word with one written word.

Onset Rime-Blending. Everything before the vowel and RIME (the vowel and everything after it). For example, the word "sleep" can be broken into /sl/ and /eep/. Word families are built using rimes. The /eep/ word family would include *jeep, keep,* and *weep.*

Orthography. A method of representing spoken language through letters and diacritics.

Percentile. If a child scores at the 56th percentile for his/grade level, his/her score is equal to or above that of 56 percent of the children taking that standardized test and below that of 46 percent of the children on whose scores the test was normed.

Performance Assessment. Having children do a task that demonstrates their knowledge, skills, and competency. Having children author their own alphabet book on a particular topic would be a performance assessment for knowledge of the alphabet.

Phoneme. The speech sound units that make a difference in meaning. The word "rope" has three phonemes /r/, /o/, and /p/. Change one phoneme, say /r/ to /n/, and you have a different word: *nope.*

Phonemic Awareness. The understanding that words are composed of sounds. Phonemic awareness is a specific type of phonological awareness dealing only with phonemes in a *spoken* word.

Phonics. The study of relationships between phonemes (speech sounds) and graphemes (letters) that represent the phonemes. It is also decoding or the sounding out of unknown written words.

Phonological Awareness. The ability to recognize the sounds of spoken language and how they can be blended together, segmented, and switched/manipulated to form new combinations and words.

Phonological Cues. Readers use their knowledge of letter/sound and sound/letter relationships to predict and confirm meaning.

Phonology. The study of speech structure in language that includes both the patterns of basic speech units (phonemes) and the tacit rules of pronunciation.

Portfolios. Collections of a child's work over time. They include a cover letter, reflections from the child and teacher, and other supportive documents including standards, performance-task examples, prompts, and sometimes peer comments.

Primary Language (an ELL term). The language an individual is the most fluent in and at ease with. This is usually, but not always, the individual's first language.

Prompts. When the teacher intervenes in the child's independent reading to help with pronouncing or comprehending a specific word or prompt. On a reading record, the teacher notes the prompt. When the teacher wants to match a child with a particular book or determine the child's stage/level of reading, the teacher does not use prompts.

Question-Generating Strategy for an Expository Text. First the child previews the text by reading titles, subheads, looking at pictures or illustrations, and reading the first paragraph. Next the child asks a "think" question, which he or she records. Then the child reads to find information that might answer the "think" question. The child may write down the information found or think about another question that is answered by what is being read. The child continues to read, using this strategy.

Reading for Information. Reading with the purpose of extracting facts and expert opinion from the text. Children should be introduced to the following information reading resources: web resources that are age and grade appropriate for children, the concept of the table of contents, chapter headings, glossaries, pictures, maps, charts, diagrams and text structures in an information text. They should be taught to use notes, graphs, organizers, and mind maps to share information extracted from a text.

Recode. To change information from one code into another, as recoding writing into oral speech.

Recognition Vocabulary. The group of words that children are able to correctly pronounce, read orally, and understand on sight.

Record of Reading Behavior (Running Record). An objective observation during which the teacher records, using a standard set of symbols, everything the child reader says as the child reads a book selected by the teacher.

Reflection. To analyze, discuss, and react to one's learning on any grade or age level.

Retelling. Can be written or oral. Children are expected and encouraged to tell as much of a story as they can remember. Retelling is far more extensive than just summarizing. Children should include the beginning, middle, and end plot lines and should be able to tell about the book's characters.

Rubric. A set of guidelines or acceptable responses for the completion of any task. Usually a rubric ranges from 0 to 4 with 4 being the most detailed response and 0 indicating a response to the task that lacked detail or was in other ways insufficient.

Scaffolding. Refers to the teacher support necessary for the child to accomplish a task or to achieve a goal that the child could not accomplish on his/her own. Vygotsky termed this window of opportunity the "zone of proximal development." Ultimately, as the child becomes more proficient or capable, the scaffold is withdrawn. The goal of scaffolding is to help the child perform the reading task independently and internalize the behavior. During *shared reading*, the task is scaffolded by the teacher's reading to the children aloud. As the teacher reads, the teacher scaffolds the initial decoding and helps with the meaning making/construction.

Searching. Children pause to search in the picture, print, or their memory for known information. This can happen as the child tackles an unknown word or after an error.

Second Language (ELL term). A language acquired or learned simultaneously with or after a child's acquisition of a first language.

Segmenting. The process of hearing a spoken word and identifying its separate phonemes or syllables.

Self-Correction. Children begin to correct some of their own reading errors. Generally, this behavior is accompanied by the rereading of the previous phrase or sentence.

Semantic Cues. Children use their prior knowledge, sense of the story, and pictures to support their predicting and confirming the meaning of the text.

Semantic Web. A visual graphic organizer that the teacher can use to introduce a reading on a specific topic. It visually represents many other words associated with a target word. The web can help activate the children's prior knowledge and extend or clarify it. It can also serve to check new learning after guided or independent reading.

Spatial Learning. Using images, color, or layout to help readers whose learning style is spatial.

Standard Score. How far a child's grade on a standardized test is from the average score (mean) on the test in terms of the standard deviation. If a child scores 70 on a standardized test and the standard deviation is 5 and the average (mean) score is 65, the child is one standard deviation above the average.

Standardized Test. A test given under specified conditions allowing comparisons to be made. A set of norms or average scores on this test will be used for comparisons.

Stop-and-Think Strategy. A balanced-literacy strategy for constructing meaning. As the text is being read, the child asks himself or herself, does this make sense to me? If it does not make sense to me, I should then try to reread it or read ahead. I can also look up words that I don't know or ask for help. Generally the teacher models this strategy with the whole class as a mini-lesson and then it is posted prominently in the classroom for continued reference by the children.

Strategic Readers. As defined by researchers Marie Clay and Sharon Taberski, strategic readers are self improving and do the following as they read:

(A lengthy glossary explanation of this term has been provided because it can appear in a variety of multiple-choice questions on the examination as well as part of a constructed-response question).

- Monitor their reading to see if it makes sense semantically, syntactically, and visually.
- Look for and use semantic, syntactic, and visual clues.
- Uncover and identify new things about the text.
- Cross check and use one cueing system against another.
- Self-correct their reading when what they first read does not match the semantic, syntactic, and visual clues
- Solve for and identify new words using multiple cueing systems

Beyond these behaviors, strategic or self-improving readers use many strategies to construct meaning. When their reading experience is going well—they know the words and understand the text or story—they are working continuously (even if they are not conscious of it) at maintaining meaning. If and when the strategic or self-improving reader runs into an unfamiliar word, many strategies are available to him or her to identify that word. Becoming a successful strategic reader is a goal that can and should be shared with children as early as the middle of the first grade although the term "self-improving reader" might be used at that point.

Text Features. Children need to be alerted to the following text features that may initially appear strange to them:
1. a period that marks the end of a "telling sentence"
2. a question mark that is at the end of a sentence that asks a question
3. an exclamation mark used to express surprise or excitement at the end of a sentence
4. capital letters that begin a sentence and the names of persons, places, and things
5. bold, italicized, or underlined text to highlight key ideas
6. quotation marks that show dialogue
7. a hyphen used to break a long word up into its syllables
8. a dash used to show a break in an idea, a parenthetical element. or an omission an ellipse that shows an omission or break in the text
9. a paragraph in nonfiction which shows a new point being made.

Transitional Readers. Recognize an increasing number of "hard" words that are content related. They can provide summaries of the stories they read. They are more at ease with handling longer, more complex, connected text with short chapters. Transitional readers can read independent-level texts with correct phrasing, expression, and fluency. When they encounter unfamiliar words, they have a variety of strategies to figure out the unfamiliar words. Their reading demonstrates that they are able to integrate meaning, syntax, and phonics in a consistent manner so they can understand the texts they are reading.

Venn Diagram. A diagram consisting of two or three intersecting circles to visually represent similarities and differences for texts, characters, and topics. No author study is complete without VENN DIAGRAMS comparing different authors' works. This is the most commonly-used graphic organizer in elementary schools today. It can be used effectively as part of an answer to a constructed response question.

Visual Cues. Readers use their knowledge of graphemes to predict and confirm text. The graphemes may be words, syllables, or letters.

Word Analysis. The analysis of words employing letters, phonic structures, contextual clues, or dictionary skills.

Word Identification. How the reader determines the pronunciation and the meaning of an unknown word.

Word Recognition. The process of determining the pronunciation and some degree of the meaning of an unknown word.

Word Work. The term the balanced-literacy approach uses for the study of vocabulary.

Directory of Theorists and Researchers

Introduction

Many questions on the teacher certification examinations can only be correctly answered if you know the theorist or the research that is referenced. The teaching of reading owes much to the work, principles, and guidelines of teacher educators and university field researchers who have changed the style, methods, and practice of teaching reading. While those listed in this directory are by no means all the major researchers (page constraints would make a complete listing impossible), the individuals listed below are those whose contributions are frequently referenced on the certification tests and whose work is evident in today's elementary classroom teaching and learning of reading.

PHONICS CENTERED APPROACH

In 1955, Rudolph Flesch gained national prominence when he published *Why Johnny Can't Read*. This book went on to become a best seller and has now become a classic. It is readable and does speak to current concerns. Flesch became the spokesperson for a war that periodically resurfaces in the reading world.

Flesch, Chall (1967), Stahl (1992), Adams (1990), and Johnson and Bauman (1984) believe that a phonics-based approach is crucial for reading success. Flesch and others feel that the balanced-literacy advocates are seriously undermining the crucial role that phonics plays in the children's development as successful decoding readers. However, it must be noted that while balanced literacy does emphasize the use of literature-based reading programs, it in no way dismisses phonics from its reading program; indeed, phonics is included in the crucial "word work" component of the reading and writing workshop.

The phonics advocates point to the fact that most research shows that early and systematic instruction in phonics skills results in superior reading achievement in elementary school and beyond.

Adams (1990) detailed what type of phonics instruction is needed: To learn to read skillfully, children need practice in seeing and understanding decodable words in real reading situations and with connected text. . . phonics instruction {needs to be} part of a reading program that provides ample practice in reading and writing. Encouraging children with connected text can also show them the importance of what they are learning and make the lessons in phonics relevant and sensible. Phonics-centered advocates believe that children should begin to learn letter associations in kindergarten with most useful phonics skills being taught by first grade. These basic skills should then be reviewed in second grade and beyond.

Consonant sounds should be taught first, since they are more reliable in their letter-sound associations.

Short vowel sounds appear more frequently in beginning reading materials, so they should be introduced before long vowels. Phonics advocates believe that most beginning readers need to be taught letter/sound associations explicitly. Phonics advocates also believe that beginning readers need to read stories that have words to which phonics skills apply. This allows them to practice their phonics skills as they write and spell words. They should also play lots of letter/sound association games.

Phonics advocates claim that when phonics is abandoned, reading scores drop; balanced-literacy advocates counter with the fact that they have never advocated abandoning the teaching of phonics.

As Jeanne Chall, a professor at Harvard's Graduate School of Education notes: "a beginning reading program that does not give children knowledge and skill in recognizing and decoding words will have poor results."

Theorists and Researchers:

Adams, Marilyn Jager

Noted for her research on early reading, Adams lists five basic types of phonemic-awareness tasks that should be covered by the end of first grade. These include the ability to hear rhymes and alliterations, to do oddity tasks, to orally blend words, to orally segment words, and to do phonemic manipulation tasks.

Clay, Marie M.

A New-Zealand-born researcher in the field of special needs emergent literacy and in the development of assessment tools for these children. Her research in this field is felt throughout the Reading Recovery movement and involves the use of her *Reading Recovery: A Guidebook for Teachers in Training,* in the majority of graduate emergent literacy courses and in many classrooms in the US including those that do not have a Reading Recovery teacher.

Her doctoral thesis focused on what was to become her life's work, emergent reading behavior. At the crux of her research for the dissertation, Clay reviewed and detailed the week-by-week progress of one hundred children during their first year of school (1966). An important outcome of the dissertation was her development of reliable observation tools for the assessment and analysis of changes over time in children's literacy learning. These assessments are the crux of *An Observation Survey of Early Literacy Achievement* (1993) which is an essential work for the primary school educator. The assessments have been validated and reconstructed for learners from the Spanish, Maori, and French languages. A special appendix in this guide includes the *Record of Reading Behavior* tool she created with Kenneth Goodman.

Reading Recovery is a key Clay contribution to the field of foundations of reading teaching. The movement, which is discussed in detail in this section, was born out of the concerns of classroom educators who were upset that even with excellent programs and expert teaching, they were not able to positively influence the literacy progress of some of their young children. Clay posed the question of investigating what would happen if the design and delivery of traditional reading education were changed for these struggling young learners.

The whole thrust of the Reading Recovery movement has been to improve the early identification and instructional delivery for these struggling young readers. Her goal was to develop a system that would bring those children scoring the lowest in assessment measures to the level of the average readers within their classes.

With the support of Barbara Watson and others, the program was developed in three years. The first field tests took place in the late 1970's in Auckland schools. By 2005, the program was operating in most English-speaking countries and has been restructured for use in Spanish and French.

Janet S. Gaffey and Billie Askew have said of Marie Clay (1991) that her contribution "has been to change what is possible for individual learners when teaching permits different routes to be taken for desired outcomes."

Reading Recovery has been identified by the International Reading Association as a program that not only teaches children how to read but also reduces the number of children who are labeled as "learning disabled." It further lowers the number of children who are placed in remedial reading programs and classes.

Clay Reading Recovery lessons are designed to promote accelerated learning so that children can catch up to their peers and continue to learn independently.

The hallmark of the Reading Recovery program is that the Reading Recovery teacher works with one student at a time over a 12-to-20-week period. Each daily 30-minute lesson is tailored to address the needs of the individual student. Therefore, Reading Recovery teachers generally teach no more than four or five students per day in individual lessons.

The Clay Observation of Early Childhood Achievement (1993) is used to assess children's strengths and weaknesses. Reading Recovery teachers devote the first ten minutes of their sessions with individual children to assessment as the children engage in reading and writing. A running record of the child's progress is taken every day and is used to plan future lessons.

The lessons themselves include the use of familiar stories. Children engage in assembling and in sequencing cut-up stories. They work with letters or write a story. Teaching style involves the teacher's demonstrating strategies and the child then developing effective strategies to continue reading independently. Key components of each lesson include phonemic awareness, phonics, spelling, and comprehension study. Much time is devoted to problem solving so that the children's decoding is purposeful. Children are given time to practice and demonstrate fluency skills.

Ultimately, what sets Reading Recovery apart is the fact that it is one-to-one tutoring. This is also what makes it effective for children. Of course, what raises issues about it are costs for the school systems that may want to adopt it. Obviously, the districts and education systems must decide whether they want to pay the costs of this effective program and other individualized tutoring systems now available for the primary school years or pay later as these children become adults whose literacy skills are not sufficient for proactive citizenship.

Fountas, Irene C and Gay Su Pinnell

These two researchers have developed a leveling system for reading texts, which arranges them by level of difficulty. Beyond a specific analysis of set titles, the theorists have explained in several published works how to use their leveling system to meet and assess the progress of various readers. They also provide detailed explanations and support for reading teachers of young children K-3 in using reading records and benchmark texts.

They are the key articulators of the balanced-literacy model that includes reading and writing workshops. Among their other contributions to the field are guidelines for creating sets of leveled books, assessment rubrics, strategies for fostering "word solver" skills in child readers, and methods for teaching phonics and spelling in the literacy classroom.

Routman, Regie

Routman's contributions to Reading Foundations are the result of over three decades of experience as an elementary school teacher, a reading specialist, a learning disabilities tutor, a Reading Recovery teacher, a language arts and mentor teacher, and a staff developer. Due to these various experiences, her insights into reading resonate with a broad spectrum of school community members.

Routman's works are conversational, teacher-to-teacher sharings of her daily experiences in classrooms. In her published books on the teaching of reading (i.e. *Reading Essentials*, Heinemann, 2002), Regie shows teachers how to teach consistent with the findings in reading research, yet also with highly practical "scripted lessons" and teaching tips that make the classroom come alive. She advocates literature-based teaching and meaning-centered approaches for learning.

In addition, she is a strong advocate of using poetry from grades one and beyond as an integral thread for a reading program. She is the author of *Kids' Poems: Teaching Children to Love Writing Poetry*, Scholastic, 2000, which includes separate volumes of poetry for grades K-4.

Routman believes in teaching reading to meet specific children's needs regardless of the particular reading program in place. She is a strong advocate for the use of small, guided reading groups and reading for understanding. Phonics and other word-analysis strategies are part of her reading framework, but not at its core. Her focus for the reading classroom is on the development and the use of the classroom library as the center for an independent reading program, shared reading and reading aloud.

Routman has designed informal reading evaluations on books/texts her students are reading (her published works are known for their appendices replete with templates for evaluation, projects, reports, book lists, suggested texts by topics, etc.). Her classroom model includes matching children with specific library books as well as linking assessment with instruction. Finally, she is a researcher who sees reading as intimately linked to writing.

Routman is also involved with the politics of literacy. This vision of literacy involves the image of the teacher as an informed professional who regularly reads the latest professional books, collaborates with colleagues in school and beyond, and deals with the most recent research developments. Interestingly, Routman is one researcher who also feels that an informed professional can and should know when to question research. Other aspects of the politics of literacy as Routman conceptualizes them are communicating effectively with parents and dealing with testing and standards mandates.

Two of her published works, *Conversations: Strategies for Teaching, Learning, and Evaluating*, Heinemann, 2000, and *Invitations: Changing as Teachers and Learners k-12*, Heinemann, 1991 and 1994, are essential for the elementary reading teacher's bookshelf and can take the teacher through several years of work.

Taberski, Sharon

Taberski is an experienced elementary teacher educator who is also a member of the Primary Literacy Standards Committee run by the National Center on Education and the Economy and the University of Pittsburgh. Her works in the field are served up as wonderfully accessible and necessary advice from "the veteran teacher across the hall" who loves her students and is delighted to help a new colleague.

Unlike many theorists in the field of reading, Taberski's work is not focused on a prescribed set of skills, but rather on a series of interconnected interactions with the learner.

Among these interactions, which are detailed and clearly communicated in her book *On Solid Ground*, Heinemann, 2000, are:

- Assessment. Procedures for assessing children's reading, and to inform teaching, scheduling, and managing reading conferences, taking oral reading records, and using retellings as discussion tools.
- Demonstration. Taberski developed and field-tested strategies for using shared reading and read-aloud as platforms for figuring out words and comprehending texts. She is a strong advocate of small-group work-guided reading, word-study groups, and teaching children one on one.
- Practice. In the Taberski framework, independent reading is used as a time for practice. Students play key roles in this practice and Sharon has a set of detailed and easily-adaptable guidelines for matching children with books for independent reading. Her work includes booklists and ready-to-use information that is available for reproduction.
- Response. It's important for students to know that they are doing well and where they must focus their efforts to improve skills. Taberski explains how her students use writing and dialogue as tools for independent reading.

Vail, Priscilla

Noted for her research in the study of dyslexia and its myths, Vail has articulated ways in which children can develop their reading skills as they cope with this disorder and techniques parents and educators can use to support reading development. She has also worked on specific test-taking skills for children coping with dyslexia and other special needs. Her strategies can be included in the regular education program to enhance all students' reading achievement. She is a proponent of phonics instruction and skills within the context of an integrated whole-language approach (once called integrated language arts).

Another focus of Vail's research is the link between language and thinking. She is concerned with how a child's receptive language, expressive language, and metacognition can be fostered. She has developed assessment methods for each of these capacities and activities to help strengthen them in children grades K-4.

BIBLIOGRAPHY OF PRINT RESOURCES

PROFESSIONAL BOOKS:

Adams, M. (1990). *Beginning to read:Thinking and Learning about Print.* Cambridge, MA: MIT Press.

Anders, P., & Bos, C. (l986). Semantic Feature Analysis: An Interactive Strategy for Vocabulary Development and Reading Comprehension, *Journal of Reading, 29,* 610-616.

Blevins, W. (l997). *Phonemic Awareness Activities for Early Reading Success.* New York: Scholastic.

Boyd-Bastone, P. (2004). Focused Anecdotal Record Assessment (ARA): A Tool for Standards Based Authentic Assessment. *Reading Teacher, 58* (3), pp. 230-239.

Calkins, Lucy McCormick. (2001). *The Art of Teaching Reading.* New York: Longman.
(This is the woman who beautifully explains the reading workshop and its relationship to the writing workshop as she shares wonderful snapshots of mini-lessons, conferring, conferencing, independent reading, guided reading, book talks, prompts, coaching, and classroom library use. Exceedingly readable and direct.)

Campbell, Robin. (2004). *Reading and Writing for Real Purposes.* Portsmouth, NH: Heinemann.
(This work focuses on how children who deftly absorb and interconnect symbols and sounds of their universes can be supported in K-1 classes to extend this ability into phonics learning. Campbell demonstrates how immersion in a highly-literate classroom filled with print and language stimuli allows kids to build accurate letter-sound relationships. The book provides a framework for teaching phonics using proven field-tested Campbell strategies. Among these strategies are early mark making, read-alouds, playing with language in rhyme and song, writing and reading in a variety of genres, exploring environmental and classroom print, and using students' own names. Samples of student work are included.)

Chancey, C. (l994). Language development, metalinguistic awareness, and emergent literacy skills of 3 year old children in relation to social class. *Applied Psycholinguistics, 15,* 371-394.

Clay, Marie M. (1993). *An Observation Survey of Early Literacy Achievement.* Portsmouth, NH: Heinemann.

Clay, Marie M. (l993). *Reading Recovery: A Guidebook for Teachers in Training.* Portsmouth, NH: Heinemann.

Cooper, J. David. (2004). *Literacy: Helping Children Construct Meaning.* (5th Edition). Boston, MA: Houghton Mifflin.
(This book explains, with numerous charts, tables, templates, and excerpts from actual texts, what the balanced-literacy approach to the teaching of reading and writing is. It offers the new teacher exact schedules, strategies, guidelines, assessment tools, bibliographies, research, and even scripts for conferring with children. Cooper is a clear and crisp writer who does not overwhelm but rather engages the reader. Even veteran teachers return again and again to this text for support and refreshing insights.)

Cox, Carole. (2005). *Teaching Language Arts.* Boston, MA: Pearson.
(A compendium of state-of-the-art lesson plans, web resources, online case studies, teaching ideas, and extensive templates. All of these materials are aligned with the balanced-literacy reading-and-writing workshop model. It includes teaching ideas for the ELL reader, children with learning disabilities, and speakers of non-standard dialects. The book also features snapshots of second language learners as well as bi-literacy web resources.)

Cullinan, Bernice E. (1998). *Three Voices:An Invitation to Poetry Across the Curriculum.* New York: Stenhouse. For K-6 and beyond.
(Two classroom educators and a noted researcher in children's literature demonstrate how poetry can be used in the classroom to teach various aspects of reading and to nurture lifelong literacy. Thirty-three grade-and–age-appropriate strategies are included, which have been field tested in classrooms across the country.

Ezell, H. K., & Justice, L. M. (2000). Increasing the Print Focus of Adult -Child Shared Book Reading through Observational Learning. *American Journal of Speech Pathology, 9,* 36-37.

Flesch, Rudolf. (1985). *Why Johnny Can't Read.* New York: Harper and Row.

Fountas, Irene C., & Pinnell, Gay Su. (2001). *Guiding Readers and Writers 3-6.* Portsmouth, NH: Heinemann.
(This work includes 1,000 leveled books with guidelines for using them as part of a reading and writing workshop. The book explains how to use various genres in the classroom and how to use visual graphic organizers for the teaching of reading and writing.

Fountas, Irene. C., & Pinnell, Gay Su. (1999). *Matching Books to Readers Using Leveled Books in Guided Reading K-3.* Portsmouth, NH: Heinemann. (This major contribution to the field has a list of 7,500 grade-and-age-appropriate books. In addition, the authors include word counts to be used for keeping running records, text characteristics, guidelines for leveling of additional books and suggestions for developing classroom library collections.Other works by these researchers also published by Heinemann include *Voices on Word Matters: Learning about Phonics and Spelling in the Literacy Classroom* (1999) and *Word Matters:Teaching Phonics and Spelling in the Reading/Writing Classroom* (1998).

Fry, Edward Bernard; Kress, Jacqueline; Fountakidis, Dona Lee. (2000). *The Reading Teacher's Book of Lists.* San Francisco, CA: Wiley Press. (This book is an invaluable one for the working classroom educator. It includes ready-to-use lists that cover a multiplicity of teacher needs. Among them are spelling demons, readability graphs, phonics, useful words, reading math, vowel lists, anagrams, portmanteaus (do you know what they are and how well they can work in word study?), web sites, classic children's literature, etc. Even a veteran teacher educator will find useful and new resources. Also wonderful for developing independent word-study investigations and literature explorations.)

Ganske, Kathy. (2000). *Word Journeys:Assessment-Guided Phonics, Spelling, and Vocabulary Instruction.* New York, NY: Guilford Press. (This book offers a practical approach for assessing children's spelling. The author has created a DSA (Development Spelling Analysis) tool which teachers can use to evaluate individual children's spelling progress and to differentiate instruction. The book includes snapshots of children at different levels of spelling development.)

Hall, Susan. (1994). *Using Picture Books to Teach Literary Devices.* Westport, CT: Oryx Press.

Labov, L. (2003). When Ordinary Children Fail to Read. *Reading Research Quarterly*, 38, 128-31.

Macmillan, B. M. (2002). Rhyme and Reading. A Critical Review of the Research Methodology. *Journal of Research in Reading,* 25(1), 4-42.

Makor, Barbara. *Primary Phonics Readers.* (Short storybooks that K-2 can own and read independently.They feature phonetically controlled texts, sounds, and spellings that are grade and age appropriate with high-interest child-centered themes. As children progress through the series of twenty titles, they review and enhance their mastery of phonetic elements, sight words, and sequences at a more rapid pace. This material is compatible with the majority of phonics programs.)

Munro, J. (l998). Phonological and Phonemic Awareness: Their Impact on Learning to Read Prose and Spell. *Australian Journal of Learning Disabilities*, 3, 2, 15-21.
(Paperback Nursery Rhyme Sampler. Essential for a Pre-K-1 classroom and useful even in grades 1 and 2. These classic nursery rhymes promote phonemic and phonological awareness and children's ownership of their reading through song and movement.

Routman, Regie. (l994). *Invitations: Changing as Teachers and Learners K-12.* Portsmouth, NH. Heinemann.

Routman, Regie. (l996). *Literacy at the Crossroads: Crucial Talk About Reading, Writing, and Other Teaching Dilemmas.* Portsmouth, NH: Heinemann.

Routman, Regie. (2000). *Conversations: Strategies for Teaching, Learning, and Evaluating.* Portsmouth, NH: Heinemann.

Routman, Regie. (2002). *Reading Essentials.* Portsmouth, NH: Heinemann.

Statman, Ann.(ongoing). *Handprints: Leveled Storybooks for Early Readers* Cambridge, MA: Educators Publishing Service.Grades K-2.
(These fifty titles that come with five teacher's guides were leveled using the Fountas and Pinnell Guided Reading Leveling System. The stories reflect real-world situations and people young readers know. They include sentence structure, pictures, and cues that focus strategic reading. Print size, sentence positioning, and word spacing is appropriate for the level of the particular storybook. The titles build a strong sight vocabulary through the use of high frequency words. Language used within the series progresses from natural to formal book language.)

Pernu, Caryn; Schumm, Gerald E.; Schumm, Jeanne Shay. (1999). *The Reading Tutor's Handbook.* Minneapolis, MN: Free Spirit. K-6 and beyond.
(This guide offers step-by-step instructions, templates. and handouts for providing differentiated reading support for children. It is not only helpful for teachers but also can be shared with paraprofessionals, teachers, interns, and parents as a support framework for the classroom reading program.)

Taberski, Sharon. (2000). *On Solid Ground: Creating a Literacy Environment in Your K-3 Classroom.* Portsmouth, NH: Heinemann.

Terban, Marvin. (1994). *Time to Rhyme:A Rhyming Dictionary.* Honesdale, PA: Boyd Mills Press. Grades 1-3.
(This book is easily-enough formatted so that it can be used to introduce children in the early elementary grades to the use of a rhyming dictionary as a reference tool. Its simple word groupings encourage writing that can also reinforce and reciprocally enhance reading skills through the reading and writing workshop.)

U.S. Department of Education. (2000). *How to Help Every Child Become a Reader.* K-6 and beyond.
(This accessible text draws on materials developed by the U.S. Department of Education to share research, resources, referrals, and suggestions for supporting all children to become lifelong and engaged readers. It offers specific suggestions and resources for assisting struggling readers including those with special needs and those from ELL backgrounds.)

Vail, Patricia.(1999). *Reading Comprehension: Students' Needs and Teachers' Tools.* Modern Learning Programs. K-6 and beyond.
(This is a compendium of explanations of specific instructional practices, terms, student projects, learning games and resources which are critical for successfully teaching reading.)

ALPHABET BOOKS

A major genre of fiction and non-fiction for the teacher of reading is the alphabet book. These books' appeal, concepts, and efficiency as models for reading and writing merit them a special section in this bibliography. Even those whose text is simple enough for Pre-K-2, can serve as anchor books and models for writing workshop in grades 3-6.

Aigner-Clark, Julie. (2002). *Baby Einstein: The ABCs of Art.* (Illustrations by Nadeen Zaidi). New York: Hyperion Books.

Beaton, Clare. *Zoe and Her Zebra.* Cambridge, MA: Barefoot Books. Prek-1.
(This board book features a character young children can identify with named Zoe. Her adventures are told in a simple, repetitive text with soft "touchy" felt art.)

Bunting, Eve. (2002). *Girls A to Z.* Honesdale, PA: Boyd Mills Press. PreK-1.
(This book uses the alphabetic format to promote opportunities for girls to select various professions and careers ranging from astronaut to zookeeper. Bunting's text is breezy and rhyming.)

Cheney, Lynne. (2002). *America: A Patriotic Primer.* (Illustrated by Robin Priess Glasser). New York: Simon and   Schuster Books..

Cheney, Lynne. (2003). *A Is For Abigail: An Almanac of Amazing American Women.* New York: Simon and Schuster Books. Ages 4-8.

Cummings, Pat. (2002). *C is for City.* Honesdale, PA: Boyd Mill Press. K-3.
(This alphabet rhyme book doubles as a guide to city activities. With its built-in invitations to readers to search for alphabetical items, it is perfect for use as an informal assessment tool or an interactive/paired reading anchor text.)

Glaser, Shirley. (2003). *The Alphazeds*. New York: Hyperion. Ages 4-8.

Inkpen, Mick. (2000). *Kipper's A to Z*. San Diego, CA: Harcourt. Ages 3-7.

Isadora, Rachel. (1999). *ABC Pops!* (Picture Books). New York: Disney Press. Ages 4-8.

Johnson, Stephen. (1995). *Alphabet City*. New York, NY: Penguin Books. All ages.

Kelley, Marty. (2001). *Summer Stinks*. Madison, WI: Zino Press. Prek-1.
(This work describes the summer season in terms of things that "stink" about it, including ants, bugs, and sweat. Fun to read and add to as the alphabet letters are learned and vocabulary is built up.)

Martin, Mary Jane. (1996). *From Anne to Zach*. Honesdale, PA: Boyd Mills Press.
(In this captivating book, which can serve as a touchstone text for model collaborative authoring, children learn the letters of the alphabet through other children's names.)

Melmed, Laura Krauss and Frane Lesser. (2003). *Capital! Washington DC from A to Z*. New York: Harper Collins.

Musgrove, Margaret. (l976). *Ashanti to Zulu. African Traditions.* (Illustrated by Leo and Diane Dillon.) New York: Dial Books for Young Readers.
(This is a Caldecott-winning book. which uses the alphabetic format for a richly-detailed researched study of 26 African Peoples. It includes a map and pronunciation guide and illustrations that were researched in the Schomberg Center and the American Museum of Natural History. Even the frame design for each illustration reflects the African Kano knot which signifies endless searching.)

Paratore, Colleen. *26 Big Things Small Hands Can Do*. Minneapolis, MN: Free Spirit.
(What is delightful about this alphabet book is that it presents the alphabet letters as positive actions children can perform with their own small hands to help others. These actions include applauding, giving gifts, planting, and volunteering. Of course, alphabet study can continue with adding other "helping actions" to the word wall or substituting for them in the text.)

Pelham, David, (1991). *A is for Animals*. New York: Simon and Schuster

Seeley, Lorna. (1990). *The Book of Shadow Boxes*. Atlanta, GA: Peachtree.
(Within the shadow of each letter's shadow box lies a hidden treasure for the young reader to find. The book is intricately and exquisitely designed and conceptualized by Ms. Seeley. Its visual fascination extends well beyond the elementary grades; it fosters not only the alphabetic principle, but also reading comprehension and literacy response.)

Sneed, Brad. (2002). *Picture a Letter*. New York: Penguin Books.

Seuss, Dr. *Dr. Seuss's ABC: An Amazing Alphabet Book*. New York:Random House. Ages 2-up.

Thornhill, Jim. (2004). *The Wildlife ABC and 123: A Nature Alphabet and Counting Book*. Berkeley, CA:Maple Tree Press. K-1 with additional nature notes on the species for the teacher/parent.
(In addition to fostering the alphabetic principle, the book nicely mixes geographic, multicultural, and scientific knowledge into a beautifully-designed text. It uses children's fascination with nature to foster reading and math literacy.

Zschock, Martha. (2001). *Journey Around Boston from A to Z*. Beverly Mass: Commonwealth Editions.

Zschock, Martha and Heather. (2002). *Journey Around New York from A to Z*. Beverly, Mass: Commonwealth Editions

TRADE BOOKS

These books foster particular aspects of reading skills, fluencies and competencies.

Blackstone, Stella. *Where's the Cat?* Ontario: Barefoot Books. Pre-K-K.
(This book, which focuses its primary school readers on searching for a lost cat, provides excellent use of repetitive language and encourages interactive reading.)

Campbell, Bebe Moore. (2003). *Sometimes My Mommy Gets Angry*. New York: G. P. Putnam's Sons.
(This is a moving story about a young girl whose mother suffers from mental illness. It is told in a way that is easy to read, along with beautiful illustrations. The main character is Annie. Sometimes her mother is very happy and other times very angry and sad. Annie has learned what to do when her mom is having a bad episode. She has books to read, a special stuffed animal and some secret snacks. Annie also has a strong support system in place with friends, neighbors, her teacher, and grandmother.

This book is a good introduction to the issue of mental illness. It is especially important in that students see how this young girl is able to cope with this difficult part of her life. "Sometimes my mommy has a dark cloud inside of her. I can't stop the rain from falling, but I can find sunshine in my mind."

Teachers can introduce students to this issue with this poignant book. Students can brainstorm different scenarios and discuss how they can be resolved. They can discuss who their support network includes and what it takes for a person to be strong enough to weather such a storm.

The book is a much-needed resource for children nowadays when Annie's situation is far more common than is generally known. Annie's capacity to make effective, affirming social decisions makes the work an inspirational touchstone for other peers who need to confront their parents' emotional crises. Children might be inspired to author poetry or create deliberately fictionalized narrative accounts about how they have confronted various crises.

In offering an upper-elementary-grade and age-appropriate narrative of a peer dealing with an emotionally ill parent, this book provides readers confronting similar family and caregiver issues with an opening for discussion and for hopeful outreach. Just reading this account may well be the first step toward assisting a youngster in acknowledging a "hidden problem" and getting crucial adult assistance in dealing with the crisis.)

Garza, Carmen Lomas. (1990). *Family Pictures Cuadros de familia*. San Francisco, CA:Children's Book Press.
(This book tells the story of the author's childhood growing up in a Hispanic community in Texas. Written in both Spanish and English, the story is accompanied by the author's incredible paintings. The paintings are unique, somewhat folksy, colorful, and totally entrancing. They bring you into Carmen's world. Once inside it, you don't want to leave.

There is so much to explore in this book; it works well with the study of "myself and family," community, communities around the world, Mexico, and family traditions and customs. It emphasizes social and emotional learning and how a young girl can find her way in the world. The traditions followed by her community and family were not necessarily accepted or understood by white America. Yet these values gave her the strength to be her own person and to rely both on her relationships and rich inner life to express herself.

There are so many activities that this book inspires. Children can study the origins of the piñata and make one. They can make a cookbook of recipes from Mexico or from their own homes. Children can also be encouraged to design their own book of family pictures. They can emphasize special occasions they celebrate or focus on family traditions that reflect their cultural backgrounds. The richness and lushness of the paintings invites the readers to construct meaning and to create their own narratives, procedural accounts, poetry, and dialogues inspired by one or more of the paintings.

Picture walk through the illustrations. Given the Spanish/English text, this strategy can be an engaging spatial entry point for descriptive and narrative spoken and written presentations. The lushly-detailed illustrations of family rites and celebrations can be springboards for children's literary and artistic renditions of equivalent family pictures and events that are prompted by Carmen's selections.

Use of dual language text for the book validates children's and family member's responses in languages other than English. Obviously, this book and its format are inspirational for ELL/bilingual learners and for special-needs learners who can be captivated by the paintings.

Glaser, Shirley, & Glaser, Milton. (2003). *The Alphazeds*. New York: Hyperion Books.
(This book is incredible in so many ways! It is an alphabet book that can be read by or to little ones and not-so-little ones. It starts with an empty room. One by one, each letter of the alphabet enters the room, each with its own distinct look, fantastic illustrations, and typography by the designer, Milton Glaser. Each of these letters also has its own distinct personality. A is angry, B is bashful, J is jealous, and so on. The room gets quite crowded. How do all of these different personalities manage to get along and coexist? Not too well apparently, as there is shouting, pushing, hitting, and kicking. In the midst of all the chaos, the light in the room goes out and there is silence.

> When the light came back on, something extraordinary had happened. Four letters had gotten together to comfort one another. Together they had managed to create something larger and more important than themselves.
> *They had made the first word.*

This is a great lesson on how each of us can be an individual, yet when we work together, something wonderful can happen. This book illustrates an incredible lesson in social and emotional maturity, and helps the child realize that it isn't just about "me."

There are many different activities that a teacher can use with this book. The children can work in groups to make their own alphabet book of emotions. They can then present the book as a group, discussing the roles each of them played, and how they used their unique talents to make the book.

Older children grades 3 and up can research and present as a group some important discoveries that were made more special because they involved people working together. They can also work on a project about cooperative learning, perhaps surveying class and schoolmates on how they feel they learn the best.)

Hest, Amy. (1985). *The Purple Coat*. New York: Macmillan Publishing Co.
(In the autumn of every year, Gabrielle travels with her mother to New York City to visit her Grandpa, who owns a tailor shop. Once there, he always makes her a new coat, but this year Gabrielle decides the usual navy blue coat won't do. *The Purple Coat* follows Gabrielle in her attempt to establish her own identity.)

Lionni, Leo. (1980). *Inch by Inch*. New York: Astor-Honor Publishing Co. Inc.
(In *Inch by Inch*, an inchworm (a caterpillar, or larval stage, of the fall cankerworm, which becomes a moth) keeps itself from being eaten by various birds by proving its worth as a measuring device.)

Lupton, Hugh. *The Story Tree-Tales to Read Aloud*. Ontario: Barefoot Books. K-3
(These seven multicultural stories are accessible enough to children to encourage their eventually taking over the read-aloud sharing on their own. This book is also a good one for family literacy sessions and for parent volunteers to read aloud in the classroom.)

Martin Jr., Bill, & John Archambault. (1966). *Knots on a Counting Rope*. New York: Henry Holt and Company.
(This beautifully-illustrated book reaches out in so many different directions, and we can all learn so much from it. *Knots on a Counting Rope* is the story of a Native-American boy who is blind and is learning from his grandfather how to survive in the world. Boy-Strength-of-Blue-Horses insists on hearing the story of his birth over and over again. Every time his grandfather retells the story of the boy's birth, he adds a knot to his counting rope. Each time he hears the story, Boy-Strength-of-Blue-Horses gains more confidence in himself. The story emphasizes the Native-American tradition of storytelling, and there are numerous art, math. and social studies lessons that offshoot from this book.

Of course, the telling and retelling of the story celebrate the young blind hero's strengths and weaknesses and ability to set goals with optimism. Stories of one's birth related by others are powerful demonstrations of social skills of the highest order.

This book also deals extensively with social and emotional learning. Children learn that those with disabilities need to be treated with sensitivity while learning to find their places in the world. One way in which children's social and emotional learning is strengthened is by understanding themselves and those around them. In order to facilitate this, each child will interview at least one family member about when he/she was born. The accounts collected with appropriate photos or memorabilia can then be shared in class and perhaps even authored into a *Knots on a Counting Rope*-style book format.

Children can also retell the story of the boy using the counting system of cultures other than Native American. This literary response will incorporate cultural study, respect. and empathy into ongoing reading and writing workshop efforts.)

McCully, Emily Arnold. (1992). *Mirette on the High Wire*. New York: G.P. Putnam's Sons.
(Mirette helps her mother run a boardinghouse for acrobats, jugglers, actors, and mimes. Her life changes when she discovers a boarder crossing the courtyard on air. She begs him to teach her how he does it. He refuses to teach her, but she begins practicing on her own. As she improves, he begins to help her. In the end she helps him overcome his fear of the high wire.)

Rabe, Bernice. (1981). *The Balancing Girl*. New York: E.P. Dutton.
(Margaret, a girl in a wheel chair, is excellent at balancing all kinds of objects. Margaret shows her friend Tommy how good she is at balancing at the school carnival.)

Ringgold, Faith. (1991). *Tar Beach*. New York: Crown Publishers.
(This book is one of my favorites, and it is moving in its words, art, and the beautiful story it tells. This is an effective book to use for younger grades to help the children connect with themselves, their families and their communities. It can also be used in connection with a mapmaking unit. The children can be encouraged to make a map of their neighborhoods from an aerial view.

A starting point for a discussion would be why the author portrayed New York from such a vantage point. In this beautiful book, the narrator, Cassie Louise Lightfoot, lets her dreams and ambitions take her to places in New York City that she ordinarily would not be able to be part of because of her circumstances. As a result of her self-motivation and self-awareness, Cassie is able to go as far as her dreams will let her. In this book, Cassie also shows strengths in the areas of emotional sensitivity, as well as inter- and intra-personal relationships.)

Children can author their own Tar Beach equivalent night fantasies and then share them with one another through an exhibit or big books. Although Cassie's family is obviously poor since they have to picnic on their roof, Cassie's dreamlike, lushly-illustrated flight over Harlem validates the beauty of their family life and of the city landscape, which is accessible to all. This is an invaluable lesson in the importance of the wealth inherent in the appreciation of family connections and the beauty of nature and public architectural designs! A song of family and of the city!

Schories, Pat. (2004). *Breakfast for Jack/Jack and the Missing Piece*. Honesdale, PA: Front Street Books.
(These wordless stories help pre-literate children, ELL learners new to this country, and special-needs children explore the basic elements of story: character, setting, and plot. The absence of words allows the children to construct their own meaning and create their own different stories to fit the illustrations.)

Steinberg, Laya. (2003). *Thesaurus Rex*. Ontario: Barefoot Books.
(This book introduces a dinosaur with an interest in words whose story is told through a wonderful rhyming text that can be used for fostering phonemic awareness and for choral readings.)

Uhlberg, Myron. (2003) *The Printer*. Atlanta, GA: Peachtree Press.
(This story celebrates the conventions of print in that the boy narrator's father is a deaf man who speaks with his hands and as a job chooses to turn lead type letters into words and sentences. An excellent book to support family literacy and an appreciation for the conventions of print.)

Van Allsburg, Chris. (1988). *Two Bad Ants*. New York: Houghton Mifflin Co.
(In *Two Bad Ants*, news comes to the ant world of a great discovery in a faraway place. A delicious crystal has been found. A group of ants set out to bring back this crystal to their queen. Two ants are overwhelmed by the treasure and stay behind in this dangerous alien world. It is a tale of choices, consequences, and the discovery of life's real treasures.)

Walter, Mildred Pitts. (2004). *Alec's primer*. (Illustrated by Larry Johnson). Lebanon, NH: University Press of New England.
(This is the true account of a Virginian slave who was taught to read by his owner's daughter. He later fought in the Civil War on the Union side and became a landowner himself in Vermont. The beautifully written narrative is complemented by the vibrant paintings of Larry Johnson, which include authentic period details.)

Webliography

Reading Online
http://www.readingonline.org
This online web resource sponsored by the International Reading Association is full of specific reading teaching ideas, lessons, and new research. It includes summaries of conference presentations and even tips on how to use technology to teach reading.

Balanced Literacy
http://www.thekcrew.net/balancedliteracy.html
Established in 1996, this site is organized according to the components of the balanced literacy approach. It also has an excellent listing of professional books that can assist with various aspects of teaching reading.

Carol Hurst
http://www.carolhurst.com/index.html
This is a terrific resource for exploring the children's literature works that are at the crux of author and genre study. It can be used for material to supplement period studies and discussions of authors' lives. Older children will be able to explore it on their own.

Read, Write, Think
http://www.readwritethink.org/lessons/
This resource maintained by the NCTE, National Council of Teachers of English, has a growing database of age- and grade-specific literacy lesson plans. It also includes all the graphic organizers cited in this book and many more, ready to download.

Inspiration Software
http://www.inspiration.com
http://www.inspiration.com/freetrial/index.cfm
This is the home site for the Inspiration and Kidspiration mind-mapping software. These online templates and capacities assist the reading teacher with customizing the various graphic organizers discussed throughout the book, and with gaining the ability to design customized graphic organizers for a particular theme, study, or student group. A free trial version of this resource, which is child friendly, can be downloaded.

Visual Thesaurus
http://www.visualthesaurus.com/online/
This is both an online dictionary and a thesaurus.

Resources for Read Aloud, Shared Reading, and Independent Reading available on the Internet include the following:

http:// www.mightybook.com/library_4to6.htm.
This is a library of books read aloud by the computer. Children can listen to these books or practice reading with a buddy as the computer broadcasts the text. Of course, this type of read-aloud would only be used in addition to the read-aloud of the teacher.

http://www.enchantedlearning.com/Rhymes.html
These are online nursery rhymes ready for reading to the children and posting throughout for room or for literacy center display.

SEDL-RCI Framework of Reading
http://www.sedl.org/reading/framework/assessment.html
This is an excellent resource for readings in the theories and methods of foundations. There are topic-aligned links to specific theorists that can be included at the close of your lesson planning and may be reviewed before certification tests.

TOOLS TO HELP YOU TEACH THE FOUNDATIONS OF READING AND TO SUCCEED IN CONSTRUCTED RESPONSE CERTIFICATION EXAMINATIONS

Appendix 1- The Record of Reading Behavior- A close up look at a key assessment tool.

Often in the constructed-response question on a foundations-of-education certification test or on a general-elementary certification test; the educator is asked to analyze a record of reading behavior or to construct an appropriate one from data given in an anecdote. Furthermore, with the current accountability climate, it is a good idea for new teachers and for career changers to examine closely the basic elements in recording reading behavior.

While there are various acceptable formats for emergent literacy assessment used throughout the country, the one selected for use here is based on the work of Marie Clay and Kenneth Goodman. These two are key researchers in the close observation and documentations of children's early reading miscues (reading mistakes).

It is important to emphasize that the teacher should not just "take the Record of Reading Behavior " and begin filling it out as the child reads from a random book prior to beginning of the observation. There are specific steps for taking the record and analyzing its results.

1. Select a text
If you want to see if the child is reading at instructional level, choose a book that the child has already read. If the purpose of the test is to see whether the child is ready to advance to the next level, choose a book from that level that the child has not yet seen.

2. Introduce the text
If the book is one that has been read, you do not need to introduce the text other than by saying the title. But if the book is new to the child, you should briefly share the title and tell the child a bit about the plot and style of the book.

3. Take the record
Generally, with emergent readers' grades 1-2, there are only 100-150 words in a passage used to take a record. Make certain that the child is seated beside you, so that you can see the text as the child reads it.

If desired, you may want to photocopy the text in advance for yourself so you can make direct notations on your text while the child reads from the book. After you introduce the text, make certain that the child has the chance to read the text independently. Be certain that you do not "teach" or help the child with the text other than to supply an unknown word that the child requests you to supply. The purpose of the record is to see what the child does on his or her own. As the child reads the text, you must be certain to record the reading behaviors the child exhibits using the following notations.

READING K-12

In taking the record, keep in mind the following: Allow enough time for the child to work independently on a problem before telling or supplying the word. If you wait too long, you could run the risk of having the child lose the meaning and his/her interest in the story as he or she tries to identify the unknown word.

It is recommended that when a child is way off track, you tell him or her to "Try that again" (TTA). If a whole phrase is troubling, put it into square brackets and score it as only one error.

The notation for filling out the Record of Reading behavior involves noting the child's response on the top with the actual text below it.

Comprehension Check

This can and should be done by inviting the child to retell the story. This retelling can then be used to ask further questions about characters, plot, setting, and purpose, which allow you to observe and to record the child's level of comprehension.

Calculating the Reading Level and the Self-Correction Rate

Calculating the reading level lets you know if the book is at the level on which the child can read it independently or comfortably with guidance or if the book is at a level where reading it frustrates the child.

Generally, an accuracy score of 95-100% suggests that the child can read the text and other books or texts on the same level.

An accuracy score of 90-94% indicates that the text and texts likely will present challenges to the child, but with guidance from you, a tutor or parent, the child will be able to master these texts and enjoy them. This is instructional level.

However, an accuracy score of less than 89% tells you that the material you have selected for the child is too hard for the child to control alone. Such material needs to be shared with the child in a shared reading situation or read to the child.

KEEPING SCORE ON THE RECORD

Insertions, omissions, substitutions, and teacher-told responses, all count as errors. Repetitions are not scored as errors. Corrected responses are scored as self corrections.

No penalty is given for a child's attempts at self correction that results in a finally incorrect response but the attempts should be noted. Multiple unsuccessful attempts at a word score as one error only.

The lowest score for any page is zero. If a child omits a line or lines, each word omitted is counted as an error. If the child omits a page, deduct the number of words omitted from the total number of words that you have used for the record.

Calculating the Reading Level

Note the number of errors made on each line on the Record of Reading Behavior in the column marked E (for Error).

Total the number of errors in the text and divide this number into the number of words that the child has read. This will give you the error rate.

If a child read a passage of 100 words and made 10 errors, the error rate would be 1 in 10. Convert this to an accuracy percentage, or 90%.

Calculating the Self Correction Rate

Total all the self-corrections.
Next, add the number of errors to the number of self-corrections and divide by the number of self-corrections.

A self correction rate of 1 in 3 to 1 in 5 is considered good. This rate indicates that the child is able to help himself or herself as problems are encountered in reading.

Analyzing the record

This record should assist the educator in developing a detailed date-specific picture of the child's progress in reading behavior. It should be used to help the educator individualize instruction for the specific child.

As the errors are reviewed, consider whether the child made the error because of semantics (cues from meaning), syntactic (language structure), or visual information difficulties.

As self-corrections are analyzed, consider what led the child to make that self-correction. Check out and consider what cues the child does use effectively and which the child does not use well.

Consider the ways in which the child tackles a word that is unknown. Characterize that behavior and consider how the teacher can assist the child with this issue.

If a child can retell at least three quarters of a story, this is considered adequate for retelling.

Analysis of reading behavior records can and should support the educator in designing appropriate mini-lessons and strategies to help the child with his or her recorded errors and miscues.

Sample Test

1) There are two basic types of text structure:
(Easy) (Skill 1.1)

A) Fiction and non-fiction.

B) Primary and pre-k.

C) Expository and narrative.

D) Wordless and text rich.

2) A "decodable text" is:
(Average Rigor) (Skill 1.1)

A) A text that a child can read aloud with correct pronunciations.

B) A text that a child can answer comprehension questions about with a high percentage of accuracy.

C) Text written to match the sequence of letter-sound relationships that have been taught.

D) None of the above.

3) The major difference between phonemic and phonological awareness is:
(Average Rigor) (Skill 1.2)

A) One deals with a series of discrete sounds and the other with sound-spelling relationships.

B) One is involved with teaching and learning alliteration and rhymes.

C) Phonemic awareness is a specific type of phonological awareness that deals with separate phonemes within a given word.

D) Phonological awareness is associated with printed words.

4) The theorist in early reading (emergent reading) who has identified five tasks for phonemic awareness is:
(Average Rigor) (Skill 1.2)

A) John Munro

B) Brian Cambourne

C) Marilyn Jager Adams

D) Lucy Calkins

5) **An oddity task is one in which children:**
(Rigorous) (Skill 1.2)

A) Identify the odd number in a mathematical series and talk about how they did it.

B) Perform a creative exercise designed for differentiated learning styles.

C) Recognize which sound is odd in a series of like sounds.

D) Design a different activity for themselves.

6) **All of the following are true about phonological awareness EXCEPT:**
(Average Rigor) (Skill 1.2)

A) It may involve print.

B) It is a prerequisite for spelling and phonics.

C) Activities can be done by the children with their eyes closed.

D) It starts before letter recognition is taught.

7) **"Beautiful Beth is the Best Girl in the Bradley Bay area." This sentence could be used to help children learn about:**
(Easy) (Skill 1.2)

A) Assonance.

B) Alliteration.

C) Rhyming pairs.

D) None of the above

8) **Phonological awareness includes all of the following skills except:**
(Average Rigor) (Skill 1.2)

A) Rhyming and syllabification

B) Blending sounds into words

C) Understanding the meaning of the root word

D) Removing initial sounds and substituting others

9) Paul is a new teacher. He has just started his logs and assessments for his children's phonemic awareness. He asks a reading teacher to look over his log, but the log is returned to him:
(Average Rigor) (Skill 1.2)

A) Paul gave the log to the wrong colleague.

B) The colleague would not help him out by reviewing it.

C) The log did not have the dates the child's behavior was observed and had no stated performance standards.

D) The log didn't have a cover letter from Paul.

10) As a parent walked through the first grade floor of her school, she kept hearing repeated clapping. Most likely the children were:
(Average Rigor) (Skill 1.2)

A) Clapping to show respect for one another.

B) Rehearsing for how they would clap at a play.

C) Clapping out syllables of multi-syllabic words.

D) All of the above.

11) A key theorist whose work has helped teacher's document children's oral reading progress throughout the school year is:
(Average Rigor) (Skill 2.1)

A)   Jerome Bruner.

B)   Daniel J. Chard.

C)   J. David Cooper.

D)   Marie Clay.

12) Most of the children in first-year teacher Ms. James's class are really doing well in their phonemic awareness assessments. However, Ms. James is very concerned about three children who do not seem to be able to distinguish between spoken words that "sound alike," but are different. Since she is a first year teacher, she feels her inexperience may be to blame. In truth, the reason these three children have not yet demonstrated phonemic awareness is most likely that:
(Rigorous) (Skill 2.1)

A) They are not capable of becoming good readers.

B) They are bored in class.

C) They may be from an ELL background.

D) Ms. James does not pronounce the different phonemes clearly enough.

13) **To decode is to:**
    (Easy) (Skill 2.1)

    A) Construct meaning.

    B) Sound out a printed
       sequence of letters.

    C) Use a special code to
       decipher a message.

    D) None of the above.

14) **To help students develop as
    readers it is important to do
    all of the following except:**
    (Average Rigor) (Skill 2.2)

    A) Surround children with
       books

    B) Have students participate in
       daily read aloud activities

    C) Have students read only the
       books that have been picked
       out for them by the teacher

    D) Have students read their
       favorite books over and over

15) **Characteristics of difficulties
    seen in emergent readers
    include:**
    (Rigorous) (Skill 2.3)

    A) High interest in reading

    B) Clear, concise speech

    C) Ability to follow directions
       accurately

    D) None of the above

16) **In terms of a balanced
    literacy classroom, a "leveled
    bin" indicates:**
    (Easy) (Skill 2.4)

    A) A plant set at child's eye
       level for descriptive writing
       purposes.

    B) A bin with books the child
       has selected.

    C) A bin with books leveled by
       the teacher.

    D) A bin with all kinds of
       reading materials including
       magazines and packaging
       on a child's level.

17) **The term graphophenemic
    awareness refers to:**
    (Easy) (Skill 2.4)

    A) Handwriting skills.

    B) Letter to sound
       recognition.

    C) Alphabetic principle.

    D) Phonemic awareness

18) Gracie seems to be struggling with her reading, even in first grade, although her mother works at a publishing firm and her dad is an editor. Her speech is also full of mispronunciations, although her parents were born in the school neighborhood. Gracie should be checked by:
(Average Rigor) (Skill 2.4)

A) A reading specialist.

B) A speech therapist or an audiologist

C) A pediatrician.

D) A psychologist.

19) Ability grouping means:
(Rigorous) (Skill 2.4)

A) Grouping of children according to the results of an IQ test.

B) Grouping of children with similar test results for instructional purposes.

C) Grouping of children according to their oral reading accuracy rate.

D) Grouping of children wit similar needs for instructional purposes.

20) The teacher is very concerned about identifying a book that is "just right" for Jay to read independently. This means that Jay should be able to read this book with:
(Average Rigor) (Skill 2.4)

A) Below 92% accuracy

B) 100% accuracy

C) 95-100% accuracy

D) 92-97% accuracy

21) Jay really wants to read a book that he can only read with 94% accuracy. He could get to read this book as:
(Average Rigor) (Skill 2.4)

A) An independent reading.

B) A guided reading.

C) A shared reading.

D) All of the above.

22) Dictionary study:
(Average Rigor) (Skill 2.4)

A) can begin in grades 1 or 2.

B) can begin in pre-K using the lush picture dictionaries.

C) should start on grade three level.

D) a and b.

23) **Mrs. Young is a first grade teacher trying to select a books that are "just right" for her students to read independently. She needs to consider which of the following:**
(Rigorous) (Skill 2.4)

A) Illustrations should support the meaning of the text.

B) Content that relates to student interest and experiences

C) Predictable text structures and language patterns

D) All of the above

24) **Greg Ball went to an author signing where Faith Ringgold gave a talk about one of her many books.He was so inspired by her presence and by his reading of her book *TAR BEACH*, that he used the book for his reading and writing workshop activities. His supervisor wrote in his plan book, that he was pleased that Greg had used the book as an/a _____ book.**
(Average Rigor) (Skill 3.1)

A) Basic book.

B) Feature book.

C) Anchor book.

D) Focus book.

25) **Environmental print is available at all of the following except:**
(Easy) (Skill 3.1)

A) Within a newspaper.

B) On the page of a library book.

C) On a supermarket circular.

D) In a commercial flyer.

26) **The best way for a teacher to track a student's progress in demonstrating the alphabetic principal/ graphophonemic awareness is to:**
(Rigorous) (Skill 3.1)

A) Provide group assessments

B) Maintain individual records

C) Assess with standardized tests

D) Have the student assessed by a team of teachers

27) Author's viewpoint questions stump Gary. His teacher can help him by asking him during their reading conferences:
(Average Rigor) (Skill 3.1)

A) If Gary feels the book he is reading, is it just right for him.

B) What the author would say about what the character is doing in the story.

C) How the story can be changed to another genre.

D) If Gary wants to read more books by this author.

28) Bill has been called up to the teacher for an individual conference. She asks him to retell one of the books he has listed on his weekly log. He begins and is still talking 7 minutes later. Most probably, Bill:
(Average Rigor) (Skill 3.1)

A) Told the entire story with all its details and minor characters.

B) May or may not have really gotten the main points and perspectives of the story.

C) May have really liked the Story.

D) None of the above.

29) The work of Chard and Osborn (l999) in establishing guidelines for children with reading disabilities has shown that it is essential for them to:
(Rigorous) (Skill 3.2)

A) Read wordless picture books.

B) Learn at least 10 sight words.

C) Work intensely on the alphabetic principle.

D) Focus on using syntactic clues.

30) An observer enters Julia's first grade classroom. Children are working with oaktag strips and placing the word letters on these strips on a sentence strip holder. Then they seem to be involved in some kind of counting. The observer is confused. This activity is taking place during the reading block. Julia explains: *(Rigorous) (Skill 3.2)*

A) The children are counting letters.

B) This is word sorting and the children are grouping words by length, common letters and sound.

C) The children are combining mathematics counting and word study.

D) The children are doing a strategy sheet based on a particular word family

31) As he walks up and down the hallway, Mr. Adams, the new Assistant Principal, continually hears Ms. Brown telling her children to go to the wall. Mr. Adams looks briefly at the literacy block schedule and continues on his walk through the building. He realizes that Ms. Brown's children are at work on: *(Rigorous) (Skill 3.2)*

A) A new hall display.

B) Taking down an old display and then redoing it for a new theme.

C) Adding words to their spelling word wall.

D) Measuring the height of plants for a mathematics lesson.

32) Randy is proud of how many new vocabulary words he has learned. He enjoys playing with a device his teacher has, since it helps him to show all the words he can create from various letters. The device is a: *(Rigorous) (Skill 3.2)*

A) Word strip.

B) Letter holder for making words.

C) Word mask.

D) None of the above.

33) A delegation from the United Kingdom has come to the United States and since they are considering adapting the balanced literacy approach, they are very interested in seeing the small group demonstrated. Mr. Adams knows that he should bring them into Greg's room when Greg is doing which activity? *(Rigorous) (Skill 3.2)*

A) A mini lesson.

B) A conference with individual students.

C) A time when children are divided into small and independent study groups.

D) A read-aloud.

34) Ronald's parents are hearing impaired. He probably will need: *(Average Rigor) (Skill 3.2)*

A) Extensive work with the use of picture cues

B) Work with songs, rhymes and read alouds to promote phonemic awareness.

C) No extra work or support.

D) None of the above.

35) The best ways to select words students need to learn to spell include all of the following except: *(Rigorous) (Skill 3.2)*

A) Misspelled words from student writing

B) Lists of theme words

C) Lists from a spelling textbook

D) Lists of words from content areas

36) As Ms. Maxwell enters a first grade class, the teacher is busily writing down what the children are saying. The teacher is probably doing this to: *(Easy) (Skill 3.2)*

A) Demonstrate how to copy down speech.

B) Make a connection and promote awareness of the relationship between spoken and written language.

C) Authenticate the children's comments.

D) Raise the children's self esteem.

37) **The best way for a primary grade teacher to model directionality and one to one word matching would be:**
(Easy) (Skill 3.2)

A) Using a regular library or classroom text book.

B) Using her own person reading book.

C) Using a big book.

D) Using a book dummy.

38) **Children "own" words when all of the following happen except:**
(Average Rigor) (Skill 3.2)

A) They find these words on their own.

B) The teacher provides a mandated word list.

C) They use the words in their own writings.

D) The words appear in literature that interests them.

39) **In order to get children to compile specialized vocabulary, they can use:**
(Rigorous) (Skill 3.2)

A) Newspapers.

B) Internet resources and approved web-sites that focus on the special interest.

C) Experts they can interview.

D) All of the above.

40) **If children are engaged in creating a museum within classroom project to exhibit their work, they are:**
(Average Rigor) (Skill 3.2)

A) Not doing any reading or writing.

B) Doing many authentic reading, writing, and researching tasks.

C) Not likely to visit a real museum.

D) All of the above.

41) A district observer notes that fifth graders are showing younger peers in the third grade how to hold a book and walk around with it, they assume:
(Rigorous) (Skill 3.3)

A) That the fifth graders are particularly theatrical.

B) That the fifth graders are proud of how they read stories aloud.

C) That the fifth graders are training the younger children in book holding.

D) That this has nothing to do with instruction.

42) At a faculty meeting Ms. Riley found out that she might have crisscrossers in her class and that Mr. Brown had them and he was happy about it:
(Rigorous) (Skill 3.3)

A) Crisscrossers are students who have skipped a grade.

B) Crisscrossers are students with excellent skills in reading and in Math.

C) Crisscrossers are second language learners who have a positive attitude toward first and second language learning.

D) Crisscrossers are second language learners who are only positive about English Language Learning.

43) Cues in reading are:
(Easy) (Skill 3.3)

A) Vowel sounds.

B) Digraphs.

C) Sources of information used by readers to help them construct meaning.

D) None of the above.

44) A teacher is asking children to look at the beginning letters of words. She then asks the child to connect the beginning letter to the text and story and to think about what word would make sense there. This is an example of:
(Average Rigor) (Skill 3.3)

A) A balanced literacy approach.

B) A phonemic approach.

C) A phonic approach.

D) AN ELL differentiated approach.

45) As the child is reading and has made an incorrect attempt, the teacher prompts:
(Average Rigor) (Skill 3.3)

A) That is a mistake, do it again.

B) No, you are stupid. .. why can't you get it?

C) Does that make sense to you?

D) Forget it, this is too hard for you.

46) Asking a child if what he or she has read makes sense to him or her, is prompting the child to use:
(Easy) (Skill 3.3)

A) Phonics cues.

B) Syntactic cues.

C) Semantic cues.

D) Prior knowledge.

47) When you ask a child, if what he or she has just read "sounds right" to him or her, you are trying to get that child to use:
(Average Rigor) (Skill 3.3)

A) Phonics cues.

B) Syntactic cues.

C) Semantic cues.

D) Prior knowledge.

48) To encode means that you:
(Average Rigor) (Skill 3.3)

A) Decode a second time.

B) Construct meaning from a code.

C) Tell someone a message.

D) None of the above.

49) A natural role for a highly proficient reader would be: (Rigorous) (Skill 3.3)

A) To assist the teacher with cleaning the classroom and organizing the student folders.

B) To develop charts for the teacher by copying needed poems for full class study.

C) Tutor and support struggling readers.

D) Work on his/her own interests while the teacher works with the rest of the class.

50) "Ballgame" is a _____word. Its meaning is derived from the combination of "Ball" and "Game": (Easy) (Skill 3.3)

A) Contraction.

B) Compound.

C) Portmanteau.

D) Palindrome.

51) Two consonants placed together in a word to make a unique sound is a : (Easy) (Skill 3.3)

A) Consonant digraph

B) Consonant blend

C) Morpheme

D) Phoneme

52) Reading expression, appropriate phrasing, and good inflection are characteristics of: (Rigorous) (Skill 4.1)

A) Prosody

B) Fluency

C) Modeling

D) Accuracy

53) Reader's Theater is: (Average Rigor) (Skill 4.2)

A) Reading as a group or with the teacher

B) When students use scripts that have different parts for different characters

C) When students read aloud daily

D) When students work together to provide instruction for each other

54) **Factual book features children should learn include:** *(Average Rigor) (Skill 5.1)*

A) Captions.

B) Glossaries.

C) Diagrams.

D) All of the above.

55) **The Stop and Think Strategy means that the child reader will:** *(Rigorous) (Skill 5.1)*

A) Read through until the end of the story or text.

B) Ask himself or herself if what he or she has read makes sense to him or her.

C) Stop after reading some text and write down his/her concerns.

D) All of the above

56) **To help children with "main idea" questions, the teacher should:** *(Rigorous) (Skill 5.1)*

A) Give out a strategy sheet on the main idea for children to place in their reader's notebooks.

B) Model responding to such a question as part of guided reading.

C) Have children create "main idea questions" to go with their writings.

D) All of the above.

57) **By definition, which children in a classroom will have trouble with syntactic cues?** *(Rigorous) (Skill 5.1)*

A) Those from families who do not have household libraries.

B) Those not in a top reading group.

C) Those from ELL backgrounds.

D) All of the above.

58) **Making inferences from the text means that the reader:** *(Average Rigor) (Skil 5.1)*

A) Is making informed judgments based on available evidence.

B) Is making a guess based on prior experiences.

C) Is making a guess based on what the reader would like to be true of the text.

D) All of the above.

59) **Mr. Mark is a brand new teacher who is not from the neighborhood where his school is located. He is a bit nervous as this is his first teaching assignment. He does not yet know how to relax enough to get his students to activate prior experience. He should:** *(Average Rigor) (Skill 5.1)*

A) Try a free recall question: Tell us what you know about...

B) Try an unstructured Question: Let's talk About...

C) Use word association: What do you associate X with?

D) All of the above.

60) **Among the literary strategies that teachers can use to activate prior knowledge are:** *(Easy) (Skill 5.1)*

A) Predicting and previewing a story.

B) Story mapping.

C) Venn diagramming.

D) Linear arrays.

61) **In a balanced literacy classroom, new vocabulary would most likely appear on:** *(Easy) (Skill 5.1)*

A) An experiential chart.

B) A class newspaper.

C) The word wall.

D) Outside the room on a bulletin board.

62) **Based on individual conferences with many children, the teacher realizes that although they are all self-improving readers, they need help in better use of the context to define words. The teacher decided to try the use of:**
(Rigorous) (Skill 5.1)

A) A dictionary to look up words.

B) A thesaurus to use with the dictionary.

C) Contextual redefinition training.

D) Instruction in how to effectively use a dictionary.

63) **A theorist who believes that there is a finite body of approved literature children should be taught on various grade levels and has produced books about what everyone needs to know to be literate on various grade levels is:**
(Rigorous) (Skill 5.2)

A) Rudolf Flesch

B) J. David Cooper

C) John Dewey

D) E. D. Hirsch

64) **To promote word study, children can:**
(Average Rigor) (Skill 5.2)

A) Be required to go to the dictionary at least once or twice a day.

B) Collect and share words of interest they find in their readings.

C) Do vocabulary work sheets from a basal reader or commercial vocabulary book.

D) Do all of the above.

65) **Teachers should select at least ___words for pre-reading vocabulary discussion:**
(Rigorous) (Skill 5.2)

A) 12.

B) 15.

C) 2-3.

D) 8-10.

66) **The teacher should choose words for pre-story discussion and exploration based on:**
(Average Rigor) (Skill 5.2)

A) The teacher's interest.

B) Whether the teacher feels the children have prior knowledge of or experience with the words.

C) A pre-existing grade level required vocabulary list.

D) Words that will impress his or her supervisor.

67) **Two steps a teacher might take before selecting words for study are:**
(Rigorous) (Skill 5.2)

A) Reading the story and story mapping.

B) Asking advice from a veteran teacher and the grade leader.

C) Looking in a teacher's guide and copying out the words listed there.

D) All of the above are Correct

68) **A teacher discovers after considering his class's prior knowledge of the story material that he would need to teach 12 words at least before he starts teaching the story to the whole group. This indicates:**
(Rigorous) (Skill 5.2)

A) The children will need a read-aloud.

B) The children will need independent reading.

C) The children will need guided reading.

D) The children will need shared reading.

69) **Vocabulary should be introduced after reading if:**
(Average Rigor) (Skill 5.2)

A) The children have identified words from their reading which were difficult and which they need explained.

B) The text is appropriate for vocabulary building.

C) The teacher would like to teach vocabulary after the reading.

D) a and b

70) Taking responsibility for a child's own learning, will usually involve the child in: *(Average Rigor) (Skill 5.2)*

   A) Reading and writing on his/her own.

   B) Developing a personal literacy project which will later be shared with the teacher and peers and family.

   C) Putting away books and materials when directed.

   D) a and b.

71) The word "bat" is a ___word for "batter-up": *(Easy) (Skill 5.2)*

   A) Suffix.

   B) Prefix.

   C) Root word.

   D) Inflectional ending.

72) Four of Ms. Wolmark's students have lived in other countries. She is particularly pleased to be studying Sumerian proverbs with them as part of the sixth grade unit in analyzing the sayings of other cultures because: *(Rigorous) (Skill 5.2)*

   A) This gives her a break from teaching and the children can share sayings from other cultures they and their families have experienced.

   B) This validates the experiences and expertise of ELL learners in her classroom.

   C) This provides her children from the US with a lens on other cultural values.

   D) All of the above.

73) An effective way to build vocabulary and to make connections with mandated science and mathematics material is to teach Greek and Latin roots using: *(Average Rigor) (Skill 5.2)*

   A) Semantic maps.

   B) Hierarchical arrays.

   C) Linear arrays.

   D) Word webs.

74) A bound morpheme is:
(Easy) (Skill 5.2)

A) A prefix.

B) A contraction.

C) An inflectional ending that can be added to a base word to change its case, gender, number, tense or form.

D) A root word.

75) Direct teaching of a concept or strategy means:
(Average Rigor) (Skill 5.2)

A) The teacher teaches the concept or strategy as part of a genre lesson.

B) The teacher teaches the concept as part of the writing workshop.

C) The teacher explicitly announces to the class that this strategy will be taught.

D) The teacher teaches the strategy to a small group of children or to an individual child.

76) The theorist who believes children should not be "taught" vocabulary and structural analysis is:
(Rigorous) (Skill 5.2)

A) Cooper

B) Flesch

C) Hirsch

D) Calkins

77) Structural analysis is:
(Rigorous) (Skill 5.2)

A) the "sounding out" a printed sequence of letters based on knowledge of letter sound correspondences

B) when the teacher keeps a detailed recording of the errors or inaccurate attempts of a child reader during a reading assessment

C) the process of hearing a spoken word and identifying its separate phonemes or syllables.

D) the process of examining the words in the text for meaningful word units (affixes, base words, inflected endings).

78) One of the many ways in which a child can demonstrate comprehension of a story is by:
(Average Rigor) (Skill 5.3)

A) Filling in a strategy sheet.

B) Retelling the story orally.

C) Retelling the story in writing.

D) All of the above.

79) Ms. James is seated with a child by her side. The child is reading aloud from an open book. Ms. James is teaching in a school that has embraced the Balanced Literacy Approach. Therefore it is most likely that Ms. James is writing and recording:
(Average Rigor) (Skill 6.1)

A) The child's use of expression in reading aloud.

B) The child's errors and miscues.

C) Her observations of the child's attitude toward reading.

D) The child's feelings about the particular passage being read.

80) Andrew is just starting school, but it looks like he will be successful in reading because:
(Average Rigor) (Skill 6.1)

A) He comes from a family which cares about his progress.

B) He is phonemically aware and knows his alphabet.

C) He has been in pre-school.

D) He is well behaved.

81) Ms. James is seated with a child by her side. The child is reading aloud from an open book. Ms. James is teaching in a school that has embraced the Balanced Literacy Approach. Therefore it is most likely that Ms. James is writing and recording:
(Rigorous) (Skill 6.1)

A) The child's use of expression in reading aloud.

B) The child's errors and miscues.

C) Her observations of the child's attitude toward reading.

D) The child's feelings about the particular passage being read.

82) **"Self correct" in reading means:**
(Easy) (Skill 6.1)

A) The teacher corrects on the record the errors the child makes.

B) The child goes back and corrects errors made in a running record.

C) The reading specialist teaches this to the child.

D) a and b.

83) **When taking a child's running record, the kinds of self corrections the child makes:**
(Average Rigor) (Skill 6.1)

A) Are not important, but the percentage of accuracy is important.

B) May show something about which cueing systems the child relies on.

C) Can be meaningful if analyzed over several records.

D) Both b and c

84) **Once a teacher has carefully recorded and documented a running record:**
(Rigorous) (Skill 6.1)

A) There is nothing further to do as long as the teacher keeps the running record for conferences and documentation of grades.

B) The teacher should review the running record and other subsequent ones taken for growth over time.

C) The teacher should differentiate instruction for that particular student as indicated by growth over time and evidence of other needs.

D) Both b and c

85) **A strategy is:**
(Average Rigor) (Skill 6.1)

A) A practice or routine the teacher can continually refer to.

B) A practice or routine a child can continually refer to or use.

C) A sheet or template for a practice the child can continually fill out.

D) All of the above.

86) "Sounds right" can sound wrong to:
(Rigorous) (Skill 6.1)

A) Any reader who is not a fluent or early reader.

B) AN ELL reader.

C) A struggling reader.

D) None of the above.

87) An excellent research project that can combine dictionary study with science research would be:
(Average Rigor) (Skill 6.1)

A) A student authored dictionary terms and phrases about earthworms.

B) A teacher developed specialized dictionary of words and phrases about. earthworms.

C) A collection of articles on earthworms put together by the school librarian.

D) b and c.

88) Ways a paragraph may be organized include:
(Average Rigor) (Skill 6.2)

A) Sequence of events

B) Statement Support

C) Classification

D) All of the above

89) Andrew is just starting school, but it looks like he will be successful in reading because:
(Average Rigor) (Skill 6.3)

A) He comes from a family which cares about his progress.

B) He is phonemically aware and knows his alphabet.

C) He has been in pre-school.

D) He is well behaved.

90) A fifth grade teacher as subscribed to an online version of a local newspaper. She can help the students examine this resource and how it compares to the print version by noting which of the following differences: *(Rigorous) (Skill 6.4)*

A) Use of video to document events.

B) Use of sound clips in addition to written text

C) Links to other web resources

D) all of the above

91) Nonfiction genres include all of the following except: *(Easy) (Skill 7.1)*

A) Essays

B) Poetry

C) Speech

D) Biography

92) Historical Fiction, Mythology, Folklore, Realistic Fiction, Mystery, and Legends are known as: *(Easy) (Skill 7.1)*

A) Reading styles

B) Young Adult topics

C) Genres

D) Booklists

93) The Developing Readers Assessment System for leveling books was developed by: *(Rigorous) (Skill 7.2)*

A) Calkins and Clay

B) Fountas and Pinnell

C) Wylie and Durrell

D) Flesch and Clay

94) Sometimes children can be asked to demonstrate their understanding of a text in a non-written format. This might include all of the following except: *(Easy) (Skill 8.1)*

A) A story map.

B) A Venn diagram.

C) Storyboarding a part of the story with dialogue bubbles.

D) Retelling or paraphrasing.

95) **Ms. Angel has to be certain that her fourth graders know the characteristics of the historical fiction genre. She can best support them in becoming comfortable with this genre by:**
(Rigorous) (Skill 8.2)

A) Providing sequel and prequel writing opportunities using that genre.

B) Reading them many different works from that genre.

C) a and b.

D) Having them look up the definition of that genre in a literary encyclopedia.

96) **Ms. James is seated with a child by her side. The child is reading aloud from an open book. Ms. James is teaching in a school that has embraced the Balanced Literacy Approach. Therefore it is most likely that Ms. James is writing and recording:**
(Average Rigor) (Skill 9.1)

A) The child's use of expression in reading aloud.

B) The child's errors and miscues.

C) Her observations of the child's attitude toward reading.

D) The child's feelings about the particular passage being read.

97) **The work of Chard and Osborn (1999) in establishing guidelines for children with reading disabilities has shown that it is essential for them to:**
(Rigorous) (Skill 9.2)

A) Read wordless picture books.

B) Learn at least 10 sight words.

C) Work intensely on the alphabetic principle.

D) Focus on using syntactic clues.

98) **Miscue analysis assists the teacher in determining which of the following:**
(Average Rigor) (Skill 9.3)

A) Methods a student uses to figure out unknown words

B) Student ability to monitor their own reading

C) Strategies that students are using with the greatest success

D) All of the above

99) **A key theorist who supports a phonics centered approach is:**
(Rigorous) (Skill 9.4)

A) Marie Clay.

B) Sharon Taberski.

C) Shelley Harwayne.

D) Rudolf Flesch.

100) **The reliability of a test is measured by:**
(Rigorous) (Skill 9.5)

A) The number of children who can pass it.

B) The number of children who fail it.

C) The degree to which it measures what it is supposed to measure over time.

D) None of the above

101) **A quartile on a test is:**
(Average Rigor) (Skill 9.5)

A) A quarter of the grades grouped.

B) The division of the percentiles into four segments each of which is called a quartile.

C) 25 of the tests scored.

D) b and c

102) **Validity in assessment means:**
(Rigorous) (Skill 9.5)

A) The test went off without any previewing of the questions or leaks on its contents.

B) The majority of test takers passed.

C) The correct time was allowed for the children to complete the test.

D) The test assessed what it was supposed to assess and measure.

103) "Bias" in testing occurs when:
(Rigorous) (Skill 9.5)

A) The assessment instrument is not an objective, fair and impartial one for a given cultural, ethnic, or special needs participant.

B) The testing administrator is biased.

C) The same test is given with no time considerations or provisions for those in need of more time or those who have handicapping conditions.

D) All of the above

104) Norm-referenced tests:
(Average rigor) (Skill 9.5)

A) Give information only about the local samples results.

B) Provide information about the local test takers did compared to a representative sampling of national test takers.

C) Make no comparisons to national test takers.

D) None of the above.

105) When helping students locate and evaluate information, you may want to solicit the help of your school's:
(Average Rigor) (Skill 10.1)

A) library media specialist.

B) speech therapist.

C) counselor.

D) reading teacher.

106) When considering a core reading program, it should adhere to all of the following characteristics except:
(Rigorous) (Skill 11.1)

A) Based on current research and methods.

B) Provides explicit instruction in phonemic awareness, phonics, decoding, word recognition, spelling, vocabulary, comprehension, and writing.

C) Contain student workbooks.

D) Provide opportunities for students to discuss reading in class.

107) A small group of students choose a book to read. Each person in the group is assigned a role, which changes so that each person gets to play each role is called a:
(Rigorous) (Skill 11.2)

A) Literature circle

B) Workshop

C) Reading Center

D) None of the above.

108) Book handling skills include ALL of the following except:
(Easy) (Skill 11.3)

A) Putting a cellophane or plastic cover on a book.

B) Identifying the back cover of the book.

C) Reading the book jacket.

D) Reading dedication page and the title page of the book.

109) Mr. Mandrake is subbing for Ms. Matley. He sees by the schedule that he is supposed to start the day after the morning meeting with a Read-Aloud. He notes a large picture on the easel and grabs the book just two minutes before the Read-Aloud is to start. He shouldn't heave a sigh of relief because:
(Rigorous) (Skill 11.3)

A) He needs to be familiar with the book so that he can plan the read-aloud.

B) He does not know if the class has already heard this book.

C) He has not planned vocabulary, themes, or activities to go with the book.

D) All of the above.

110) Author's viewpoint questions stump Gary. His teacher can help him by asking him during their reading conferences:
(Average Rigor) (Skill 11.3)

A) If Gary feels the book he is reading, is it just right for him.

B) What the author would say about what the character is doing in the story.

C) How the story can be changed to another genre.

D) If Gary wants to read more books by this author.

111) Young children often spell words they write according to the way the letters sound. This is called:
(Average Rigor) (Skill 11.3)

A) Spelling lists

B) Incorrect spelling

C) Developmental spelling

D) Invented spelling

112) Ms. Clark is seen by outside observers from her district, seated in front of her class of sixth graders with a notebook in her lap and an easel. She reads aloud from a book and then writes down a series of questions. As she reads along, she sometimes writes down the answers to her own questions. This is most likely:
(Rigorous) (Skill 11.3)

A) A sign that Ms. Clark is uncertain of her own comprehension capacity.

B) She is modeling self questioning for the children.

C) She is aware that she is being watched and wants to make a good impression.

D) All of the above.

113) If you get your raw score on a test, you will get:
(Average Rigor) (Skill 12.1)

A) The actual number of points you scored on the test.

B) The percentage score of the number of questions you answered correctly.

C) A letter grade for your work on the test.

D) An aggregated score for your performance on the text.

114) To keep abreast of reading trends and research, a reading specialist should subscribe to which of the following periodicals:
(Average Rigor) (Skill 12.3)

A) *The Reading Teacher*

B) *Educational Leadership*

C) *Reading Research Quarterly*

D) All of the above

115) Teacher research that is carried out by a teacher practitioner in the classroom to help a teacher evaluate his/her performance in the classroom is which type of research?
(Rigorous) (Skill 12.4)

A) Qualitative Research

B) Quantitative Research

C) Action Research

D) Both A and B

116) Strategies for educating parents and family include providing:
(Average Rigor) (Skill 13.1)

A) Workshops

B) Newsletters

C) Parent Nights

D) All of the above

117) Ms. Rivers is preparing for a parent teacher conference. She does all of the following EXCEPT:
(Average Rigor) (Skill 13.1)

A) Collects individual child running records.

B) Puts away all the book bags and leveled pots so the classroom will be more spacious.

C) Puts out by each child's seat the child's weekly log and spelling folder.

D) Sets up work samples by each child's place.

118) It is 4 PM, yet Francine is still in her classroom. The seats in her classroom are filled with adults of various ages who are holding books. They are seated two by two with both holding copies of the same book. Francine probably is:
(Rigorous) (Skill 13.1)

A) Explaining to parents how she will teach a particular story.

B) Demonstrating shared reading with a buddy for volunteer parents.

C) Hosting a parents organization meeting for her grade level.

D) Distributing old books from the class library to parents.

119) Tasks a reading specialist can use to determine student's level of comprehension include:
(Rigorous) (Skill 13.2)

A) Listening to passages.

B) Oral Reading

C) Written Response

D) All of the above.

120) As teachers work to determine the strengths and weaknesses of individual students it is important that they:
(Rigorous) (Skill 13.3)

A) Apply a variety of assessments.

B) Utilized information provided from standardized tests only.

C) Utilize tests found in the textbook.

D) None of the above.

121) Which theorist(s) developed a readability formula and graph?
(Rigorous) (Skill 13.4)

A) Cooper

B) Frye

C) Fountas and Pinnel

D) Clay

122) It is important for students to have an opportunity to read silently or on their own:
(Average Rigor) (Skill 13.5)

A) hourly.

B) daily.

C) weekly.

D) monthly

123) Commercially developed products are meant to reach the majority of students and provide them with the necessary skills to be successful readers is known as a:
(Average Rigor) (Skill 13.6)

A) Specialized Reading Program

B) Core Curriculum Program

C) Basel Reading Program

D) None of the above

124) It is important to stay in close contact with a paraprofessional to monitor their progress. Ways to provide feedback as to their progress include:
(Easy) (Skill 13.7)

A) Observation

B) Praise

C) Schedule regular meeting times

D) All of the above.

125) Mrs. Young is a first grade teacher trying to select a books that are "just right" for her students to read independently. She needs to consider which of the following:
(Rigorous) (Skill 13.8)

A) Illustrations should support the meaning of the text.

B) Content that relates to student interest and experiences

C) Predictable text structures and language patterns

D) All of the above

Answer Key:

1. C	45. C	89. B
2. A	46. C	90. D
3. C	47. B	91. B
4. C	48. B	92. C
5. C	49. C	93. B
6. A	50. B	94. D
7. B	51. A	95. C
8. C	52. A	96. B
9. C	53. B	97. C
10. C	54. D	98. D
11. D	55. B	99. D
12. C	56. D	100. C
13. B	57. C	101. B
14. C	58. A	102. D
15. D	59. B	103. D
16. C	60. A	104. B
17. C	61. C	105. A
18. B	62. C	106. C
19. D	63. B	107. A
20. D	64. D	108. A
21. A	65. C	109. D
22. D	66. B	110. B
23. D	67. D	111. D
24. C	68. C	112. B
25. B	69. D	113. B
26. B	70. D	114. D
27. B	71. C	115. C
28. A	72. D	116. D
29. C	73. D	117. B
30. B	74. C	118. B
31. C	75. D	119. D
32. B	76. A	120. A
33. C	77. D	121. B
34. B	78. D	122. B
35. C	79. B	123. B
36. B	80. B	124. D
37. C	81. B	125. D
38. B	82. B	
39. D	83. D	
40. B	84. C	
41. C	85. D	
42. C	86. B	
43. C	87. A	
44. C	88. D	

Rigor Table

	Easy %20	Average Rigor %40	Rigorous %40
Question #	1, 7, 13, 16, 17, 25, 36, 37, 43, 46, 50, 51, 60, 61, 71, 74, 78, 79, 80, 82, 91, 92, 94, 108, 111	2, 3, 4, 6, 8, 9, 10, 11, 14, 18, 20, 21, 22, 24, 27, 28, 34, 38, 40, 44, 45, 47, 48, 49, 53, 54, 55, 57, 58, 59, 64, 66, 69, 70, 73, 75, 83, 85, 87, 88, 89, 96, 98, 101, 104, 105, 110, 111, 113, 114, 117, 122, 123,	5, 12, 15, 19, 23, 26, 29, 30, 31, 32, 33, 35, 41, 42, 49, 52, 55, 56, 57, 62, 63 ,65, 67, 68, 72, 76, 77, 81, 84, 86, 90, 93, 95, 97, 99, 100, 102, 103, 106, 107, 109, 112, 115, 116, 118, 119, 120, 121, 125

Rationales with Sample Question

1) **There are two basic types of text structure:**
   (Easy) (Skill 1.1)

   A) Fiction and non-fiction.

   B) Primary and pre-k.

   C) Expository and narrative.

   D) Wordless and text rich.

Answer: C) Expository and narrative.

EXPOSITORY TEXT-. is non-fiction that provides information and facts. This text type is what newspapers, science, mathematics and history texts use. Currently there is much focus, even in elementary schools, on teaching children how to comprehend and author expository texts. They must produce brochures, guides, recipes, and procedural accounts on most elementary grade levels. The teaching of reading of expository texts requires working with a particular vocabulary and concept structure that is very different from that of the narrative text. Therefore time must be taken to teach the reading of expository texts and contrast it with the reading of narrative texts.

NARRATIVE TEXT- one of the two basic text structures. The narrative text tells or communicates a story. Narrative texts are novels, short stories and plays. Some poems are narratives as well. The narrative text needs to be taught differently than the expository text because of its structure.

2) **A "decodable text" is:**
   (Average Rigor) (Skill 1.1)

   A) A text that a child can read aloud with correct pronunciations.

   B) A text that a child can answer comprehension questions about with a high percentage of accuracy.

   C) Text written to match the sequence of letter-sound relationships that have been taught.

   D) None of the above.

Answer: A) A text that a child can read aloud with correct pronunciations.

Decodable books are vocabulary-controlled using language from word families with high predictability. Thus we get sentences like "Nan has a tan fan." Reading is seen as skills-based, and the skills are taught one at a time.

3) **The major difference between phonemic and phonological awareness is:**
(Average Rigor) (Skill 1.2)

   A) One deals with a series of discrete sounds and the other with sound-spelling relationships.

   B) One is involved with teaching and learning alliteration and rhymes.

   C) Phonemic awareness is a specific type of phonological awareness that deals with separate phonemes within a given word.

   D) Phonological awareness is associated with printed words.

Answer: C) Phonemic awareness is a specific type of phonological awareness that deals with separate phonemes within a given word.

Phonemic awareness is a specific type of phonological awareness which focuses on the ability to distinguish, manipulate and blend specific sounds or phonemes within an individual word.

4) **The theorist in early reading (emergent reading) who has identified five tasks for phonemic awareness is:**
(Average Rigor) (Skill 1.2)

   A) John Munro

   B) Brian Cambourne

   C) Marilyn Jager Adams

   D) Lucy Calkins

Answer: C) Marilyn Jager Adams

Theorist Marilyn Jager Adams who researches early reading has outlined five basic types of phonemic awareness tasks. Task 1- Ability to hear rhymes and alliteration. Task 2- Ability to do oddity tasks (recognize the member of a set that is different.) Task 3 –The ability to orally blend words and split syllables. Task 4 –The ability to orally segment word. Task 5- The ability to do phonics manipulation tasks

5) An oddity task is one in which children:
(Rigorous) (Skill 1.2)

A) Identify the odd number in a mathematical series and talk about how they did it.

B) Perform a creative exercise designed for differentiated learning styles.

C) Recognize which sound is odd in a series of like sounds.

D) Design a different activity for themselves.

Answer: C) Recognize which sound is odd in a series of like sounds.

The ability to detect an oddity is the ability to recognize the member of a set that is different [odd] among the group. For example, the children would look at the pictures of grass, a garden and a rose, answering, Which one starts with a different sound?

6) All of the following are true about phonological awareness EXCEPT:
(Average Rigor) (Skill 1.2)

A) It may involve print.

B) It is a prerequisite for spelling and phonics.

C) Activities can be done by the children with their eyes closed.

D) It starts before letter recognition is taught.

Answer: A) It may involve print.

PHONOLOGICAL AWARENESS- the ability to recognize the sounds of spoken language and how they can be blended together, segmented, and switched/manipulated to form new combinations and words.

7) **"Beautiful Beth is the Best Girl in the Bradley Bay area." This sentence could be used to help children learn about:**
(Easy) (Skill 1.2)

A) Assonance.

B) Alliteration.

C) Rhyming pairs.

D) None of the above

Answer: B) Alliteration

Alliteration is the term for a series of words that begin with the same sound as in "Beautiful Beth is the Best Girl in the Bradley Bay area."

8) **Phonological awareness includes all of the following skills except:**
(Average Rigor) (Skill 1.2)

A) Rhyming and syllabification

B) Blending sounds into words

C) Understanding the meaning of the root word

D) Removing initial sounds and substituting others

Answers: C) Understanding the meaning of the root word

Phonological awareness involves the recognition that spoken words are composed of a set of smaller units such as onsets and rimes, syllables, and sounds.

9) **Paul is a new teacher. He has just started his logs and assessments for his children's phonemic awareness. He asks a reading teacher to look over his log, but the log is returned to him:**
(Average Rigor) (Skill 1.2)

A) Paul gave the log to the wrong colleague.

B) The colleague would not help him out by reviewing it.

C) The log did not have the dates the child's behavior was observed and had no stated performance standards.

D) The log didn't have a cover letter from Paul.

Answer: C. The log did not have the dates the child's behavior was observed and had no stated performance standards.

Records of independent Reading and Writing: These can include the children's journals, notebooks or logs of books read with the names of the authors, titles of the books, date completed, and pieces related to books completed or in progress.

10) **As a parent walked through the first grade floor of her school, she kept hearing repeated clapping. Most likely the children were:**
(Average Rigor) (Skill 1.2)

A) Clapping to show respect for one another.

B) Rehearsing for how they would clap at a play.

C) Clapping out syllables of multi-syllabic words.

D) All of the above.

Answer: C) Clapping out syllables of multi-syllabic words.

The objective of this activity is for children to understand that there are every syllable in a polysyllabic word can be studied for its spelling patterns in the same way that monosyllabic words are studied for their spelling patterns.

First the teacher reads the poem with the children. As they are reading it aloud, the children clap the beats of the poem and the teacher uses a colored marker to place a tic (/) above each syllable.

11) **A key theorist whose work has helped teacher's document children's oral reading progress throughout the school year is:**
(Average Rigor) (Skill 2.1)

    A)   Jerome Bruner.

    B)   Daniel J. Chard.

    C)   J. David Cooper.

    D)   Marie Clay.

Answer: D. Marie Clay

Understanding the value and importance of the concepts of print for beginning readers developed out of the work of Marie Clay in New Zealand. Assessment of these skills typically occurs in kindergarten and into first grade as necessary.

12) **Most of the children in first-year teacher Ms. James's class are really doing well in their phonemic awareness assessments. However, Ms. James is very concerned about three children who do not seem to be able to distinguish between spoken words that "sound alike," but are different. Since she is a first year teacher, she feels her inexperience may be to blame. In truth, the reason these three children have not yet demonstrated phonemic awareness is most likely that:**
(Rigorous) (Skill 2.1)

    A) They are not capable of becoming good readers.

    B) They are bored in class.

    C) They may be from an ELL background.

    D) Ms. James does not pronounce the different phonemes clearly enough.

Answer: C) They may be from an ELL background.

Not all English phonemes are present in various ELL native languages; for example, the sound of /th/ does not appear in Spanish. Some native language phonemes may and do conflict with English phonemes.

13) **To decode is to:**
(Easy) (Skill 2.1)

A) Construct meaning.

B) Sound out a printed sequence of letters.

C) Use a special code to decipher a message.

D) None of the above.

Answer: B) Sound out a printed sequence of letters.

To decode means to change communication signals into messages. Reading comprehension requires that the reader learn the code within which a message is written and be able to decode it to get the message.

14) **To help students develop as readers it is important to do all of the following except:**
(Average Rigor) (Skill 2.2)

A) Surround children with books

B) Have students participate in daily read aloud activities

C) Have students read only the books that have been picked out for them by the teacher

D) Have students read their favorite books over and over

Answer: C) Have students read only the books that have been picked out for them by the teacher

To develop a love of reading, it is important for students to be able to choose their own reading material as well as reading assigned texts.

15) Characteristics of difficulties seen in emergent readers include: (Rigorous) (Skill 2.3)

A) High interest in reading

B) Clear, concise speech

C) Ability to follow directions accurately

D) None of the above

Answer: D) None of the above

Students with reading difficulties generally display other difficulties as well. They often do not have a high interest in reading. They may have speech problems and may not follow directions well.

16) In terms of a balanced literacy classroom, a "leveled bin" indicates: (Easy) (Skill 2.4)

A) A plant set at child's eye level for descriptive writing purposes.

B) A bin with books the child has selected.

C) A bin with books leveled by the teacher.

D) A bin with all kinds of reading materials including magazines and packaging on a child's level.

Answer: C) A bin with books leveled by the teacher

The classroom library in the context of the balanced literacy approach to reading instruction is focused on leveled books. These are books which have been leveled with the support of Fountas and Pinnell's Guided Reading: *Good First Teaching for All Children* and *Matching Books to Readers: Using Leveled Reading in Guided Reading,* K-3.

17) **The term graphophonemic awareness refers to:**
    (Easy) (Skill 2.4)

    A) Handwriting skills.

    B) Letter to sound recognition.

    C) Alphabetic principle.

    D) Phonemic awareness

Answer: C) Alphabetic principle

Graphophonemic involves:
- Match all consonant and short vowel sounds.
- Read one's own name.
- Read one syllable words and high frequency words.
- Demonstrate ability to read and understand that as letters in words change, so do the sounds.
- Generate the sounds from all letters including consonant blends and long vowel patterns. Blend those different sounds into recognizable words.
- Read common sight words.
- Read common word families.

18) **Gracie seems to be struggling with her reading, even in first grade, although her mother works at a publishing firm and her dad is an editor. Her speech is also full of mispronunciations, although her parents were born in the school neighborhood. Gracie should be checked by:**
    (Average Rigor) (Skill 2.4)

    A) A reading specialist.

    B) A speech therapist or an audiologist

    C) A pediatrician.

    D) A psychologist.

Answer: B) A speech therapist or an audiologist.

A speech therapist or an audiologist works with students who show difficulties in pronouncing words to improve the quality of their speech.

19) **Ability grouping means:**
(Rigorous) (Skill 2.4)

A) Grouping of children according to the results of an IQ test.

B) Grouping of children with similar test results for instructional purposes.

C) Grouping of children according to their oral reading accuracy rate.

D) Grouping of children wit similar needs for instructional purposes.

Answer: D) Grouping of children with similar needs for instructional purposes.

It is often difficult to meet each child's needs individually in a large classroom. Therefore, teachers often group students with similar needs to make the most efficient use of time and to provide students with others to work with.

20) **The teacher is very concerned about identifying a book that is "just right" for Jay to read independently. This means that Jay should be able to read this book with:**
(Average Rigor) (Skill 2.4)

A) Below 92% accuracy

B) 100% accuracy

C) 95-100% accuracy

D) 92-97% accuracy

Answer: D) 92-97% accuracy

For a book to be considered on a child's independent level the student must be able to read it with 92-97% accuracy. A higher percentage would be too easy and a lower percentage would mean the text was too difficult.

21) **Jay really wants to read a book that he can only read with 94% accuracy. He could get to read this book as:**
(Average Rigor) (Skill 2.4)

    A) An independent reading.

    B) A guided reading.

    C) A shared reading.

    D) All of the above.

Answer: A) An independent reading.

For a book to be considered on a child's independent level the student must be able to read it with 92-97% accuracy. A higher percentage would be too easy and a lower percentage would mean the text was too difficult.

22) **Dictionary study:**
(Average Rigor) (Skill 2.4)

    A) can begin in grades 1 or 2.

    B) can begin in pre-K using the lush picture dictionaries.

    C) should start on grade three level.

    D) a and b.

Answer: D) a and b.

Dictionary skills should be taught at an early age to assist students in discovering meaning of words. The use of a dictionary is often used to support the reading of a particular text.

23) Mrs. Young is a first grade teacher trying to select a books that are "just right" for her students to read independently. She needs to consider which of the following:
(Rigorous) (Skill 2.4)

A) Illustrations should support the meaning of the text.

B) Content that relates to student interest and experiences

C) Predictable text structures and language patterns

D) All of the above

Answer: D) All of the above.

It is important that all of the above factors be considered when selecting books for young children.

24) Greg Ball went to an author signing where Faith Ringgold gave a talk about one of her many books.He was so inspired by her presence and by his reading of her book *TAR BEACH,* that he used the book for his reading and writing workshop activities. His supervisor wrote in his plan book, that he was pleased that Greg had used the book as an/a _____ book.
(Average Rigor) (Skill 3.1)

A) Basic book.

B) Feature book.

C) Anchor book.

D) Focus book.

Answer: C) Anchor book.

ANCHOR BOOK- a balanced literacy term for a book that is purposely read repeatedly and used as part of both the reading and writing workshop.

25) **Environmental print is available at all of the following except:**
(Easy) (Skill 3.1)

A) Within a newspaper.

B) On the page of a library book.

C) On a supermarket circular.

D) In a commercial flyer.

Answer: B) On the page of a library book.

Environmental print involves print from items such as signs, boxes, etc. Magazines and catalogues are another source of environmental print that is accessible with ads for child centered products. Supermarket circulars and coupons from the newspaper are also excellent for engaging children in using environmental print as reading, especially when combined with dramatic play centers or prop boxes.

26) **The best way for a teacher to track a student's progress in demonstrating the alphabetic principal/ graphophonemic awareness is to:**
(Rigorous) (Skill 3.1)

A) Provide group assessments

B) Maintain individual records

C) Assess with standardized tests

D) Have the student assessed by a team of teachers

Answer: B) Maintain individual records

The teacher will want to maintain individual records of children's reading behaviors demonstrating alphabetic principle/graphophonemic awareness

27) **Author's viewpoint questions stump Gary. His teacher can help him by asking him during their reading conferences:**
   (Average Rigor) (Skill 3.1)

   A) If Gary-feels the book he is reading, is it just right for him.

   B) What the author would say about what the character is doing in the story.

   C) How the story can be changed to another genre.

   D) If Gary-wants to read more books by this author.

Answer: B) What the author would say about what the character is doing in the story.

Author's viewpoint refers to what the author was thinking or feeling as they wrote the book. Questions may include: What do you think the author meant by having the character say that statement?

28) **Bill has been called up to the teacher for an individual conference. She asks him to retell one of the books he has listed on his weekly log. He begins and is still talking 7 minutes later. Most probably, Bill:**
   (Average Rigor) (Skill 3.1)

   A) Told the entire story with all its details and minor characters.

   B) May or may not have really gotten the main points and perspectives of the story.

   C) May have really liked the Story.

   D) None of the above.

Answer: A) Told the entire story all its details and minor characters.

A retell should only take a couple of minutes. In a retell, the student should only relay major event, major characters, and provide a summary of key points.

29) **The work of Chard and Osborn (1999) in establishing guidelines for children with reading disabilities has shown that it is essential for them to:**
(Rigorous) (Skill 3.2)

   A) Read wordless picture books.

   B) Learn at least 10 sight words.

   C) Work intensely on the alphabetic principle.

   D) Focus on using syntactic clues.

Answer: C) Work intensely on the alphabetic principle.

David J. Chard and Jean Osborn (1999) have reflected on the guidelines necessary for teachers to use in selecting supplemental phonics and word-recognition materials for addressing students with learning disabilities.
They note that an important way to help children with reading disabilities figure out the system underlying the printed word is leading them to understand the alphabetic principle.

30) **An observer enters Julia's first grade classroom. Children are working with oaktag strips and placing the word letters on these strips on a sentence strip holder. Then they seem to be involved in some kind of counting. The observer is confused. This activity is taking place during the reading block. Julia explains:**
(Rigorous) (Skill 3.2)

   A) The children are counting letters.

   B) This is word sorting and the children are grouping words by length, common letters and sound.

   C) The children are combining mathematics counting and word study.

   D) The children are doing a strategy sheet based on a particular word family

Answer: B) This is word sorting and the children are grouping words by length, common letters and sound.

This activity allows children to focus closely on the specific features of words and to begin to understand the basic elements of letter sound relationships. Start with one syllable (monosyllabic) words. Have the children group them by their length, common letters, sound, and/or spelling pattern.

31) **As he walks up and down the hallway, Mr. Adams, the new Assistant Principal, continually hears Ms. Brown telling her children to go to the wall. Mr. Adams looks briefly at the literacy block schedule and continues on his walk through the building. He realizes that Ms. Brown's children are at work on:**
(Rigorous) (Skill 3.2)

A) A new hall display.

B) Taking down an old display and then redoing it for a new theme.

C) Adding words to their spelling word wall.

D) Measuring the height of plants for a mathematics lesson.

Answer: C) Adding words to their spelling word wall.

Teachers often use a word wall to reinforce new vocabulary and assist with writing. A teacher would have a child go to the wall to add new words or to use the wall to help with spelling words during writing.

32) **Randy is proud of how many new vocabulary words he has learned. He enjoys playing with a device his teacher has, since it helps him to show all the words he can create from various letters. The device is a:**
(Rigorous) (Skill 3.2)

A) Word strip.

B) Letter holder for making words.

C) Word mask.

D) None of the above.

Answer: B) Letter holder for making words

Through use of this letter holder, children can experience how letters can be rearranged, added, or removed to make new words. They can use these cards also to focus as needed on letter sequences and to support them in recognizing spelling patterns in words.

33) **A delegation from the United Kingdom has come to the United States and since they are considering adapting the balanced literacy approach, they are very interested in seeing the small group demonstrated. Mr. Adams knows that he should bring them into Greg's room when Greg is doing which activity?**
(Rigorous) (Skill 3.2)

A) A mini lesson.

B) A conference with individual students.

C) A time when children are divided into small and independent study groups.

D) A read-aloud.

Answer: C) A time when children are divided into small and independent study groups.

In a balanced literacy approach, small group time is when small groups of students are pulled to work independently with focused direction from the teacher.

34) **Ronald's parents are hearing impaired. He probably will need:**
(Average Rigor) (Skill 3.2)

A) Extensive work with the use of picture cues

B) Work with songs, rhymes and read alouds to promote phonemic awareness.

C) No extra work or support.

D) None of the above.

Answer: B) Work with songs, rhymes and read alouds to promote phonemic awareness.

Because of his parent's impairment, Ronald may not have been exposed to normal auditory communication that would be necessary to have a strong sense of phonemic awareness. He may need additional work to strengthen those skills.

35) **The best ways to select words students need to learn to spell include all of the following except:**
(Rigorous) (Skill 3.2)

A) Misspelled words from student writing

B) Lists of theme words

C) Lists from a spelling textbook

D) Lists of words from content areas

Answer: C) Lists from a spelling textbook

Some of the techniques teachers use to determine the words students need to spell include:

- Lists of misspelled words from student writing
- Lists of theme words
- Lists of words from the content areas
- Word banks

36) **As Ms. Maxwell enters a first grade class, the teacher is busily writing down what the children are saying. The teacher is probably doing this to:**
(Easy) (Skill 3.2)

A) Demonstrate how to copy down speech.

B) Make a connection and promote awareness of the relationship between spoken and written language.

C) Authenticate the children's comments.

D) Raise the children's self esteem.

Answer: B) Make a connection and promote awareness of the relationship between spoken and written language.

By writing down what the children are saying, the teacher promotes the awareness of the relationship between the spoken and written word. Other strategies include:
- Reading together big-print and oversized books to teach print conventions such as directionality.
- Practicing how to handle a book: How to turn pages, to find the top and bottom of pages, and how to tell the difference between the front and back covers.

- Discussing and comparing with children the length, appearance and boundaries of specific words. For example, children can see that

37) **The best way for a primary grade teacher to model directionality and one to one word matching would be:**
(Easy) (Skill 3.2)

A) Using a regular library or classroom text book.

B) Using her own person reading book.

C) Using a big book.

D) Using a book dummy.

Answer: C) Using a big book.

Teachers often use big books to model reading skills for children. Teaching directionality and one to one word matching are just two of the skills that can be taught.

38) **Children "own" words when all of the following happen except:**
(Average Rigor) (Skill 3.2)

A) They find these words on their own.

B) The teacher provides a mandated word list.

C) They use the words in their own writings.

D) The words appear in literature that interests them.

Answer: B) The teacher provides a mandated word list.

When students take ownership of words this generally means that the words are of special significance to the child. This could mean that they use the words frequently in their writing, they appear in favorite books, or they discover the words on their own.

39) In order to get children to compile specialized vocabulary, they can use:
(Rigorous) (Skill 3.2)

A) Newspapers.

B) Internet resources and approved web-sites that focus on the special interest.

C) Experts they can interview.

D) All of the above.

Answer: D) All of the above

Vocabulary lists can be compiled from just about any source possible.

40) If children are engaged in creating a museum within classroom project to exhibit their work, they are:
(Average Rigor) (Skill 3.2)

A) Not doing any reading or writing.

B) Doing many authentic reading, writing, and researching tasks.

C) Not likely to visit a real museum.

D) All of the above.

Answer: B) Doing many authentic reading, writing, and researching tasks.

By creating a museum within the classroom students take ownership in the creation of their project. The project would generally involve a topic meaningful to the student. The student would be more motivated to create a quality product.

41) **A district observer notes that fifth graders are showing younger peers in the third grade how to hold a book and walk around with it, they assume:**
(Rigorous) (Skill 3.3)

A) That the fifth graders are particularly theatrical.

B) That the fifth graders are proud of how they read stories aloud.

C) That the fifth graders are training the younger children in book holding.

D) That this has nothing to do with instruction.

Answer: C) That the fifth graders are training the younger children in book holding.

Students often learn better from other students. It is important to provide opportunities for students of various ages or levels to work together to learn from each other.

42) **At a faculty meeting Ms. Riley found out that she might have crisscrossers in her class and that Mr. Brown had them and he was happy about it:**
(Rigorous) (Skill 3.3)

A) Crisscrossers are students who have skipped a grade.

B) Crisscrossers are students with excellent skills in reading and in Math.

C) Crisscrossers are second language learners who have a positive attitude toward first and second language learning.

D) Crisscrossers are second language learners who are only positive about English Language Learning.

Answer: C) Crisscrossers are second language learners who have a Positive attitude toward first and second language learning.

CRISSCROSSERS- an ELL term for second language learners who have a positive attitude toward both first language and second language learning. These second language learners, children from ELL backgrounds, are comfortable navigating back and forth between the two languages as they learn.

43) **Cues in reading are:**
(Easy) (Skill 3.3)

A) Vowel sounds.

B) Digraphs.

C) Sources of information used by readers to help them construct meaning.

D) None of the above.

Answer: C) Sources of information used by readers to help them construct meaning.

Cuing systems assist readers to construct meaning. These include: Syntactic and Semantic.

44) **A teacher is asking children to look at the beginning letters of words. She then asks the child to connect the beginning letter to the text and story and to think about what word would make sense there. This is an example of:**
(Average Rigor) (Skill 3.3)

A) A balanced literacy approach.

B) A phonemic approach.

C) A phonic approach.

D) AN ELL differentiated approach.

Answer: C) A phonic approach.

Instruction begins with a strong phonics approach, learning letter-sound relationships and often using basal readers or *decodable books*.

45) As the child is reading and has made an incorrect attempt, the teacher prompts:
(Average Rigor) (Skill 3.3)

A) That is a mistake, do it again.

B) No, you are stupid. .. why can't you get it?

C) Does that make sense to you?

D) Forget it, this is too hard for you.

Answer: C) Does that make sense to you?

Students will need use their base knowledge of word meanings, semantics, to help them decipher unknown words or text as well as to clarify reading when it does not seem to make sense. Some prompts the teacher can use which will alert the children to semantic cues include:
- Does that sentence make sense?
- Which word in that sentence does not seem to fit?
- Why doesn't it fit?
- What word might make sense in that sentence?

46) Asking a child if what he or she has read makes sense to him or her, is prompting the child to use:
(Easy) (Skill 3.3)

A) Phonics cues.

B) Syntactic cues.

C) Semantic cues.

D) Prior knowledge.

Answer: C) Semantic cues.

SEMANTIC CUES- children use their prior knowledge, sense of the story, and pictures to support their predicting and confirming the meaning of the text.

47) **When you ask a child, if what he or she has just read "sounds right" to him or her, you are trying to get that child to use:**
(Average Rigor) (Skill 3.3)

A) Phonics cues.

B) Syntactic cues.

C) Semantic cues.

D) Prior knowledge.

Answer: B) Syntactic cues.

Syntactic cues use the order of words and the student's knowledge of the oral English language to help determine if what was read could be accurate.

48) **To encode means that you:**
(Average Rigor) (Skill 3.3)

A) Decode a second time.

B) Construct meaning from a code.

C) Tell someone a message.

D) None of the above.

Answer: B) Construct meaning from a code.

ENCODE- to change a message into symbols. For example, readers encode oral language into writing.

49) **A natural role for a highly proficient reader would be:**
(Rigorous) (Skill 3.3)

A) To assist the teacher with cleaning the classroom and organizing the student folders.

B) To develop charts for the teacher by copying needed poems for full class study.

C) Tutor and support struggling readers.

D) Work on his/her own interests while the teacher works with the rest of the class.

Answer: C) Tutor and support struggling readers.

Highly proficient readers can sometimes support early readers through a partner relationship. Some children, particularly the emergent and beginning early readers, benefit from reading books with partners. The partners sit side by side and each one takes turns reading the entire text.

50) **"Ballgame" is a _____word. Its meaning is derived from the combination of "Ball" and "Game":**
(Easy) (Skill 3.3)

A) Contraction.

B) Compound.

C) Portmanteau.

D) Palindrome.

Answer: B) Compound

Compound Words occur when two or more base words are connected to form a new word. The meaning of the new word is in some way connected with that of the base word. Examples are *firefighter, newspaper,* and *pigtail*.

51) **Two consonants placed together in a word to make a unique sound is a :**
(Easy) (Skill 3.3)

A) Consonant digraph

B) Consonant blend

C) Morpheme

D) Phoneme

Answer: A) Consonant digraph

<u>Consonant Digraph</u> – a consonant digraph are two consonants of the English language who when placed together in a word make a unique sound, neither makes when alone. Examples: ch, th, sh, and wh.

52) **Reading expression, appropriate phrasing, and good inflection are characteristics of:**
(Rigorous) (Skill 4.1)

A) Prosody

B) Fluency

C) Modeling

D) Accuracy

Answer: A) Prosody

Prosody is defined as the stress and intonation in a language.

53) Reader's Theater is:
(Average Rigor) (Skill 4.2)

A) Reading as a group or with the teacher

B) When students use scripts that have different parts for different characters

C) When students read aloud daily

D) When students work together to provide instruction for each other

Answer: B) When students use scripts that have different parts for different characters

Reader's theater is just as it sounds. It is when students act out a story.

54) Factual book features children should learn include:
(Average Rigor) (Skill 5.1)

A) Captions.

B) Glossaries.

C) Diagrams.

D) All of the above.

Answer: D) All of the above

Factual books may contain the items listed above as well as others. In order for students to successfully read factual books it is important that they learn to utilize various features.

55) **The Stop and Think Strategy means that the child reader will:**
(Rigorous) (Skill 5.1)

A) Read through until the end of the story or text.

B) Ask himself or herself if what he or she has read makes sense to him or her.

C) Stop after reading some text and write down his/her concerns.

D) All of the above

Answer: B) Ask himself or herself if what he or she has read makes sense to him or her.

When a student is reading, it is helpful for them to periodically stop and question themselves to see if what that have just read makes sense.

56) **To help children with "main idea" questions, the teacher should:**
(Rigorous) (Skill 5.1)

A) Give out a strategy sheet on the main idea for children to place in their reader's notebooks.

B) Model responding to such a question as part of guided reading.

C) Have children create "main idea questions" to go with their writings.

D) All of the above.

Answer: D) All of the above

Identifying main ideas can be improved when the children have an explicit strategy for identifying important information. All of the above strategies can be beneficial in identifying the main idea.

57) By definition, which children in a classroom will have trouble with syntactic cues?
(Rigorous) (Skill 5.1)

A) Those from families who do not have household libraries.

B) Those not in a top reading group.

C) Those from ELL backgrounds.

D) All of the above.

Answer: C) Those from ELL backgrounds.

By definition a child from an ELL background does not have a strong accurate sense of what "sounds right" in English. Not all English phonemes are present in various ELL native languages; for example, the sound of /th/ does not appear in Spanish. Some native language phonemes may and do conflict with English phonemes.

58) Making inferences from the text means that the reader:
(Average Rigor) (Skil 5.1)

A) Is making informed judgments based on available evidence.

B) Is making a guess based on prior experiences.

C) Is making a guess based on what the reader would like to be true of the text.

D) All of the above.

Answer: A) Is making informed judgments based on available evidence.

Inferencing is a process that involves the reader making a reasonable judgment based on the information given and engages children to literally construct meaning.

59) **Mr. Mark is a brand new teacher who is not from the neighborhood where his school is located. He is a bit nervous as this is his first teaching assignment. He does not yet know how to relax enough to get his students to activate prior experience. He should: (Average Rigor) (Skill 5.1)**

A) Try a free recall question: Tell us what you know about...

B) Try an unstructured Question: Let's talk About...

C) Use word association: What do you associate X with?

D) All of the above.

Answer: B) Try and unstructured question: Let's talk about...

An unstructured question is open-ended and can lead to great discussion. This type of question can also provide the teacher with more insight into the student's thoughts.

60) **Among the literary strategies that teachers can use to activate prior knowledge are:**
(Easy) (Skill 5.1)

A) Predicting and previewing a story.

B) Story mapping.

C) Venn diagramming.

D) Linear arrays.

Answer: A) Predicting and previewing a story.

By predicting the events or preview a story the teacher can help students connect with and not only activate prior knowledge, but build vocabulary as well.

61) In a balanced literacy classroom, new vocabulary would most likely appear on:
(Easy) (Skill 5.1)

A) An experiential chart.

B) A class newspaper.

C) The word wall.

D) Outside the room on a bulletin board.

Answer: C) The Word Wall

A word wall is a classroom display of high frequency and/or grade level specific words available for student reference.

62) Based on individual conferences with many children, the teacher realizes that although they are all self-improving readers, they need help in better use of the context to define words. The teacher decided to try the use of:
(Rigorous) (Skill 5.1)

A) A dictionary to look up words.

B) A thesaurus to use with the dictionary.

C) Contextual redefinition training.

D) Instruction in how to effectively use a dictionary.

Answer: C) Contextual redefinition training.

This strategy encourages children to use the context more effectively by presenting them with sufficient context BEFORE they begin reading. It models for the children the use of contextual clues to make informed guesses about word meanings.

63) **A theorist who believes that there is a finite body of approved literature children should be taught on various grade levels and has produced books about what everyone needs to know to be literate on various grade levels is:**
(Rigorous) (Skill 5.2)

A) Rudolf Flesch

B) J. David Cooper

C) John Dewey

D) E. D. Hirsch

Answer: B) J. David Cooper

J. David Cooper (2004) and other advocates of the Balanced Literacy Approach, feel that children become literate, effective communicators and able to comprehend, by learning phonics and other aspects of word identification through the use of engaging reading texts. Engaging text, as defined by the balanced literacy group, are those texts which contain highly predictable elements of rhyme, sound patterns, and plot.

64) **To promote word study, children can:**
(Average Rigor) (Skill 5.2)

A) Be required to go to the dictionary at least once or twice a day.

B) Collect and share words of interest they find in their readings.

C) Do vocabulary work sheets from a basal reader or commercial vocabulary book.

D) Do all of the above.

Answer: D) Do all of the above.

All of the answers listed could be used to promote word study in the classroom.

65) **Teachers should select at least ___words for pre-reading vocabulary discussion:**
   (Rigorous) (Skill 5.2)

   A) 12.

   B) 15.

   C) 2-3.

   D) 8-10.

Answer: C) 2-3

The number of words that require explicit teaching should only be two or three. If the number is higher than that, the children need guided reading and the text needs to be broken down into smaller sections for teaching. When broken down into smaller sections, each text section should only have two to three words which need explicit teaching.

66) **The teacher should choose words for pre-story discussion and exploration based on:**
   (Average Rigor) (Skill 5.2)

   A) The teacher's interest.

   B) Whether the teacher feels the children have prior knowledge of or experience with the words.

   C) A pre-existing grade level required vocabulary list.

   D) Words that will impress his or her supervisor.

Answer: B) Whether the teacher feels the children have prior knowledge of or experience with the words.

It is up to the teacher to determine when vocabulary needs to be introduced. If vocabulary is selected to by introduced prior to reading the story it is generally done to assist students in developing prior knowledge.

67) **Two steps a teacher might take before selecting words for study are:** *(Rigorous) (Skill 5.2)*

A) Reading the story and story mapping.

B) Asking advice from a veteran teacher and the grade leader.

C) Looking in a teacher's guide and copying out the words listed there.

D) All of the above are correct

Answer: D) All of the above are correct.

It may be beneficial for the teacher to utilize all of these resources when planning reading instruction.

68) **A teacher discovers after considering his class's prior knowledge of the story material that he would need to teach 12 words at least before he starts teaching the story to the whole group. This indicates:** *(Rigorous) (Skill 5.2)*

A) The children will need a read-aloud.

B) The children will need independent reading.

C) The children will need guided reading.

D) The children will need shared reading.

Answer: C) The children need guided reading.

Stories that include so many words to be taught may prove difficult for a student to read independently. They would need assistance in attacking these words. The best way to complete this lesson is through guided reading.

69) **Vocabulary should be introduced after reading if:**
(Average Rigor) (Skill 5.2)

A) The children have identified words from their reading which were difficult and which they need explained.

B) The text is appropriate for vocabulary building.

C) The teacher would like to teach vocabulary after the reading.

D) a and b

Answer: D) a and b

Introduce vocabulary AFTER READING if. . .
- The children themselves have shared words which they found difficult or interesting
- The children need to expand their vocabulary
- The text itself is one that is particularly suited for vocabulary building.

70) **Taking responsibility for a child's own learning, will usually involve the child in:**
(Average Rigor) (Skill 5.2)

A) Reading and writing on his/her own.

B) Developing a personal literacy project which will later be shared with the teacher and peers and family.

C) Putting away books and materials when directed.

D) a and b.

Answer: D) a and b

While keeping ones area neat and tidy is important, it does not directly engage students in taking responsibility for their own learning. When students are involved in they are able to select meaningful projects and take and active role in planning their leaning.

71) **The word "bat" is a ___word**
for "batter-up":
(Easy) (Skill 5.2)

   A) Suffix.

   B) Prefix.

   C) Root word.

   D) Inflectional ending.

Answer: C) Root word.

This is a word from which another word is developed. The second word can be said to have its "root" in the first, such as *vis, to see,* in visor or vision.

72) **Four of Ms. Wolmark's students have lived in other countries. She is**
particularly pleased to be studying Sumerian proverbs with them
as part of the sixth grade unit in analyzing the sayings of other
cultures because:
(Rigorous) (Skill 5.2)

   A) This gives her a break from teaching and the children can share
       sayings from other cultures they and their families have experienced.

   B) This validates the experiences and expertise of ELL learners in her
       classroom.

   C) This provides her children from the US with a lens on other cultural
       values.

   D) All of the above.

Answer: D) All of the above.

It is recommended that all teachers of reading and particularly those who are working with ELL students use meaningful, student centered, and culturally customized activities. These activities may include: language games, word walls, and poems. Some of these activities might, if possible, be initiated in the child's first language and then reiterated in English.

73) **An effective way to build vocabulary and to make connections with mandated science and mathematics material is to teach Greek and Latin roots using:**
(Average Rigor) (Skill 5.2)

A) Semantic maps.

B) Hierarchical arrays.

C) Linear arrays.

D) Word webs.

Answer: D) Word Webs

For example, during readings on rodents (a favorite of first and second graders), the teacher draws her class's attention to the fact that beavers, gnaw at things with their teeth. She then connects the "dent" root or derivative to the children's lives, other words they are familiar with or experiences. The children then volunteer *"dentist," "dental," "denture."* The teacher begins to place these in a graphic organizer, or word web.

74) **A bound morpheme is:**
(Easy) (Skill 5.2)

A) A prefix.

B) A contraction.

C) An inflectional ending that can be added to a base word to change its case, gender, number, tense or form.

D) A root word.

Answer: C) An inflectional ending that can be added to a base word to change its case, gender, number, tense or form.

MORPHEMES- the smallest units of meaning in words. There are two types of morphemes; free morphemes, which can stand alone such as *love,* and bound morphemes, which must be attached to another morpheme to carry meaning such as *ed* in *loved*.

75) **Direct teaching of a concept or strategy means:**
(Average Rigor) (Skill 5.2)

   A) The teacher teaches the concept or strategy as part of a genre lesson.

   B) The teacher teaches the concept as part of the writing workshop.

   C) The teacher explicitly announces to the class that this strategy will be taught.

   D) The teacher teaches the strategy to a small group of children or to an individual child.

Answer: D) The teacher teaches the strategy to a small group of children or to an individual child.

Direct teaching occurs when the teacher specifically teaches or explains a skill to a student or group of students.

76) **The theorist who believes children should not be "taught" vocabulary and structural analysis is:**
(Rigorous) (Skill 5.2)

   A) Cooper

   B) Flesch

   C) Hirsch

   D) Calkins

Answer: A) Cooper

Cooper (2004) believes that children should not be "taught" vocabulary and structural analysis skills.

77) Structural analysis is:
(Rigorous) (Skill 5.2)

A) the "sounding out" a printed sequence of letters based on knowledge of letter sound correspondences

B) when the teacher keeps a detailed recording of the errors or inaccurate attempts of a child reader during a reading assessment

C) the process of hearing a spoken word and identifying its separate phonemes or syllables.

D) the process of examining the words in the text for meaningful word units (affixes, base words, inflected endings).

Answer: D) the process of examining the words in the text for meaningful word units (affixes, base words, inflected endings).

Structural analysis of words as defined by J. David Cooper (2004) involves the study of significant word parts. This analysis can help the child with pronunciation and constructing meaning.

78) One of the many ways in which a child can demonstrate comprehension of a story is by:
(Average Rigor) (Skill 5.3)

A) Filling in a strategy sheet.

B) Retelling the story orally.

C) Retelling the story in writing.

D) All of the above.

Answer: D) All of the above.

All are examples of ways a child can demonstrate that they understand what they have read.

79) **Ms. James is seated with a child by her side. The child is reading aloud from an open book. Ms. James is teaching in a school that has embraced the Balanced Literacy Approach. Therefore it is most likely that Ms. James is writing and recording:**
(Average Rigor) (Skill 6.1)

A) The child's use of expression in reading aloud.

B) The child's errors and miscues.

C) Her observations of the child's attitude toward reading.

D) The child's feelings about the particular passage being read.

Answer: B) The child's errors and miscues.

Running records taken of children help the teacher learn about the cueing systems that children use. It is important for the teacher to adjust reading instruction based on the pattern of miscues gathered from several successive reading records. When the teacher carefully reviews a given student's substitutions and self corrections, certain patterns begin to surface

80) **Andrew is just starting school, but it looks like he will be successful in reading because:**
(Average Rigor) (Skill 6.1)

A) He comes from a family which cares about his progress.

B) He is phonemically aware and knows his alphabet.

C) He has been in pre-school.

D) He is well behaved.

Answer: B) He is phonemically aware and knows his alphabet

Since the ability to distinguish between individual sounds, or phonemes, within words is a prerequisite to association of sounds with letters and manipulating sounds to blend words—a fancy way of saying "reading," the teaching of phonemic awareness is crucial to emergent literacy (early childhood K-2 reading instruction). Children need a strong background in phonemic awareness in order for phonics instruction (sound –spelling relationship-printed materials) to be effective.

81) **Ms. James is seated with a child by her side. The child is reading aloud from an open book. Ms. James is teaching in a school that has embraced the Balanced Literacy Approach. Therefore it is most likely that Ms. James is writing and recording:**
(Rigorous) (Skill 6.1)

   A) The child's use of expression in reading aloud.

   B) The child's errors and miscues.

   C) Her observations of the child's attitude toward reading.

   D) The child's feelings about the particular passage being read.

Answer: B) The child's errors and miscues.

Running records taken of children help the teacher learn about the cueing systems that children use. It is important for the teacher to adjust reading instruction based on the pattern of miscues gathered from several successive reading records. When the teacher carefully reviews a given student's substitutions and self corrections, certain patterns begin to surface

82) **"Self correct" in reading means:**
(Easy) (Skill 6.1)

   A) The teacher corrects on the record the errors the child makes.

   B) The child goes back and corrects errors made in a running record.

   C) The reading specialist teaches this to the child.

   D) a and b.

Answer: B) The child goes back and corrects errors made in a running record.

SELF-CORRECTION- children begin to correct some of their own reading errors. Generally this behavior is accompanied by the re-reading of the previous phrase or sentence.

83) **When taking a child's running record, the kinds of self corrections the child makes:**
(Average Rigor) (Skill 6.1)

A) Are not important, but the percentage of accuracy is important.

B) May show something about which cueing systems the child relies on.

C) Can be meaningful if analyzed over several records.

D) Both b and c

Answer: D) Both b and c

A running record provides the teacher with insight into what a child is thinking and how they are approaching a text as they read. Teachers are better able to understand a student's strengths and weaknesses.

84) **Once a teacher has carefully recorded and documented a running record:**
(Rigorous) (Skill 6.1)

A) There is nothing further to do as long as the teacher keeps the running record for conferences and documentation of grades.

B) The teacher should review the running record and other subsequent ones taken for growth over time.

C) The teacher should differentiate instruction for that particular student as indicated by growth over time and evidence of other needs.

D) Both b and c

Answer: C) The teacher should differentiate instruction for that particular student as indicated by growth over time and evidence of other needs.

After the completion of a running record, the teacher should analyze the record to determine the next teaching step that should occur for the student.

85) **A strategy is:**
(Average Rigor) (Skill 6.1)

A) A practice or routine the teacher can continually refer to.

B) A practice or routine a child can continually refer to or use.

C) A sheet or template for a practice the child can continually fill out.

D) All of the above.

Answer: D) All of the above

All of the answers refer to types of strategies.

86) **"Sounds right" can sound wrong to:**
(Rigorous) (Skill 6.1)

A) Any reader who is not a fluent or early reader.

B) AN ELL reader.

C) A struggling reader.

D) None of the above.

Answer: B) An ELL reader

The English language contains sounds that are not found in other languages and some letters have more than one sound. Because ELL students are not native to English then many of the words will not sound right.

87) **An excellent research project that can combine dictionary study with science research would be:**
(Average Rigor) (Skill 6.1)

A) A student authored dictionary terms and phrases about earthworms.

B) A teacher developed specialized dictionary of words and phrases about. earthworms.

C) A collection of articles on earthworms put together by the school librarian.

D) b and c.

Answer: A. A student authored dictionary terms and phrases about earthworms.

It is always more meaningful to a student if they can take ownership of any part of their learning. A student authored dictionary would include terms of interest to the student.

88) **Ways a paragraph may be organized include:**
(Average Rigor) (Skill 6.2)

A) Sequence of events

B) Statement Support

C) Classification

D) All of the above

Answer: D) All of the above.

Paragraphs may contain all of the items listed above.

89) **Andrew is just starting school, but it looks like he will be successful in reading because:**
(Average Rigor) (Skill 6.3)

A) He comes from a family which cares about his progress.

B) He is phonemically aware and knows his alphabet.

C) He has been in pre-school.

D) He is well behaved.

Answer: B) He is phonemically aware and knows his alphabet

Since the ability to distinguish between individual sounds, or phonemes, within words is a prerequisite to association of sounds with letters and manipulating sounds to blend words—a fancy way of saying "reading," the teaching of phonemic awareness is crucial to emergent literacy (early childhood K-2 reading instruction). Children need a strong background in phonemic awareness in order for phonics instruction (sound –spelling relationship-printed materials) to be effective

90) **A fifth grade teacher as subscribed to an online version of a local newspaper. She can help the students examine this resource and how it compares to the print version by noting which of the following differences:**
(Rigorous) (Skill 6.4)

A) Use of video to document events.

B) Use of sound clips in addition to written text

C) Links to other web resources

D) all of the above

Answer: D) All of the above

Online resources contain other forms of media that go beyond the printed word. Audio and video clips can be used to enhance the experience of the learner.

91) **Nonfiction genres include all of the following except:**
(Easy) (Skill 7.1)

A) Essays

B) Poetry

C) Speech

D) Biography

Answer: B) Poetry

Nonfiction genres include:
- Essays
- Narrative Nonfiction
- Biography
- Speech
- Autobiographies

92) **Historical Fiction, Mythology, Folklore, Realistic Fiction, Mystery, and Legends are known as:**
(Easy) (Skill 7.1)

A) Reading styles

B) Young Adult topics

C) Genres

D) Booklists

Answer: C) Genres

A genre is a particular category of literature.

93) **The Developing Readers Assessment System for leveling books was developed by:**
(Rigorous) (Skill 7.2)

   A) Calkins and Clay

   B) Fountas and Pinnell

   C) Wylie and Durrell

   D) Flesch and Clay

Answer: B) Fountas and Pinnell

Fountas and Pinnell created a leveling system for books. Knowing these levels will be helpful in meeting the instructional needs of the students in a more efficient manner.

94) **Sometimes children can be asked to demonstrate their understanding of a text in a non-written format. This might include all of the following except:**
(Easy) (Skill 8.1)

   A) A story map.

   B) A Venn diagram.

   C) Storyboarding a part of the story with dialogue bubbles.

   D) Retelling or paraphrasing.

Answer: D) Retelling or paraphrasing.

Children are expected and encouraged to tell as much of a story as they can remember. Re-telling is far more extensive than just summarizing. Children should include the beginning, middle and end plot lines and should be able to tell about the book's characters.

95) **Ms. Angel has to be certain that her fourth graders know the characteristics of the historical fiction genre. She can best support them in becoming comfortable with this genre by:**
(Rigorous) (Skill 8.2)

    A) Providing sequel and prequel writing opportunities using that genre.

    B) Reading them many different works from that genre.

    C) a and b.

    D) Having them look up the definition of that genre in a literary encyclopedia.

Answer: C) a and b

Providing students with writing experiences based upon particular genres and reading various works are good ways to introduce a particular genre.

96) **Ms. James is seated with a child by her side. The child is reading aloud from an open book. Ms. James is teaching in a school that has embraced the Balanced Literacy Approach. Therefore it is most likely that Ms. James is writing and recording:**
(Average Rigor) (Skill 9.1)

    A) The child's use of expression in reading aloud.

    B) The child's errors and miscues.

    C) Her observations of the child's attitude toward reading.

    D) The child's feelings about the particular passage being read.

Answer: B) The child's errors and miscues.

Running records taken of children help the teacher learn about the cueing systems that children use. It is important for the teacher to adjust reading instruction based on the pattern of miscues gathered from several successive reading records. When the teacher carefully reviews a given student's substitutions and self corrections, certain patterns begin to surface

97) **The work of Chard and Osborn (1999) in establishing guidelines for children with reading disabilities has shown that it is essential for them to:**
(Rigorous) (Skill 9.2)

A) Read wordless picture books.

B) Learn at least 10 sight words.

C) Work intensely on the alphabetic principle.

D) Focus on using syntactic clues.

Answer: C) Work intensely on the alphabetic principle.

David J. Chard and Jean Osborn (1999) have reflected on the guidelines necessary for teachers to use in selecting supplemental phonics and word-recognition materials for addressing students with learning disabilities.
They note that an important way to help children with reading disabilities figure out the system underlying the printed word is leading them to understand the alphabetic principle.

98) **Miscue analysis assists the teacher in determining which of the following:**
(Average Rigor) (Skill 9.3)

A) Methods a student uses to figure out unknown words

B) Student ability to monitor their own reading

C) Strategies that students are using with the greatest success

D) All of the above

Answer: D) All of the above

As a teacher observes a child's reading and analyzes the data, then can determine how a student attempts to figure out words, how students check for comprehension and the strengths and weaknesses of the child.

99) A key theorist who supports a phonics centered approach is:
(Rigorous) (Skill 9.4)

A) Marie Clay.

B) Sharon Taberski.

C) Shelley Harwayne.

D) Rudolf Flesch.

Answer: D) Rudolf Flesch

Researchers, such as Flesch (1981), support a phonics-centered foundation before the use of engaging reading texts. This is at the crux of the phonics versus whole language/ balanced literacy/ integrated language arts, teaching of reading controversy.

100) The reliability of a test is measured by:
(Rigorous) (Skill 9.5)

A) The number of children who can pass it.

B) The number of children who fail it.

C) The degree to which it measures what it is supposed to measure over time.

D) None of the above

Answer: C. The degree to which it measures what it is supposed to measure over time.

Reliability is the consistency of the test. This is measured by whether the test will indicate the same score for the child who takes it more than once.

101) A quartile on a test is:
(Average Rigor) (Skill 9.5)

A) A quarter of the grades grouped.

B) The division of the percentiles into four segments each of which is called a quartile.

C) 25 of the tests scored.

D) b and c

Answer: B) The division of the percentile into four segment each of which is called a quartile.

One of four segments of a distribution that has been divided into quarters. For example, the second-from-the-bottom quartile of an income distribution is those whose income exceeds the incomes of from 25% to 50% of the population.

102) Validity in assessment means:
(Rigorous) (Skill 9.5)

A) The test went off without any previewing of the questions or leaks on its contents.

B) The majority of test takers passed.

C) The correct time was allowed for the children to complete the test.

D) The test assessed what it was supposed to assess and measure.

Answer: D. The test assessed what it was supposed to assess and measure

Validity is how well a test measures what it is supposed to measure. Teacher made tests are therefore not generally extremely valid, although they may be an appropriate measure for the validity of the concept the teacher wants to assess for his/her own children's achievement.

103) "Bias" in testing occurs when:
(Rigorous) (Skill 9.5)

A) The assessment instrument is not an objective, fair and impartial one for a given cultural, ethnic, or special needs participant.

B) The testing administrator is biased.

C) The same test is given with no time considerations or provisions for those in need of more time or those who have handicapping conditions.

D) All of the above

Answer: D. All of the above.

Bias in testing occurs when the information within the test or the information required to respond to a multiple choice question or constructed response (essay question on the test) is information that is not available to some test takers who come from a different cultural, ethnic, linguistic or socio-economic background than do the majority of the test takers.

104) Norm-referenced tests:
(Average rigor) (Skill 9.5)

A) Give information only about the local samples results.

B) Provide information about the local test takers did compared to a representative sampling of national test takers.

C) Make no comparisons to national test takers.

D) None of the above.

Answer: B) Provide information about the local test takers did compared to a representative sampling of national test takers.

Norm-referenced –test in which the children are measured against one another. Scores on this test are reported in percentiles. Each percentile indicates the percent of the testing population whose scores were lower than or the same as a particular child's score. Percentile is defined as a score on a scale of 100 showing the percentage of a distribution that is equal to it or below it.

105) When helping students locate and evaluate information, you may want to solicit the help of your school's:
(Average Rigor) (Skill 10.1)

A) library media specialist.

B) speech therapist.

C) counselor.

D) reading teacher.

Answer: A) library media specialist

The library media specialist can play a key role in reading and literacy instruction. They are trained to assist patrons locate information.

106) When considering a core reading program, it should adhere to all of the following characteristics except:
(Rigorous) (Skill 11.1)

A) Based on current research and methods.

B) Provides explicit instruction in phonemic awareness, phonics, decoding, word recognition, spelling, vocabulary, comprehension, and writing.

C) Contain student workbooks.

D) Provide opportunities for students to discuss reading in class.

Answer: C) Contain student workbooks.

It is not necessary that a reading program contain workbooks, but it should contain quality reading materials for students.

107) A small group of students choose a book to read. Each person in the group is assigned a role, which changes so that each person gets to play each role is called a:
(Rigorous) (Skill 11.2)

   A) Literature circle

   B) Workshop

   C) Reading Center

   D) None of the above.

Answer: A) Literature Circles.

A small group of students (no more than 5) choose a book that they will read. Each person in the group is assigned a role, which changes so that each person gets to play each role. The group is temporary depending on the book. The groups meet on a regular basis to discuss the reading and they use written notes or drawings to help guide their discussions. Once students become more familiar with literature circles, they may abandon the use of roles and have an open dynamic discussion. The teacher becomes a facilitator and although he/she does evaluate the group, the students also engage in self-assessment. Once the book is read and discussed, the group members share with the whole class and a different book is chosen.

108) Book handling skills include ALL of the following except:
(Easy) (Skill 11.3)

   A) Putting a cellophane or plastic cover on a book.

   B) Identifying the back cover of the book.

   C) Reading the book jacket.

   D) Reading dedication page and the title page of the book.

Answer: A) Putting a cellophane or plastic cover on a book.

While students need to learn book handling skills such as how to hold the book, identifying key parts and pages, and directionality, it is not necessary for them to be able to put cellophane or plastic book covers on a book.

109) **Mr. Mandrake is subbing for Ms. Matley. He sees by the schedule that he is supposed to start the day after the morning meeting with a Read-Aloud. He notes a large picture on the easel and grabs the book just two minutes before the Read-Aloud is to start. He shouldn't heave a sigh of relief because:**
(Rigorous) (Skill 11.3)

A) He needs to be familiar with the book so that he can plan the read-aloud.

B) He does not know if the class has already heard this book.

C) He has not planned vocabulary, themes, or activities to go with the book.

D) All of the above.

Answer: D) All of the above.

Teachers should not only use wordless stories (books which tell their narratives through pictures alone), but can also make targeted use of Big Books for read-alouds, so that young children become habituated to the use of illustrations as an important component for constructing meaning. The teacher should model for the child how to reference an illustration for help in identifying a word in the text the child does not recognize.

110) **Author's viewpoint questions stump Gary. His teacher can help him by asking him during their reading conferences:**
(Average Rigor) (Skill 11.3)

A) If Gary-feels the book he is reading, is it just right for him.

B) What the author would say about what the character is doing in the story.

C) How the story can be changed to another genre.

D) If Gary-wants to read more books by this author.

Answer: B) What the author would say about what the character is doing in the story.

Author's viewpoint refers to what the author was thinking or feeling as they wrote the book. Questions may include: What do you think the author meant by having the character say that statement?

111) Young children often spell words they write according to the way the letters sound. This is called:
(Average Rigor) (Skill 11.3)

A) Spelling lists

B) Incorrect spelling

C) Developmental spelling

D) Invented spelling

Answer: D) Invented spelling

Spelling is of utmost importance in the writing process. At first young children will use invented spelling in which they write the words according to letter sounds.

112) Ms. Clark-is seen by outside observers from her district, seated in front of her class of sixth graders with a notebook in her lap and an easel. She reads aloud from a book and then writes down a series of questions. As she reads along, she sometimes writes down the answers to her own questions. This is most likely:
(Rigorous) (Skill 11.3)

A) A sign that Ms. Clark is uncertain of her own comprehension capacity.

B) She is modeling self questioning for the children.

C) She is aware that she is being watched and wants to make a good impression.

D) All of the above.

Answer: B) She is modeling self questioning for the children.

One of the most effective ways to teach students how to use various strategies is through modeling.

113) **If you get your raw score on a test, you will get:**
(Average Rigor) *(Skill 12.1)*

A) The actual number of points you scored on the test.

B) The percentage score of the number of questions you answered correctly.

C) A letter grade for your work on the test.

D) An aggregated score for your performance on the text.

Answer: B) The percentage score of the number of questions you answered correctly

The raw score identifies the number you answered correctly on a test.

114) **To keep abreast of reading trends and research, a reading specialist should subscribe to which of the following periodicals:**
(Average Rigor) *(Skill 12.3)*

A) *The Reading Teacher*

B) *Educational Leadership*

C) *Reading Research Quarterly*

D) All of the above

Answer: D) All of the above

All of the journals listed are key resources to any teacher that teaches reading skills.

115) Teacher research that is carried out by a teacher practitioner in the classroom to help a teacher evaluate his/her performance in the classroom is which type of research?
(Rigorous) (Skill 12.4)

A) Qualitative Research

B) Quantitative Research

C) Action Research

D) Both A and B

Answer: C) Action research

The question is the definition of action research. This type of research is used to evaluate performance. A variety of resources can be used to attain the data and conduct the research.

116) Strategies for educating parents and family include providing:
(Average Rigor) (Skill 13.1)

A) Workshops

B) Newsletters

C) Parent Nights

D) All of the above

Answer: D) All of the above

It is important to keep parents informed of school and classroom happenings. All of the tools listed above can be used to communicate and educate parents

117) Ms. Rivers is preparing for a parent teacher conference. She does all of the following EXCEPT:
(Average Rigor) (Skill 13.1)

A) Collects individual child running records.

B) Puts away all the book bags and leveled pots so the classroom will be more spacious.

C) Puts out by each child's seat the child's weekly log and spelling folder.

D) Sets up work samples by each child's place.

Answer: B) Puts away all the book bags and leveled pots so the classroom will bemore spacious.

A parent conference is a time to share student progress with parents. While it may be necessary to tidy the room or move things around to provide additional space, it is not a necessary part of the conference.

118) It is 4 PM, yet Francine is still in her classroom. The seats in her classroom are filled with adults of various ages who are holding books. They are seated two by two with both holding copies of the same book. Francine probably is:
(Rigorous) (Skill 13.1)

A) Explaining to parents how she will teach a particular story.

B) Demonstrating shared reading with a buddy for volunteer parents.

C) Hosting a parents organization meeting for her grade level.

D) Distributing old books from the class library to parents.

Answer: B) Demonstrating shared reading with a buddy for volunteer parents.

It is important to provide opportunities for the public to come into the school and participate in activities to encourage reading. During these incentive and fun programs, it is important to share tidbits of information about the methodologies and strategies being implemented. In this way, the public can begin to understand the differences in reading instruction today than perhaps what occurred when they attended school. Adults often comment on changes they see in current educational trends.

119) Tasks a reading specialist can use to determine student's level of comprehension include:
(Rigorous) (Skill 13.2)

   A) Listening to passages.

   B) Oral Reading

   C) Written Response

   D) All of the above.

Answer: D) All of the above.

In the diagnosis of reading difficulties, the specialist should use tools which measure the child's listening comprehension, oral reading skills, silent reading skills, and his/her ability to respond to reading in written form.

120) As teachers work to determine the strengths and weaknesses of individual students it is important that they:
(Rigorous) (Skill 13.3)

   A) Apply a variety of assessments.

   B) Utilized information provided from standardized tests only.

   C) Utilize tests found in the textbook.

   D) None of the above.

Answer: A) Apply a variety of assessments.

To gain a picture of the total child, a teacher must use a variety of assessments. This could include observations, formal assessments, standardized tests, etc.

121) Which theorist(s) developed a readability formula and graph? (Rigorous) (Skill 13.4)

A) Cooper

B) Frye

C) Fountas and Pinnel

D) Clay

Answer: B) Frye

The difficulty comes from determining which books students can in fact read. For decades, researchers have developed ways to examine the words in a story and determine for what level of reader it is appropriate. Frye developed his own readability formula and graph. These types of devices gave teachers a general grade level for which the books would be appropriate.

122) It is important for students to have an opportunity to read silently or on their own: (Average Rigor) (Skill 13.5)

A) hourly.

B) daily.

C) weekly.

D) monthly

Answer: B) daily

Reading specialists, administrators and teachers should take a critical look at the policies in place within the school for meeting the reading needs of all students. Part of this should include a school-wide reading initiative such as 15 minutes of silent reading in every classroom every day. During this time, the teacher can be reading as a model for the students or can be conferencing with individual students about what they are reading. This can take the form of listening to students read or asking them questions to ensure they comprehend what they are reading.

123) Commercially developed products are meant to reach the majority of students and provide them with the necessary skills to be successful readers is known as a:
(Average Rigor) (Skill 13.6)

A) Specialized Reading Program

B) Core Curriculum Program

C) Basel Reading Program

D) None of the above

Answer: B) Core Curriculum Program

Many districts have what are called Core Curriculum programs. These commercially developed products are meant to reach the majority of students and provide them with the necessary skills to be successful readers. Companies work hard to look at the state standards and have their products meet these standards. The problem occurs usually due to this all-encompassing nature of the materials. The products have so many pieces and parts that certain specific areas are not taught to the level some students need.

124) It is important to stay in close contact with a paraprofessional to monitor their progress. Ways to provide feedback as to their progress include:

A) Observation

B) Praise

C) Schedule regular meeting times

D) All of the above.

Answer: D) All of the above.

This can be a sensitive area for both the teacher and paraprofessional. It is important to provide feedback without being punitive or seeming judgmental. With proper training and the open communication previously discussed, a great working relationship with give and take can be achieved.

125) Mrs. Young is a first grade teacher trying to select a books that are "just right" for her students to read independently. She needs to consider which of the following:
(Rigorous) (Skill 13.8)

A) Illustrations should support the meaning of the text.

B) Content that relates to student interest and experiences

C) Predictable text structures and language patterns

D) All of the above

Answer: D) All of the above.

It is important that all of the above factors be considered when selecting books for young children.

Constructed Response Questions

Constructed Response Question One

Jean is a first year teacher who is taking over the classroom of a thirty-year veteran teacher who is retiring. Jean goes in to meet with the teacher. The teacher, Ms. Banks, talks about the importance of teaching the young first graders the concepts of print.

She gives Jean a list of these concepts and suggests that Jean create some assessment format so that she can be certain that all of her first graders learn these concepts. She also tells Jean that she will be volunteering her time in a neighborhood preschool program close to her home and so she will be taking her private books and materials with her. She suggests that Jean go over the list of concepts of print and consider the needs of her class as she prepares for teaching this crucial set of skills. Before Jean leaves the classroom, Ms. Banks tells her that the kindergarten teacher has let her know that three children who will be in her class next year are from ELL backgrounds where their families are not involved in oral story telling or reading from native language texts.

Ms. Banks' concepts of print list:

- STARTS ON LEFT

- GOES FROM LEFT TO RIGHT

- RETURN SWEEP

- MATCHES WORDS BY POINTING

- POINTS TO JUST ONE WORD

- POINTS TO FIRST AND LAST WORD

- POINTS TO 1 LETTER

- POINTS TO FIRST AND LAST LETTER

- PARTS of the BOOK: Cover, Title Page, Dedication page, Author and Illustrator

Jean thanks Ms. Banks for all of this help and asks if she can send Ms. Banks some of her teaching ideas for Concepts of Print and the ways she plans to differentiate instruction for her ELL students before the end of the year. Ms. Banks smiles and says she feels good to know that her classroom will be taken over by Jean. She promises to review Jean's response.

Constructed Response Answer One

First, as far as assessment for the key skills of concepts of print, I have decided that it is very important that I have a record of when and how well each of my students masters these concepts. After much thought, I realized that I will be keeping assessment notebooks for all of my students as part of my general reading and teaching. Therefore, I plan to print out all the key concepts of print on an 8" x 11" piece of paper in a grid format. This sheet will be included with other assessment grids for each individual child.

After conferencing with the child and I determine the child has demonstrated mastery of a particular concept, I will check it off on the grid and date that mastery. If I have other comments to make about the child's level of mastery or fluency, I will make an anecdotal notation about the child as well. I think that this will guarantee that I have a detailed checklist record and anecdotal record of all my children's individual progress on concepts of print.

I plan to use big books and many of the latest picture books, including Caldecott award winners in demonstrating and sharing with children many of the concepts of print. I will do much of my instruction mini-lessons. In fact I intend to use some of my own favorite alphabet books to introduce these conventions. With a book like Clare Beaton's, *Zoe and her Zebra*, I can easily and naturally cover the title page, cover, illustrator, and also manage to engage the children in the use of repetitive language.

Once I have shared that delightful book with the children as a read-aloud, we will be able to return to it again and use the repetitive language of it in its big book format to demonstrate for the children how they can point under each word as if there is a button to push. I can also demonstrate for the children how they should start at the top of the text and move from left to right. I will model going back to the left and under the previous line in a return weep.

After modeling this as part of the mini-lesson, the children can be divided in small groups or pairs and take other big book and practice the "point under each word" and the "return sweep" as part of "shared reading" or buddy reading. I should be able to identify some highly proficient readers who will be happy to serve as 'buddy' reader/tutors for the ELL children. I will ask that these "buddies" take time in small groups to work on another book from the alphabet book collection to share with the class as a whole. The use of the alphabet books also helps me to get some time in on the alphabetic principle.

I will also do a classroom writing workshop using the original alphabet book I use for the read-aloud, say *Zoe and Her Zebra* as a model for creating our own story. Perhaps we will call it *Barry and his Boxer*. In this way we will have a concrete literary product that demonstrates the children's mastery of and fluency in the concepts of print as they create an "in style of" story about a peer using illustrations, title page, dedication page, numbering of pages, back and front cover and other concepts of print.

I think that using individualized assessments, a group/class collaborative writing project, and an anchor alphabet book will help me successfully teach the concepts of print and address the needs of my ELL learners as well.

Constructed Response Question Two

Marianne has been selected as one of a team of teachers who will start teaching in a brand new school building that has been under construction for several years. While Marianne, a grade three teacher , is thrilled to be moving into new facilities, she is a bit overwhelmed to have to "set up her room" all over again at the new site. Her administrator, Mr. Adams, tells her that there are five new teachers with no previous experience teaching primary school age children who will be on staff. He tells her that these educators could really use help setting up their classrooms.

Marianne smiles and decides that she would very much like to use her set-up of her own grade three classroom as a workshop and demonstration for setting up a literacy teaching environment for these new staff members. Mr. Adams thinks that is a great idea and asks Marianne for an agenda and for a general description of what she will cover in her three hour workshop so that he can give it to the district office.

Marianne is happy to comply because she realizes that she will be assisting new colleagues and getting ten helping hands to help her set up all the materials she has accumulated over a twenty-year career.

Constructed Response Answer Two

The concept of sharing with new colleagues how to set up a classroom is very exciting to me. I know, based on my experiences, how crucial a well-planned and conceptualized space is for young learners' literacy learning. Therefore this is an agenda for what I will cover in my three hour in service session for my new colleagues.

First, I will discuss how whatever the size of the classroom space, it must be sectioned off into the following areas: a meeting area, with a sofa or "soft" setting; a chair, easel and basket to store book bags; a conference table; children's tables; and bin/basket main area for trade books; and another space for computers.

I may even give out a diagram of my classroom from my old school and some pictures. We will discuss collaboratively how I will set up my own new space as well as how they will want to set up their own spaces to allow for different uses of space within their own classrooms.

I will get into the issue of whether or not they want to have a traditional desk or use smaller tables for everyone. I think that they will need time to consider their own teaching styles in this regard. All teachers need to set up a space where they can easily confer with children and have access to individual assessment notebooks, reading folders (plus poetry/spelling, reading response, and handwriting notebooks) for all their students. I intend to show them how to prepare these folders for each child and how to store them so they can get to them when they need to make additional annotations for each child. Given the fact that I am working with new colleagues, I suspect that this will take at least an hour and a half of our time. I am also going to model for them a weekly reading log.

Most important of all, I am going to spend the major amount of time talking to them about the book bins as I place mine around the classroom. I will show them how to label the books using the Fountas and Pinnell levels and how to arrange the book bins with the spines out so that the children can see the books. Together we will examine how the bookcases should be close to the walls and the expository books should be separated from the narrative texts. I will also get together my audio-cassettes and book sets so that they can see how I set up my read-along center for all my children. I will share some dual language tapes I use with ELL students as well. I have some extra "author's hats" and author's chair slipcovers I will share with them.

I also intend to show them how to select big books for the easel display and anchor books to be shown there as well. By the way, I will also coach them how to write away for supplies and how to store supplies in common areas so that some children are not missing necessary materials for class activities.

Even though we are focusing on literacy, I am going to show them where to store mathematics materials, other texts, and art supplies. I will end the session by making sure that they know where to place their chart wall and the word wall. If I have time, I will sit down with each of them and start them on the word wall and some key charts for their first day. They will leave my room with an actual experience of setting up a literacy environment, plus viable teaching and reading suggestions for the first day. Most importantly, I will be available for an in-school classroom consultation, if necessary.

Tips and Reflections for tackling the Constructed Response Questions:

- Use as many phrases and words from the question as possible in your response.

- Be specific. Mention specific books, authors, theorists, and strategies you have studied. Even though this is a test about the teaching of reading, make specific use of children's trade books and literature if appropriate.

- Use as many details as you are given in the question to make your response. Write no more than 5-7 moderately brief paragraphs. The more you write, the larger the margin for error. Check your spelling, grammar and check to see that you answered everything that was asked, but no more than what was asked. Be positive and proactive about your ability to respond to whichever situation is presented.

- Stick with strategies, teaching ideas, and methods that are tried and true.

- Reread your writing at least twice for spelling and grammatical errors.

Additional Professional Citations

Block, Cathy Collins. (2002). *Comprehension Instruction: Research Based Practices.* New York: The Guilford Press.

Calkins, Lucy McCormick. (2001). *The Art of Teaching Reading.* New York: Longman.

Cambourne, Briane. (2002). "Conditions for Literacy Learning." *The Reading Teacher*, 55, (8): 758-62.

Cambourne, Briane. (l993). *The Whole Story: Natural Learning and the Acquisition of Literacy in the Classroom.* Auckland, NZ: Ashton, Scholastic.

Cunningham, Patricia M. (2000). *Phonics They Use: Words for Reading and Writing.* 3rd Edition. New York: Addison Wesley Longman.

Evidence Based Reading Instruction. (2002) Articles from International Reading Association. Newark, Delaware: *International Reading Association.*

Hoyt, Linda. (2002). *Make it Real-Strategies for Success with Informational Texts.* Portsmouth, NH: Heinemann.

Kimball-Lopez, Kimberley. (l999). *Connecting with Traditional Literature.* Boston: Allyn and Bacon.

Moustafa, Margaret. (l997). *Beyond Traditional Phonics.* Portsmouth, NH: Heinemann.

Owocki, Gretchen. (2003). *Strategic Instructions for K-3 Students.* Portsmouth, NH: Heinemann.

Owacki, G, and Y. Goodman. (2002*). Kidwatching-Documenting Children's Literacy Development.* Portsmouth, NH: Heinemann.

Quindlen, Anna. (1998). *How Reading Changed My Life.* New York: Ballantine Books, l998.

Routman, Regie. (2000). *Conversations.* Portsmouth, NH: Heinemann.

Schultz, C. (2000). *How Partner Reading Fosters Literacy Development in First Grade Students.* Action Research project, Saginaw Valley State University, University Center, Michigan.

Short, K., J. Harste and C. Burke. (l996). *Creating Classrooms for Authors and Inquirers.* Portsmouth, NH: Heinemann.

Trelease, Jim. (2001). *The Read-Aloud Handbook*. 4th Ed. New York: Penguin.

Wilde, Sandra. (2000). *Miscue Analysis Made Easy: Building on Student Strengths.* Portsmouth, NH: Heinemann.

Wilde, Sandra. (2000). *Reading Made Easy*. Portsmouth, NH: Heinemann.

XAMonline, INC. 21 Orient Ave. Melrose, MA 02176

Toll Free number 800-509-4128

TO ORDER Fax 781-662-9268 OR www.XAMonline.com

FLORIDA TEACHER CERTIFICATION EXAMINATIONS — FTCE - 2008

PO#   Store/School:

Bill to Address 1   Ship to address

City, State Zip

Credit card number_____-_____-_____-_____   expiration_____

EMAIL _____

PHONE   **FAX**

13# ISBN 2007	TITLE	Qty	Retail	Total
978-1-58197-900-8	Art Sample Test K-12			
978-1-58197-689-2	Biology 6-12			
978-1-58197-099-9	Chemistry 6-12			
978-1-58197-572-7	Earth/Space Science 6-12			
978-1-58197-921-3	Educational Media Specialist PK-12			
978-1-58197-347-1	Elementary Education K-6			
978-1-58197-292-4	English 6-12			
978-1-58197-274-0	Exceptional Student Ed. K-12			
978-1-58197-294-8	FELE Florida Ed. Leadership			
978-1-58197-919-0	French Sample Test 6-12			
978-1-58197-615-1	General Knowledge			
978-1-58197-586-4	Guidance and Counseling PK-12			
978-1-58197-089-0	Humanities K-12			
978-1-58197-640-3	Mathematics 6-12			
978-1-58197-597-0	Middle Grades English 5-9			
978-1-58197-662-5	Middle Grades General Science 5-9			
978-1-58197-286-3	Middle Grades Integrated Curriculum			
978-1-58197-284-9	Middle Grades Math 5-9			
978-1-58197-590-1	Middle Grades Social Science 5-9			
978-1-58197-616-8	Physical Education K-12			
978-1-58197-818-6	Physics 6-12			
978-1-58197-657-1	Prekindergarten/Primary PK-3			
978-1-58197-695-3	Professional Educator			
978-1-58197-659-5	Reading K-12			
978-1-58197-270-2	Social Science 6-12			
978-1-58197-583-3	Spanish K-12			
			SUBTOTAL	
b/handling $8.25 one title, $11.00 two titles, $15.00 three or more titles				
			TOTAL	